D1191191

critical applied linguistics:

critical
a ∧ introduction

critical applied linguistics:

a /\ *critical* introduction

Alastair Pennycook
University of Technology, Sydney

LEA LAWRENCE ERLBAUM ASSOCIATES, PUBLISHERS
2001 Mahwah, New Jersey London

Lawrence Erlbaum Associates, Inc., Publishers
10 Industrial Avenue
Mahwah, NJ 07430

Cover design by Kathryn Houghtaling Lacey

Library of Congress Cataloging-in-Publication Data

Pennycook, Alastair.
Critical applied linguistics : a critical introduction / Alastair
    Pennycook.
        p. cm.
        Includes bibliographical references and index.
    ISBN 0-8058-3791-4 (cloth : alk. paper)
    ISBN 0-8058-3792-2 (pbk. : alk. paper)
    1. Applied linguistics.   I. Title.
    P129 .P46   2001
    418—dc21   00-056213
                                                              CIP

Printed in the United States of America
10 9 8 7 6 5 4 3 2 1

#44468949

*For the many friends, colleagues, and students
who have been part of this journey*

Contents

Preface   xiii

1 Introducing Critical Applied Linguistics   1

    Critical applied linguistic concerns *2*

    Domains of Critical applied linguistics *10*

    Conclusion: Why critical applied linguistics? *20*

2 The Politics of Knowledge   24

    Critical work and animosity to theory *25*

    Knowledge of politics and the politics of knowledge *27*
        Liberal ostrichism *29*
        Anarcho-autonomy *33*
        Emancipatory modernism *36*
        Critical applied linguistics as problematizing practice *41*

    Conclusion: Outflanking Marx from the left *43*

3 The Politics of Language   46

    Sociolinguistics and power *47*
        Liberal sociolinguistics *48*

Language planning and politics: The global spread
    of English   55
  Liberal complementarity   56
  Language ecology, language rights, and linguistic
    imperialism   59

Postcolonialism and resistance   65
  Colonialism and postcolonialism   66
  Resistance, appropriation, and third spaces   68

Conclusion: Toward a postcolonial performative view
    of language   71

4 The Politics of Text   74

Critical literacy   75
  Literacies as social practices   76

Critical discourse analysis   78

Ideology, discourse, truth, and power   82
  Knowledge claims and truth   84
  Order and disorder   85
  The nonmaterial base of discourse   89
  Production and reception   93

Critical language awareness and the genres of power   94

Critical literacy and voice: The word and the world   100

From Poststructuralism to Postlinguistics   104
  Toward a postlinguistics   108

Conclusion: Toward an Applied Postlinguistics   110

5 The Politics of Pedagogy   114

Classrooms in context   115

Structure, agency, determinism, and resistance   117

Social and cultural reproduction in schooling   121
  Bourdieu and forms of capital   123
  Resistance and change   126

Critical pedagogy   130

Education, postmodernism, and ethics   *133*
Postmodernism and ethics   *136*
Toward a postcritical pedagogy   *138*

6 The Politics of Difference   141
Difference, identity, and language learning   *143*
Identity and subjectivity   *145*

Language, gender, sexuality, and difference   *151*
Dominance and difference   *151*
Performing gender through language   *155*

Dealing with difference: Inclusivity, issues, and
engagement   *157*
Toward engaged research   *160*

Conclusion: Embodied differences   *162*

7 Applied Linguistics With an Attitude   164
Critical themes   *165*

Guidelines for a critical praxis   *168*
Critical notes for the fridge door   *171*

Critical applied postlinguistics, Postcritical
applied linguistics, or applied linguistics
with an attitude   *173*

References   179

Author Index   195

Subject Index   199

List of Figures and Tables

Table 1.1: Three Approaches to Critical Work
Table 1.2: Critical Applied Linguistic Concerns
Figure 1.1: Concerns and Domains of Critical Applied Linguistics
Table 1.3: Overview of the Book
Table 2.1: Four Relations Between Knowledge and Politics
Table 3.1: Liberal and Critical Versions of Sociolinguistics
Table 3.2: Frameworks for Understanding the Global Role of English
Figure 3.1: Analysis and Action
Table 4.1: Two Different Domains of Critical Discourse Analysis (CDA)
Table 4.2: Central Concerns in Critical Discourse Analysis (CDA)
Table 4.3: Foucault and Power
Table 4.4: Approaches to Critical Literacy
Table 4.5: Applied Postlinguistic Approaches to Text
Table 5.1: Alternative Conceptions of School and Society
Table 5.2: An Overview of Bourdieu's Forms of Capital
Table 5.3: Strengths and Weaknesses of Bourdieu
Table 5.4: Features and Critiques of Critical Pedagogy
Figure 5.1: Reconfiguring the Posts
Table 6.1: Dominance, Difference, and Performativity
Table 6.2: Inclusivity, Issues, and Engagement
Table 6.3: Engaged Research
Table 7.1: Frameworks of Politics, Epistemology, and Applied Linguistics
Table 7.2: (Critical) Applied Linguistics (CALx) in the Curriculum

Preface

It was some 10 years ago that with the announcement of a new journal, *Issues in Applied Linguistics,* to be edited by graduate students at the University of California at Los Angeles (UCLA), I decided to try out the notion of critical applied linguistics (Pennycook, 1990). A graduate student myself at that time, I was on the one hand trying to express my own deep dissatisfactions with what I felt were severe limitations and blindspots in applied linguistics. Having taught for a number of years in Japan, Québec, and China, I had become concerned that the applied linguistics we taught was unable to deal with—indeed in a number of ways seemed to support—the many inequitable conditions I encountered: the frequent assumptions of privilege, authority, and superiority, from native speakers of English and the English language itself to particular approaches to teaching, cultural forms, or forms of social organization; and the constant denigration of other languages, other language speakers, and teachers and students from different backgrounds. On the other hand, I was trying to work out how different areas of critical work that I was just beginning to discover—critical pedagogy, critical discourse analysis, critical ethnography—might help develop an alternative way forward. The article I submitted received angry reviews, but in the end, the editor (thanks Antony) took a risk and published it.

Ten years on, Alan Davies' recent (1999) book, *An Introduction to Applied Linguistics: From Practice to Theory,* has just arrived on my desk. Critical applied linguistics (CAL) is now in the glossary (it exists!): "A judgmental approach by some applied linguists to 'normal' applied linguistics on the grounds that it is not concerned with the transformation of society" (p. 145). Well, not quite how I would have put it (see the rest of this book). For Davies and others from an earlier applied linguistic generation, there is a concern that the carefully constructed and nurtured discipline of applied linguistics is in danger of fragmentation. But Davies also sees this as part of a healthy debate:

> Modernist approaches (such as CDA) and postmodernist critiques (such as CAL) of applied linguistics are ... seductive. They provide a useful debate on the nature of the discipline, they need to be taken into account. But they must not be allowed to take over, cuckoo-like. (p. 142)

This book is an attempt to provide more substance to this debate, to put a bit more flesh on that "more radical, if also more nebulous CAL" (Davies, 1999, p. 143) that I apparently promote. It is not an attempt to take over applied linguistics, cuckoo-like (as if!). It is an attempt to present different domains of critical applied linguistics— critical approaches to text, language, literacy, research, language learning, teaching, and translation—and to show how they fit together. After many different versions, editings, and reeditings, the book is now organized with the following chapters:

1. Introducing Critical Applied Linguistics
2. The Politics of Knowledge
3. The Politics of Language
4. The Politics of Text
5. The Politics of Pedagogy
6. The Politics of Difference
7. Applied Linguistics With an Attitude.

I have also included a number of charts that present overviews of different domains. These have proved quite useful as a tool for the sort of mapping exercise I've been doing here. The book tries both to give an overview of critical work in these areas and to present my own particular take on this. It is therefore something of a personal account of what I understand critical applied linguistics to be. It is also an attempt not merely to present an overview of the area but also to critique it, to subject critical applied linguistics to the same sort of critical examination as "normal" applied linguistics. I hope therefore that this book will be of interest to a wide range of readers, from "normal" applied linguists to critical applied linguists, from language educators to translators, from practicing teachers to undergraduate and postgraduate students.

In some ways, this is for me the culmination of a 10-year project to figure out what critical applied linguistics might usefully look like. I had not thought this book would be as difficult as it has proved: All I needed to do was pull together my course notes and readings from the Critical Applied Linguistics course (thanks Tim) I used to teach at the University of Melbourne. Not so. I have come to understand in the writing how huge and complex this area is and how inadequate my own understanding was and still is. And of course, this won't be a culmination since it looks set to be part of an ongoing debate. This has not been a debate that has been easy to sustain and participate in over the last 10 years. The critical stance I (and others) have taken has caused resentment and anger. There have been nasty backlashes, attempts to discredit this sort of work, unpleasant parodies, refusals to discuss. But there has also been a great deal of support. I have been extremely privileged in the last few years to be invited to speak in many different parts of the world, from the Philippines to Brazil, from Germany to Japan, from Vietnam to the United States, from Singapore to Abu Dhabi, and in all these places, I have had wonderful conversations with a vast array of different people, trying to work out how our different projects intersect.

So, I owe a great debt of thanks to many, many people over the last 10 years, and I am not going to try to name them all. Quite a few turn up in the pages of this book. From the origins of these ideas among the "critical crowd" at Ontario Institute for Studies Education (OISE) in Toronto, through my many debates and discussions with colleagues and students in Hong Kong, Melbourne, and now Sydney, through all the discussions at conferences around the world, in coffee shops, sitting up late in bars, to the wonderful moments in class when we have arrived at a revelation of how different parts of the critical puzzle fit together (with a special thanks to the critical applied linguistics class of 1997—I still have my "exemplary umpiring" certificate on the wall). Many thanks to all these people. Let's keep the discussion going. And thanks to Naomi Silverman at Lawrence Erlbaum, who liked the sound of this book, and to Elsa Auerbach, who gave it its last critical reading before publication. And a final thanks again to my parents and to Dominique, who have done so much to support me and who will doubtless give this book yet another critical reading.

Introducing Critical Applied Linguistics

> Critical Applied Linguistic Concerns
> Domains of Critical Applied Linguistics
> Conclusion: Why Critical Applied Linguistics?

What is critical applied linguistics? Simply put, it is a critical approach to applied linguistics. Such a response, however, leads to several further questions: What is applied linguistics? What is meant by critical? Is critical applied linguistics merely the addition of a critical approach to applied linguistics? Or is it something more? This short introductory chapter gives an outline of what I understand critical applied linguistics to be, before I expand in much greater detail in later chapters on the domains it may cover, the theoretical issues it engages with, and the types of questions it raises. *Critical applied linguistics* is not yet a term that has wide currency, so this introduction in a sense is a performative act: Rather than introducing an already established domain of work, this introduction both introduces and produces critical applied linguistics (CALx). It is therefore also a fairly personal account of this area. And since I believe critical work should always be self-reflexive, this introduction must necessarily be critical (hence a critical introduction).

Rather than simply trying to define what I take critical applied linguistics to be, I would prefer to raise a number of important concerns and questions that can bring us closer to an understanding of this area. These concerns have to do with:

- The scope and coverage of applied linguistics
- The notion of praxis as a way of going beyond a dichotomous relation between theory and practice
- Different ways of understanding the notion *critical*
- The importance of relating micro relations of applied linguistics to macro relations of society
- The need for a critical form of social inquiry
- The role of critical theory
- Critical applied linguistics as a constant questioning of assumptions
- The importance of an element of self-reflexivity in critical work
- The role of ethically argued preferred futures
- An understanding of critical applied linguistics as far more than the sum of its parts.

CRITICAL APPLIED LINGUISTIC CONCERNS

Applied Linguistics

To start with, to the extent that critical applied linguistics is seen as a critical approach to applied linguistics, it needs to operate with a broad view of applied linguistics. Applied linguistics, however, has been a notoriously hard domain to define. The *Longman Dictionary of Applied Linguistics* gives us two definitions: "the study of second and foreign language learning and teaching" and "the study of language and linguistics in relation to practical problems, such as lexicography, translation, speech pathology, etc." (Richards, Platt, & Weber, 1985, p. 15). From this point of view, then, we have two different domains, the first to do with second or foreign language teaching (but, not, significantly, first language education), the second to do with language-related problems in various areas in which language plays a major role. This first version of applied linguistics is by and large a result historically of its emergence from applying linguistic theory to contexts of second language pedagogy in the United States in the 1940s. It is also worth observing that as Kachru (1990) and others have pointed out, this focus on language teaching has also been massively oriented toward teaching English as a second language. The second version is a more recent broadening of the field, although it is certainly not accepted by applied linguists such as Widdowson (1999), who continue to argue that applied linguists mediate between linguistic theory and language teaching.

In addition, there is a further question as to whether we are dealing with the application of linguistics to applied domains—what Widdowson (1980) termed *linguistics applied*—or whether applied linguistics has a more autonomous status. Markee (1990) termed these the *strong* and the *weak* versions of applied linguistics, respectively. As de Beaugrande (1997) and Markee (1990) argue, it is the so-called strong version—linguistics applied—that has predominated, from the classic British tradition encapsulated in Corder's (1973) and Widdowson's (1980) work through to the parallel North American version encapsulated in the second language acquisition studies of writers such as Krashen (1981). Reversing Markee's (1990) labels, I would argue that this might be more usefully seen as the weak version because it renders applied linguistics little more than an application of a parent domain of knowledge (linguistics) to different contexts (mainly language teaching). The applied linguistics that critical applied linguistics deals with, by contrast, is a strong version marked by breadth of coverage, interdisciplinarity, and a degree of autonomy. From this point of view, applied linguistics is an area of work that deals with language use in professional settings, translation, speech pathology, literacy, and language education; and it is not merely the application of linguistic knowledge to such settings but is a semiautonomous and interdisciplinary (or, as I argue later, antidisciplinary) domain of work that draws on but is not dependent on areas such as sociology, education, anthropology, cultural studies, and psychology. Critical applied linguistics adds many new domains to this.

Praxis

A second concern of applied linguistics in general, and one that critical applied linguistics also needs to address, is the distinction between theory and practice. There is often a problematic tendency to engage in applied linguistic research and theorizing and then to suggest pedagogical or other applications that are not grounded in particular contexts of practice (see Clarke, 1994). This is a common orientation in the linguistics-applied-to-language-teaching approach to applied linguistics. There is also, on the other hand, a tendency to dismiss applied linguistic theory as not about the real world. I want to resist both versions of applied linguistics and instead look at applied linguistics in all its contexts as a constant reciprocal relation between theory and practice, or preferably, as "that continuous reflexive integration of thought, desire and action sometimes referred to as 'praxis'" (Simon, 1992, p. 49). Discourse analysis is a practice that implies a theory, as are researching second language acquisition, translation and teaching. Thus, I prefer to avoid the theory- into-practice direction and instead see these as more complexly interwoven. This is why I argue that this book is an exercise in (critical) applied linguistics and also why it will not end with a version of the pedagogical implications of critical applied linguistics. I try to argue that critical applied linguistics is a way of thinking and doing, a "continuous reflexive integration of thought, desire and action."

Being Critical

If the scope and coverage of applied linguistics needs careful consideration, so too does the notion of what it means to be critical or to do critical work. Apart from some general uses of the term—such as "Don't be so critical"—one of the most common uses is in the sense of critical thinking or literary criticism. *Critical thinking* is used to describe a way of bringing more rigorous analysis to problem solving or textual understanding, a way of developing more critical distance as it is sometimes called. This form of "skilled critical questioning" (Brookfield, 1987, p. 92), which has recently gained some currency in applied linguistics (see Atkinson, 1997), can be broken down into a set of thinking skills, a set of rules for thinking that can be taught to students. Similarly, while the sense of critical reading in literary criticism usually adds an aesthetic dimension of textual appreciation, many versions of literary criticism have attempted to create the same sort of "critical distance" by developing "objective" methods of textual analysis. As McCormick (1994) explains:

> Much work that is done in "critical thinking" … —a site in which one might expect students to learn ways of evaluating the "uses" of texts and the implications of taking up one reading position over another—simply assumes an objectivist view of knowledge and instructs students to evaluate texts' "credibility," "purpose," and "bias," as if these were transcendent qualities. (p. 60)

It is this sense of *critical* that has been given some space by various applied linguists (e.g., Widdowson, 1999) who argue that critical applied linguistics should operate with this form of critical distance and objectivist evaluation rather than a more politicized version of critical applied linguistics.

Although there is of course much to be said for such an ability to analyze and critique, there are two other major themes in critical work that sit in opposition to this approach. The first may accept the possibility that critical distance and objectivity are important and achievable but argues that the most significant aspect of critical work is an engagement with political critiques of social relations. Such a position insists that critical inquiry can remain objective and is no less so because of its engagement with social critique. The second argument is one that also insists on the notion of *critical* as always engaging with questions of power and inequality, but it differs from the first in terms of its rejection of any possibility of critical distance or objectivity. I enlarge on these positions briefly below, and at greater length in later chapters (→ chap. 2), but for the moment let us call them the *modernist-emancipatory position* and the *postmodern-problematizing position* (see Table 1.1).

TABLE 1.1

Three Approaches to Critical Work

	Critical thinking	Emancipatory modernism	Problematizing practice
Politics	Liberalism	Neo-Marxism	Feminism, postcolonialism, queer theory, etc.
Theoretical base	Humanism	Critical theory	Poststructuralism
Goals	Questioning skills	Ideology critique	Discursive mapping

Micro and Macro Relations

Whichever of these two positions we take, however, it is clear that rather than basing critical applied linguistics on a notion of teachable critical thinking skills, or critical distance from social and political relations, critical applied linguistics has to have ways of relating aspects of applied linguistics to broader social, cultural, and political domains. One of the shortcomings of work in applied linguistics generally has been a tendency to operate with what I elsewhere (Pennycook, 1994a) called *decontextualised contexts*. It is common to view applied linguistics as concerned with language in context, but the conceptualization of context is frequently one that is limited to an overlocalized and undertheorized view of social relations. One of the key challenges for critical applied linguistics, therefore, is to find ways of mapping micro and macro relations, ways of understanding a relation between concepts of society, ideology, global capitalism, colonialism, education, gender, racism, sexuality, class, and classroom utterances, translations, conversations, genres, second language acquisition, media texts. Whether it is critical applied linguistics as a critique of mainstream applied linguistics, or as a form of critical text analysis, or as an approach to understanding the politics of translation, or as an attempt to understand implications of the global spread of English, a central issue always concerns how the classroom, text, or conversation is related to broader social cultural and political relations.

Critical Social Inquiry

It is not enough, however, merely to draw connections between micro relations of language in context and macro relations of social inquiry. Rather, such connections need to be drawn within a critical approach to social relations. That is to say, critical applied linguistics is concerned not merely with relating language contexts to social contexts but rather does so from a point of view that views social relations as problematic. Although a great deal of work in sociolinguistics, for example, has tended to map language onto a rather static view of society (see Williams, 1992), critical sociolinguistics (→ chaps. 2 and 3) is concerned with a critique of ways in which language perpetuates inequitable social relations. From the point of view of studies of language and gender, the issue is not merely to describe how language is used differently along gendered lines but to use such an analysis as part of social critique and transformation. A central element of critical applied linguistics, therefore, is a way of exploring language in social contexts that goes beyond mere correlations between language and society and instead raises more critical questions to do with access, power, disparity, desire, difference, and resistance. It also insists on an historical understanding of how social relations came to be the way they are.

Critical Theory

One way of taking up such questions has been through the work known as Critical Theory, a tradition of work linked to the Frankfurt School and such thinkers as Adorno, Horkheimer, Walter Benjamin, Erich Fromm, Herbert Marcuse, and currently Jürgen Habermas. A great deal of critical social theory, at least in the Western tradition, has drawn in various ways on this reworking of Marxist theory to include more complex understandings of, for example, ways in which the Marxist concept of ideology relates to psychoanalytic understandings of the subconscious, how aspects of popular culture are related to forms of political control, and how particular forms of positivism and rationalism have come to dominate other possible ways of thinking. At the very least, this body of work reminds us that critical applied linguistics needs at some level to engage with the long legacy of Marxism, neo-Marxism, and its many counterarguments. Critical work in this sense has to engage with questions of inequality, injustice, rights, and wrongs.

Looking more broadly at the implications of this line of thinking, we might say that *critical* here means taking social inequality and social transformation as central to one's work. Marc Poster (1989) suggests that "critical theory springs from an assumption that we live amid a world of pain, that much can be done to alleviate that pain, and that theory has a crucial role to play in that process" (p. 3). I am reminded here of a moment recounted by Habermas, the prolific heir to this critical tradition, when he went to visit Herbert Marcuse, his predecessor and author of such classic works as *One Dimensional Man*. Just before Marcuse's 80th birthday, the two had had a "long discussion on how we could and should explain the normative base of Critical Theory." Two years later,

Habermas visits Marcuse in the intensive care unit of a hospital. The dying Marcuse returns to the previous debate: "Look, I know wherein our most basic value judgments are rooted—in compassion, in our sense for the suffering of others" (Marcuse as cited in Habermas, 1985, p. 77). This moment is worth recalling, I think, for amid all the discussions of different critical approaches and amid the insistence that this sort of critical work has to be based on particular political beliefs, it is worth reminding ourselves that it is perhaps compassion, but a compassion grounded in a sharp critique of inequality, that grounds our work. Taking up Poster's (1989) terms, critical applied linguistics is an approach to language-related questions that springs from an assumption that we live amid a world of pain and that applied linguistics may have an important role in either the production or the alleviation of some of that pain. But, it is also a view that insists not merely on the alleviation of pain but also the possibility of change.

Problematizing Givens

While the sense of critical thinking I discussed earlier—a set of thinking skills—attempts almost by definition to remain isolated from political questions, from issues of power, disparity, difference, or desire, the sense of *critical* that I want to make central to critical applied linguistics is one that takes these as the *sine qua non* of our work. Critical applied linguistics is not about developing a set of skills that will make the doing of applied linguistics more rigorous or more objective but is about making applied linguistics more politically accountable. Nevertheless, as I suggested earlier, there are quite divergent strands within critical thought. As Dean (1994) suggests, the version of *critical* in Critical Theory is a form of critical modernism, a version of critical theory that tends to critique "modernist narratives in terms of the one-sided, pathological, advance of technocratic or instrumental reason they celebrate" only to offer "an alternative, higher version of rationality" in their place (Dean, 1994, p. 3). As I argue in later chapters, a great deal of the work currently being done in critical domains related to critical applied linguistics often falls into this category of emancipatory modernism, developing a critique of social and political formations but offering only a version of an alternative truth in its place. This version of critical modernism, with its emphasis on emancipation and rationality, has a number of limitations.

In place of Critical Theory, Dean (1994) goes on to propose what he calls a problematizing practice. This, he suggests, is a critical practice because "it is unwilling to accept the taken-for-granted components of our reality and the 'official' accounts of how they came to be the way they are" (p. 4). Thus, a crucial component of critical work is always turning a skeptical eye toward assumptions, ideas that have become "naturalized," notions that are no longer questioned. Dean (1994) describes such practice as "the restive problematization of the given" (p. 4). Drawing on work in areas such as feminism, antiracism, postcolonialism, postmodernism, or queer theory, this approach to the critical seeks not so much the stable ground of an alternative truth but rather the constant questioning of all categories. From this point of view, critical applied linguistics is not only about relating micro relations of applied linguistics to macro relations of social and political power; neither is it only concerned with relating such questions to a prior critical analysis of inequality; rather, it is also concerned with questioning what is meant by and what is maintained by many of the everyday categories of applied linguistics: language, learning, communication, difference, context, text, culture, meaning, translation, writing, literacy, assessment, and so on.

Self-reflexivity

Such a problematizing stance leads to another significant element that needs to be made part of any critical applied linguistics. If critical applied linguistics needs to retain a constant skepticism, a constant questioning of the givens of applied linguistics, this problematizing stance must also be turned on itself. As Spivak (1993) suggests, the notion of *critical* also needs to imply an awareness "of the limits of knowing" (p. 25). As I suggested earlier, one of the problems with emancipatory-modernism is its assurity about its own rightness, its belief that an adequate critique of social and political inequality can lead to an alternative reality. A postmodern-problematizing stance, however, needs to maintain a greater sense of humility and difference and to raise questions about the limits of its own knowing. This self-reflexive position also suggests that critical applied linguistics is not concerned with producing itself as a new orthodoxy, with prescribing new models and procedures for doing applied linguistics. Rather, it is concerned with raising a host of new and difficult questions about knowledge, politics, and ethics.

Preferred Futures

Critical applied linguistics also needs to operate with some sort of vision of what is preferable. Critical work has often been criticized for doing little more than criticize things, for offering nothing but a bleak and pessimistic vision of social relations. Various forms of critical work, particularly in areas such as education, have sought to avoid this trap by articulating 'utopian' visions of alternative realities, by stressing the 'transformative' mission of critical work or the potential for change through awareness and emancipation. While such goals at least present a direction for reconstruction, they also echo with a rather troubling modernist grandiosity. Perhaps the notion of preferred futures offers us a slightly more restrained and plural view of where we might want to head.

Such preferred futures, however, need to be grounded in ethical arguments for why alternative possibilities may be better. For this reason, ethics has to become a key building block for critical applied linguistics, although, as with my later discussion of politics (chap. 2), this is not a normative or moralistic code of practice but a recognition that these are ethical concerns with which we need to deal. And, as with my earlier discussion of Critical Theory, this notion suggests that it is not only a language of critique that I am trying to develop here but rather an ethics of compassion and a model of hope and possibility.

Critical Applied Linguistics as Heterosis

Using Street's (1984) distinction between autonomous and ideological approaches to literacy (→ chap. 4), Rampton (1995b) argues that applied linguistics in Britain has started to shift from its "autonomous" view of research with connections to pedagogy, linguistics, and psychology to a more "ideological" model with connections to media studies and a more grounded understanding of social processes. Critical applied linguistics opens the door for such change even wider by drawing on yet another range of "outside" work (critical theory, feminism, postcolonialism, poststructur- alism, antiracist pedagogy) that both challenges and greatly enriches the possibilities for doing applied linguistics. This means not only that critical applied linguistics implies a hybrid model of research and praxis but also that it generates something that is far more dynamic. As with the notion of synergy as the productive melding of two elements to create something larger than the sum of its parts, I am using here the notion of heterosis as the creative expansion of possibilities resulting from hybridity.[1] Put more simply, my point here is that critical applied linguistics is far more than the addition of a critical dimension to applied linguistics; rather, it opens up a whole new array of questions and concerns, issues such as identity, sexuality, or the reproduction of Otherness that have hitherto not been considered as concerns related to applied linguistics.

The notion of heterosis helps deal with a final concern, the question of normativity. It might be objected that what I am sketching out here is a problematically normative approach: By defining what I mean by *critical* and *critical applied linguistics,* I am setting up an approach that already has a predefined political stance and mode of analysis. There is a certain tension here: an overdefined version of critical applied linguistics that demands adherence to a particular form of politics is a project that is already limited; but I also cannot envision a version of critical applied linguistics that can accept any and every political viewpoint. The way forward here is this: On

---

[1] I am aware of the problems discussed by Young (1995) in this use of colonial concepts such as hybridity within a postcolonial framework. Some of these concerns are discussed later. Nevertheless, I find concepts such as hybridity, syncretic appropriation, and heterosis useful for understanding the development and potential of alternative spaces.

the one hand, I am arguing that critical applied linguistics must necessarily take up certain positions and stances; its view of language cannot be an autonomous one that backs away from connecting language to broader political concerns, and furthermore, its focus on such politics must be accountable to broader political and ethical visions that put inequality, oppression, and compassion to the fore. On the other hand, I do not want to suggest a narrow and normative vision of how those politics work. The notion of heterosis, however, opens up the possibility that critical applied linguistics is indeed not about the mapping of a fixed politics onto a static body of knowledge but rather is about creating something new. As Foucault (1980b) put it, "the problem is not so much one of defining a political 'position' (which is to choose from a pre-existing set of possibilities) but to imagine and to bring into being new schemas of politicisation" (p. 190). That is the political challenge of critical applied linguistics. These critical applied linguistic concerns are summarized in Table 1.2.

DOMAINS OF CRITICAL APPLIED LINGUISTICS

Critical applied linguistics, then, is more than just a critical dimension added on to applied linguistics: It involves a constant skepticism, a constant questioning of the normative assumptions of applied linguistics. It demands a restive problematization of the givens of applied linguistics and presents a way of doing applied linguistics that seeks to connect it to questions of gender, class, sexuality, race, ethnicity, culture, identity, politics, ideology, and discourse. And crucially, it becomes a dynamic opening up of new questions that emerge from this conjunction. In this second part of the chapter, I give a rough overview of domains that I see as comprising critical applied linguistics. This list is neither exhaustive nor definitive of the areas I cover in this book, but taken in conjunction with the issues raised earlier, it presents us with two principal ways of conceiving of critical applied linguistics—various underlying principals and various domains of coverage. The areas I summarize briefly in this section are critical discourse analysis and critical literacy, critical approaches to translation, language teaching, language testing, language planning and language rights, and language, literacy, and workplace settings.

Critical Discourse Analysis and Critical Literacy

It might be tempting to consider critical applied linguistics as an amalgam of other critical domains. From this point of view, critical applied linguistics would either be made up of, or constitute the intersection of, areas such as critical linguistics, critical discourse analysis (CDA), critical language awareness, critical pedagogy, critical sociolinguistics, and critical literacy. Such a formulation is unsatisfactory for several reasons. First, the

TABLE 1.2

Critical Applied Linguistic Concerns

Critical applied linguistic (CALx) concerns	*Centered on the following:*	*In opposition to mainstream applied linguistics (ALx):*
A strong view of applied linguistics (ALx)	Breadth of coverage, interdisciplinarity, and autonomy	The weak version of ALx as linguistic theory applied to language teaching
A view of praxis	Thought, desire, and action integrated as praxis	A hierarchy of theory and its application to different contexts
Being critical	Critical work engaged with social change	Critical thinking as an apolitical set of skills
Micro and macro relations	Relating aspects of applied linguistics to broader social, cultural, and political domains	Viewing classrooms, texts, and so on as isolated and autonomous
Critical social inquiry	Questions of access, power, disparity, desire, difference, and resistance	Mapping language onto a static model of society
Critical theory	Questions of inequality, injustice, rights, wrongs, and compassion	A view of social relations as largely equitable
Problematizing givens	The restive problematization of the given	Acceptance of the canon of received norms and ideas
Self-reflexivity	Constant questioning of itself	Lack of awareness of its own assumptions
Preferred futures	Grounded ethical arguments for alternatives	View that applied linguistics should not aim for change
Heterosis	The sum is greater than the parts and creates new schemas of politicization	The notion that: Politics + ALx = CALx

11

coverage of such domains is rather different from that of critical applied linguistics; critical pedagogy, for example, is used broadly across many areas of education. Second, there are many other domains— feminism, queer theory, postcolonialism, to name but a few—that do not operate under an explicit critical label but that clearly have a great deal of importance for the area. Third, it seems more constructive to view critical applied linguistics not merely as an amalgam of different parts, a piece of bricolage, or a metacategory of critical work but rather in more dynamic and productive terms. And finally, crucially, part of developing critical applied linguistics is developing a critical stance toward other areas of work, including other critical domains. Critical applied linguistics may borrow and use work from these other areas, but it should certainly only do so critically.

Nevertheless, there are clearly major affinities and overlaps between critical applied linguistics and other named critical areas such as critical literacy and critical discourse analysis. Critical literacy has less often been considered in applied linguistics, largely because of its greater orientation toward first language literacy, which has often not fallen within the perceived scope of applied linguistics. It is possible, however, to see critical literacy in terms of the pedagogical application of critical discourse analysis and therefore a quite central concern for critical applied linguistics. Critical Discourse Analysis (CDA) and critical literacy are sometimes also combined under the rubric of critical language awareness (CLA) since the aim of this work is to

> empower learners by providing them with a critical analytical framework to help them reflect on their own language experiences and practices and on the language practices of others in the institutions of which they are a part and in the wider society within which they live. (Clark & Ivanic, 1997, p. 217)

Critical approaches to literacy, according to Luke (1997a):

> are characterised by a commitment to reshape literacy education in the interests of marginalised groups of learners, who on the basis of gender, cultural and socioeconomic background have been excluded from access to the discourses and texts of dominant economies and cultures. (p. 143)

Luke and Freebody (1997) explain that

> although critical literacy does not stand for a unitary approach, it marks out a coalition of educational interests committed to engaging with the possibilities that the technologies of writing and other modes of inscription offer for social change, cultural diversity, economic equity, and political enfranchisement. (p. 1)

Thus, as Luke (1997a) goes on to argue, although critical approaches to literacy share an orientation toward understanding literacy (or literacies) as social practices related to broader social and political concerns, there are a number of different orientations to critical literacy, including Freirean-based critical pedagogy, feminist and poststructuralist approaches, and text analytic approaches. Critical discourse analysis would generally fall into this last category, aimed as it is at providing tools for the critical analysis of texts in context.

Summarizing work in CDA, Kress (1990) explains that unlike discourse analysis or text linguistics with their descriptive goals, CDA has "the larger political aim of putting the forms of texts, the processes of production of texts, and the process of reading, together with the structures of power that have given rise to them, into crisis." CDA aims to show how "linguistic-discursive practices" are linked to "the wider socio-political structures of power and domination" (p. 85). van Dijk (1993) explains CDA as a focus on "the role of discourse in the (re)production and challenge of dominance" (p. 249). And Fairclough (1995) explains that critical discourse analysis

> aims to systematically explore often opaque relationships of causality and determination between (a) discursive practices, events and texts, and (b) wider social and cultural structures, relations and processes; to investigate how such practices, events and texts arise out of and are ideologically shaped by relations of power and struggles over power. (p. 132)

Clearly, CDA will be an important tool for critical applied linguistics.

Critical Approaches to Translation

Other domains of textual analysis related to critical applied linguistics include critical approaches to translation. Such an approach would not be concerned so much with issues such as mistranslation in itself but rather the politics of translation, the ways in which translating and interpreting are related to concerns such as class, gender, difference, ideology and social context. Hatim and Mason's (1997) analysis of a parallel Spanish and English text published in the UNESCO *Courier* is a good example of how a form of critical discourse analysis across two texts reveals the ideological underpinnings of the translation. In this case, as they argue, the English translation of a Spanish text on ancient indigenous Mexican cultures reveals in many of its aspects a very different orientation toward other cultures, literacy, and colonialism. When *antiguos mexicanos* (ancient Mexicans) becomes *Indians, el hombre indígena* (indigenous man) becomes *pre-Columbian civilization,* and *sabios* (wise men) becomes *diviners,* it is evident that a particular discourse or ideology is at play. Hatim and Mason's analysis of lexical, cohesive, and other textual features leads them to conclude that the English translation here relays "an ideology which downplays the agency—and the value—of indigenous Mexicans and dissociates ... history from destiny" (pp. 158–159).

Looking more broadly at translation as a political activity, Venuti (1997) argues that the tendencies of translations to domesticate foreign cultures, the insistence on the possibility of value-free translation, the challenges to the notion of authorship posed by translation, the dominance of translation from English into other languages rather than in the other direction, and the need to unsettle local cultural hegemonies through the challenges of translation all point to the need for an approach to translation based on an *ethics of difference*. Such a stance, on the one hand, "urges that translations be written, read, and evaluated with greater respect for linguistic and cultural differences" (p. 6); on the other hand, it aims at "minoritizing the standard dialect and dominant cultural forms in American English" in part as "an opposition to the global hegemony of English" (p. 10). Such a stance clearly matches closely the forms of critical applied linguistics I have been outlining: it is based on an antihegemonic stance, locates itself within a view of language politics, is based on an ethics of difference, and tries in its practice to move towards change.

Work on translation and colonial and postcolonial studies is also of interest for critical applied linguistics. Niranjana (1991), for example, argues that:

> Translation as a practice shapes, and takes shape within, the asymmetrical relations of power that operate under colonialism .... In forming a certain kind of subject, in presenting particular versions of the colonized, translation brings into being overarching concepts of reality, knowledge, representation. These concepts, and what they allow us to assume, completely occlude the violence which accompanies the construction of the colonial subject. (pp. 124–125)

Postcolonial translation studies, then, are able to shed light on the processes by which translation, and the massive body of Orientalist, Aboriginalist, and other studies and translations of the Other, were so clearly complicit with the larger colonial project (Spivak, 1993). Once again, such work clearly has an important role to play in the development of critical applied linguistics.

Language Teaching

As I suggested earlier, language teaching has been a domain that has often been considered the principal concern of applied linguistics. Although my view of applied linguistics is a much broader one, language teaching nevertheless retains a significant role. In a recent edition of *TESOL Quarterly* that I edited, many of the different critical concerns in relation to language teaching were well represented. Awad Ibrahim (1999), for example, discusses how students from non-English-speaking African backgrounds studying in French schools in Canada "become Black" as they enter into the racialized world of North America. This process of becoming Black, as he demonstrates, is intimately tied up with the forms of English and popular culture with which these students start to identify. Class is the principal concern addressed by Angel Lin (1999) in her argument that particular ways of teaching English in Hong Kong (or elsewhere) may lead either to the reproduction or the transformation of class-based inequality. Ibrahim similarly asks what the implications are of his students identifying with marginality.

Gender runs as a theme through a number of other articles, including Rivera's (1999) and Frye's (1999) accounts of participatory research and curricula in immigrant women's education in the United States. Certainly, critical applied linguistics in the domain of language education would include many feminist approaches to language teaching (e.g., Sanguinetti, 1992/3; Schenke, 1991, 1996), or feminist research agendas (see Sunderland, 1994). Meanwhile, questions of sexuality and sexual identity are the focus of Cynthia Nelson's (1999) analysis of a period of discussion in an English as a second language (ESL) classroom about the implications of two women walking arm-in-arm down the street. Nelson shows the significance of Queer Theory for thinking about sexuality and identity in language classrooms. Other authors take different configurations of power and inequality as their focus. For Janina Brutt-Griffler and Keiko Samimy (1999), for example, it is the inequalities in the relation between the constructs of the Native and Nonnative speaker that need to be addressed, a concern that has become a major topic of discussion in recent years (e.g., Liu, 1999).

Other work that falls within the ambit of critical applied linguistics would be education or research that follows the work of Paulo Freire (and see also critical literacy). Auerbach and Wallerstein's (1987) or Graman's (1988) application of Freirean principles of problem posing to ESL classes are typical examples of this sort of work. Basing her work in a similar tradition, Walsh (1991) talks of *critical bilingualism* as

> the ability to not just speak two languages, but to be conscious of the sociocultural, political, and ideological contexts in which the languages (and therefore the speakers) are positioned and function, and the multiple meanings that are fostered in each. (p. 127)

Brian Morgan's (1997, 1998) work in a community center in Toronto also shows how critical practice in ESL can emerge from community concerns. As he suggests, "A community-based, critical ESL pedagogy doesn't mean neglecting language. It means organizing language around experiences that are immediate to students" (1998, p. 19).

Other critical approaches to questions around language education include Bonny Norton's (1995, 1997) work on *critical discourse research* and on particular ways in which student identities are linked to the processes of language learning. There is an increasing amount of much needed critical analysis of the interests and ideologies underlying the construction and interpretation of textbooks (see Dendrinos, 1992). There is critical analysis of curriculum design and needs analysis, including a proposal for doing "critical needs analysis" that "assumes that institutions are hierarchical and that those at the bottom are often entitled to more power than they have. It seeks areas where greater equality might be achieved" (Benesch, 1996, p. 736). Canagarajah's (1993, 1999b) use of critical ethnography to explore how students and teachers in the *periphery* resist and appropriate English and English teaching methods sheds important light on classroom processes in reaction to dominant linguistic and pedagogical forms: "It is important to understand the extent to which classroom resistance may play a significant role in larger transformations in the social sphere" (1999b, p. 196). Diverse as these studies are, they all show an interweaving of the themes discussed in the previous section with a range of concerns to do with language teaching.

Language Testing

As a fairly closely defined and practically autonomous domain of applied linguistics and one that has generally adhered to positivist approaches to research and knowledge, language testing has long been fairly resistant to critical challenges. In a plenary address to the American Association of Applied Linguistics, however, Elana Shohamy (1997) discussed what she saw as crucial features of critical language testing (CLT). CLT starts with the assumption that "the act of language testing is not neutral. Rather, it is a product and agent of cultural, social, political, educational and ideological agendas that shape the lives of individual participants, teachers, and learners" (p. 2). She goes on to suggest several key features of CLT: Test takers are seen as "political subjects in a political context"; tests are "deeply embedded in cultural, educational and political arenas where different ideological social forms are in struggle," making it impossible to consider that a test is just a test; CLT asks whose agendas are implemented through tests; it demands that language testers ask what vision of society tests presuppose; it asks whose knowledge the test is based on and whether this knowledge is negotiable; it considers the meaning of test scores and the extent to which this is open to interpretation; and it challenges psychometric traditions of language testing (and supports "interpretive" approaches). According to Shohamy, such a view of language testing signifies an important paradigm shift and puts many new criteria for understanding validity into play: consequential, systemic, interpretive, and ethical, all of which have more to do with the effects of tests than with criteria of internal validity.

Shohamy's (1997) proposal for critical language testing clearly matches many of the principles that define other areas of critical applied linguistics: Her argument is that language testing is always political, that we need to become increasingly aware of the effects (consequential validity) of tests, and that the way forward is to develop more "democratic" tests in which test takers and other local bodies are given greater involvement. Thus, there is a demand to see a domain of applied linguistics, from classrooms to texts and tests, as inherently bound up with larger social, cultural, and political contexts. This ties in with Peirce and Stein's (1995) concerns about different possible interpretations of texts in tests and the question of whose reading is acknowledged: "If test makers are drawn from a particular class, a particular race, and a particular gender, then test takers who share these characteristics will be at an advantage relative to other test takers" (p. 62). Importantly, too, Shohamy critiques not only what has gone before but also the politics of knowledge that informs previous approaches. Thus, there is a critique of positivism and psychometric testing with their emphases on blind measurement rather than situated forms of knowledge. There is a demand to establish what a preferred vision of society is and a call to make one's applied linguistic practice accountable to such a vision. And there are suggestions for different practices that might start to change how testing is done. All these are clearly aspects of CLT that bring it comfortably within the ambit of critical applied linguistics.

Language Planning and Language Rights

One domain of applied linguistics that might be assumed to fall easily into the scope of critical applied linguistics is work such as language policy and planning since it would appear from the outset to operate with a political view of language. Yet, as I suggested in the previous section, it is not enough merely to draw connections between language and the social world; a critical approach to social relations is also required. There is nothing inherently critical about language policy; indeed, part of the problem, as Tollefson (1991) observes, has been precisely the way in which language policy has been uncritically developed and implemented. According to Luke, McHoul, and Mey (1990), while maintaining a "veneer of scientific objectivity," language planning has "tended to avoid directly addressing larger social and political matters within which language change, use and development, and indeed language planning itself are embedded" (p. 27).

More generally, sociolinguistics has been severely critiqued by critical social theorists for its use of a static, liberal view of society and thus its inability to deal with questions of social justice (see Williams, 1992). As Mey (1985) suggests, by avoiding questions of social inequality in class terms and instead correlating language variation with superficial measures of social stratification, traditional sociolinguistics fails to "establish a connection between people's place in the societal hierarchy, and the linguistic and other kinds of oppression that they are subjected to at different levels" (p. 342). Cameron (1995) has also pointed to the need to develop a view of language and society that goes beyond a view that language reflects society, suggesting that:

> In critical theory language is treated as part of the explanation. Whereas sociolinguistics would say that the way I use language reflects or marks my identity as a particular kind of social subject ... the critical account suggests language is one of the things that *constitutes* my identity as a particular kind of subject. Sociolinguistics says that how you act depends on who you are; critical theory says that who you are (and are taken to be) depends on how you act. (pp. 15–16)

Taking up Mey's (1985) call for a "critical sociolinguistics" (p. 342), therefore, critical applied linguistics would need to incorporate views of language, society, and power that are capable of dealing with questions of access, power, disparity, and difference and that see language as playing a crucial role in the construction of difference.

Two significant domains of sociolinguistics that have developed broad critical analyses are first work on language and gender (Cameron, 1995; Coates, 1998; → chap. 6) and second, work on language rights. Questions about the dominance of certain languages over others have been raised most tellingly by Phillipson (1992) through his notion of (English) linguistic imperialism and his argument that English has been spread for economic and political purposes, and poses a major threat to other languages. The other side of this argument has then been taken up through arguments for language rights (e.g., Phillipson & Skutnabb-Kangas, 1996; Tollefson, 1991). As Skutnabb-Kangas (1988) argues, "we are still living with linguistic wrongs" that are a product of the belief in the normality of monolingualism and the dangers of multilingualism to the security of the nation state. Both, she suggests, are dangerous myths. "Unless we work fast," she argues, "excising the cancer of monolingual reductionism may come too late, when the patient, the linguistic (and cultural) diversity in the world, is already beyond saving" (p. 12). What is proposed, then, is that the "right to identify with, to maintain and to fully develop one's mother tongue(s)" should be acknowledged as "a self-evident, fundamental *individual* linguistic human right" (p. 22). Critical applied linguistics, then, would include work in the areas of sociolinguistics and language planning and policy that takes up an overt political agenda to establish or to argue for policy along lines that focus centrally on issues of social justice.

Language, Literacy, and Workplace Settings

Another domain of work in applied linguistics that has been taken up with a critical focus has been the work on uses of language and literacy in various workplace and professional settings. Moving beyond work that attempts only to describe the patterns of communication or genres of interaction between people in medical, legal, or other workplace settings, critical applied linguistic approaches to these contexts of communication focus far more on questions of access, power, disparity, and difference. Such approaches also attempt to move toward active engagement with and change in these contexts. Examples of this sort of work would include Wodak's (1996) study of hospital encounters:

> In doctor-patient interaction in the outpatient clinics we have investigated, discursive disorders establish certain routines and justify the actions of the powerful. Doctors exercise power over their patients, they ask the questions, they interrupt and introduce new topics, they control the conversation. (p. 170)

An important aspect of this work has been to draw connections between workplace uses of language and relations of power at the institutional and broader social levels. Recently, the rapid changes in workplace practices and the changing needs of new forms of literacy have attracted considerable attention. Gee, Hull, and Lankshear (1996), for example, look at the effects of the new work order under new capitalism on language and literacy practices in the workplace. Poynton (1993b), meanwhile, draws attention to the danger that "workplace restructuring" may "exacerbate the marginalised status of many women" not only because of the challenge of changing workplace skills and technologies but also because of the failure to acknowledge in language the character and value of women's skills. Women's interactive oral skills as well as their literacy skills have often failed to be acknowledged in workplaces. Poynton goes on to discuss a project designed to change these workplace naming practices.

One thing that emerges here is the way in which critical concerns are intertwined. Crawford's (1999) study of communication between patients, nurses, and doctors in Cape Town, South Africa, health services, for example, highlights the complexities of relations between Xhosa-speaking patients, nurses operating as interpreters, and predominantly White doctors. As Crawford explains:

> The power relations that operate to the detriment of patients in our health-care system are complex and are unlikely to be drastically modified by supplying a single "missing commodity" like paid interpretation, without the institution's actual commitment to a general strategy of changing to a more culturally sensitive patient-centered model of care (pp. 41–42)

Not only are the framing issues discussed in the previous section ever present here, but also both the domains described in this section—critical approaches to discourse, translation, bilingualism, language policy, pedagogy—and the underlying social relations of race, class, gender, and other constructions of difference are all at work together. The interrelation between the concerns (discussed earlier) and the domains (discussed here) of critical applied linguistics are outlined in Fig. 1.1.

CONCLUSION: WHY CRITICAL APPLIED LINGUISTICS?

Outline

The two main strands of this opening chapter—different aspects and domains of critical applied linguistics—have helped give a broad overview of what I consider this work to cover and to entail. This list, however, is neither complete nor discrete: It is by no means exhaustive, and the categories I have established overlap with each other in a number of ways. I do not intend in the rest of the book merely to continue to summarize areas

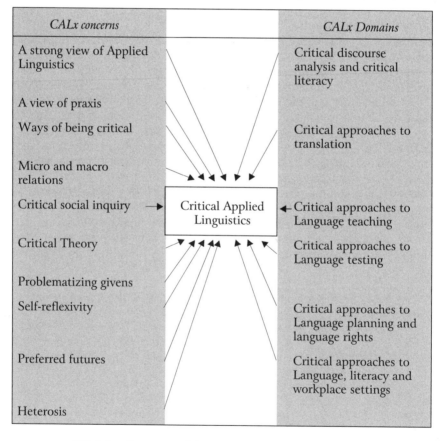

FIG. 1.1.   Concerns and domains of critical applied linguistics.

of critical applied linguistic work. Rather, the intention will be to discuss, critically, major themes than run throughout this work. A number of general concerns already emerge from the aforementioned aspects and domains: How do we understand relations between language and power? How can people resist power in and through language? How do we understand questions of difference in relation to language, education, or literacy? How does ideology operate in relation to discourse? The following chapters, therefore, deal with the politics of knowledge, the politics of language, the politics of texts, the politics of pedagogy, and the politics of difference (see Table 1.3).

Nevertheless, as I pause and reflect on the arguments, boxes, charts, structures, domains, theories, and terms that are starting to proliferate here, I also have my doubts. Is this a task with any relevance outside the academic discipline of applied linguistics? Is this a pointless exercise in positioning, defining, and explaining? So finally: Why write an introduction to critical applied linguistics? Why am I doing this? (Why indeed? I ask myself, when my eyelids droop and my head hurts, and I struggle to get my head around some of the difficult material here.) It might be suggested that my goal here is to define and claim this domain of work for myself. But while I have to acknowledge that writing this book will likely attach critical applied linguistics to my name ("Pennycook, 2001"), my goal here is not to develop a model for critical applied linguistics. Rather, my aim is to explore its complexities. The motivation comes out of 10 years of trying to relate critical work in many domains to my own fields of practice in applied linguistics. It comes out of trying to teach a course on critical applied linguistics. It comes out of the frustration of trying to figure out what is going on in different discussions or articles on critical discourse analysis, feminist pedagogy, or multiliteracies. And it also comes out of a conviction that this stuff matters, that the many discussions I have had about this work around the world suggest some significant shared struggles.

Surely, an approach to issues in language education, communication in the workplace, translation, and literacy that focuses on questions of power, difference, access, and domination ought to be central to our concerns. Two last meanings of *critical* that can also be given some space here are the notion of *critical* as important or crucial: a critical moment, a critical time in one's life, a critical illness; and critical as used in maths and physics to suggest the point that marks the change from one state to another, as in critical angle or critical mass. To the extent that I believe that this critical version of applied linguistics that I am presenting here is crucial, important, and deals with some of the central issues in language use and to the extent that it may also signal a point at which applied linguistics may finally move into a new state of being, these senses of *critical* also need to be included in an understanding of critical applied linguistics.

Discussing the broader social and political issues to do with literacy and language education, James Gee (1994) offers teachers a choice: either

TABLE 1.3

Overview of the Book

Chapter	Areas Covered	Critical Notions and Theories
Chapter 1: Introducing CALx	General overview; concerns and domains of CALx	Praxis; heterosis; problematizing practice; ways of being critical
Chapter 2: The Politics of Knowledge	The role of theory; conjunctions between knowledge and politics in relation to CALx	Power; liberalism, structuralism, emancipatory modernism; awareness; problematizing practice
Chapter 3: The Politics of Language	Critical sociolinguistics; language and power; approaches to language policy and global English	Language rights; linguistic imperialism; postcolonialism; resistance and appropriation
Chapter 4: The Politics of Texts	Critical literacy; literacy as social practice; critical discourse analysis; critical language awareness; access	Discourse and ideology; production and reception; poststructuralism and postlinguistics
Chapter 5: The Politics of Pedagogy	Critical approaches to education; theories of social reproduction; critical pedagogy	Social, cultural, and symbolic capital; structure, agency, and resistance; postmodernism and ethics
Chapter 6: The Politics of Difference	Constructions of difference; gender, identity	Performativity; queer theory; pedagogies of engagement
Chapter 7: Applied Linguistics With an Attitude	Summary and argument against reification of CALx	Diffusing a critical attitude throughout applied linguistics

to "cooperate in their own marginalization by seeing themselves as 'language teachers' with no connection to such social and political issues" or to accept that they are involved in a crucial domain of political work: "Like it or not, English teachers stand at the very heart of the most crucial educational, cultural, and political issues of our time" (p. 190). Given the significance of the even broader domain I am interested in here—language, literacy, communication, translation, bilingualism, and pedagogy—and the particular concerns to do with the global role of languages, multilingualism, power, and possibilities for the creation of difference—it would not seem too far-fetched to suggest that critical applied linguistics may at least give us ways of dealing with some of the most crucial educational, cultural, and political issues of our time.

Chapter 2

The Politics of Knowledge

Critical Work and Animosity to Theory
Knowledge of Politics and the Politics of Knowledge
    Liberal Ostrichism
    Anarcho-Autonomy
    Emancipatory Modernism
    Critical Applied Linguistics as Problematizing Practice
Conclusion: Outflanking Marx From the Left

So far, I have tried to sketch out what I understand critical applied linguistics to be by summarizing various key concerns and domains of work. But since this book is intended to be far more than just an overview of critical work and since an attempt to cover in depth all the domains outlined in the last chapter (← chap. 1) would make it too vast an enterprise, I have chosen to address key themes that cut across the different domains of critical applied linguistics. These will be discussed under the chapter headings: "The Politics of Language" (→ chap. 3), "The Politics of Texts" (→ chap. 4), "The Politics of Pedagogy" (→ chap. 5), and "The Politics of Difference" (→ chap. 6). In this chapter, I focus on some crucial background concerns to do with knowledge, politics and power. This is not, however, intended as a theoretical chapter. A typical way of doing applied linguistics, indeed a typical model for a great deal of academic writing, is to place the theory early on in a take-it-or-leave-it position before moving on to applications. The approach I have taken here, by contrast, is to interweave ideas and domains of practice throughout the book. As I suggested (← chap. 1), critical applied linguistics needs to develop ways of operating that go beyond the theory/practice divide of so much applied linguistic work. A brief discussion of theory and animosity to theory may be useful here.

CRITICAL WORK AND ANIMOSITY TO THEORY

One of the problems with discussing critical work is that for some, it may seem that we don't need to deal with theory. Such an argument may derive from a number of different positions: Critical work is a matter of critical thinking, which may be either an already culturally or educationally developed orientation about which little can be done, or a set of skills that can be taught (Atkinson, 1997; for a critique, see Benesch, 1999). A very different position suggests that critical work is merely a matter of leftist politics added to whatever domain and thus is a reasonably simple conjunction of ideology plus applied linguistics. Yet another position would suggest that critical work is basically common sense and that to critique ideological manipulation, all we need is to avoid being duped. Finally, there is the argument that doing critical work is about getting out there, working in the community, writing letters, marching; or from an applied linguistic perspective, critical work is teaching, translating, operating in workplaces. Doing theory is a waste of time. Who needs to talk about difference, poststructuralism, subjectivity, agency, and so on when the real issues are out there, on the streets, in the communities?

Weedon (1987) points out that there is feminist tradition of hostility toward theory, a position based on the one hand on the argument that theorizing, and particularly dominant forms of Western rationality, have long been part of patriarchal power and control over women and on the other hand that women need to draw on their own experiences to guide political action. Weedon's argument, however, is that while both positions need to be taken very seriously, they should not constitute an argument against theory, so that "rather than turning our backs on theory and taking refuge in experience alone, we should think in terms of transforming both the social relations of knowledge production and the type of knowledge produced" (p. 7). In other words, feminism—or, as I am arguing, critical applied linguistics—needs forms of critical theory that can help inform our thinking about social structure, knowledge, politics, pedagogy, practice, the individual, or language. But, this critical theory should be accessible and should constantly be a questioning critical theory—a restive problematization of the given—a critical theory that takes knowledge and its production as part of its critical exploration.

Roger Simon (1992) has also discussed this question of what he calls a "fear of theory," pointing out that this should not be seen as an individual reaction or inability to deal with difficult ideas but rather part of the complex social relations that surround knowledge, language, and academic institutions. Significantly, he points then to the need for education to "be directed not so much at the lack of knowledge as to resistances to knowledge" (p. 95). On the one hand, then, some may feel that critical thinking and work is already part of what they do and that dealing with texts that complicate the issues is therefore an unnecessary distraction; and on the other hand, there is a reluctance to deal with theory, a rejection of what is seen as abstruse, abstract, academic, and an unhelpful wordiness that avoids the actual issues of political engagement: an unnecessary abstraction. There is, of course, something to be said for both elements of this argument: We *do* need to stay engaged with all levels of political action, and there *is* a great deal of difficult and unnecessarily abstruse work claiming nevertheless to be somehow politically engaged. Certainly, many "critical theorists" need to accept a large measure of blame here: Far too little has been done to make critical academic work more accessible or to show, at the very least, pathways that connect theory and practice. Writers in areas such as critical pedagogy have been quite rightly criticized for their bombastic and obscurantist prose (Gore, 1993). And others have suggested that the constant use of words such as *revolutionary* and *radical* is "mere posturing. I personally do not feel the need to dress up what I do in pseudorevolutionary bluster" (Johnston, 1999, p. 563).

Nonetheless, I wish to make a case here for the importance of a level of engagement with some key issues in critical theory. Teaching a course in critical applied linguistics over the last few years, I became increasingly aware that not only did the course presuppose a knowledge of many domains of applied linguistics—second language acquisition, translation, sociolinguistics, and so on—but also a knowledge of many concepts in critical theory—determinism, agency, discourse, post-structuralism, and so on. Although we do not necessarily need to share the same political outlook on various issues, we do need ways of understanding what our differences are, to go beyond tossing around terms such as *oppression, inequality, imperialism, racism, ideology,* and so forth without a clear understanding of how such terms invoke different understandings of the world. If we are to take critical applied linguistics seriously, we need to understand the different forms of background knowledge that inform it. By analogy, if one was doing research on young children learning to write in school, one would be expected to have a good grasp of background theoretical work on areas such as literacy, primary education, and child development; similarly, if we are to take critical applied linguistics seriously, we need not only to understand key issues in applied linguistics but also to have a reasonable grasp of how concepts such as ideology, discourse, capital, sexuality, or agency can be understood. Rather than writing a chapter on critical theory, however, I have opted to try to bring it in when relevant. This book, then, will try to interweave critical theory and applied linguistics to produce a critical applied linguistic perspective.

I have given myself a tough challenge here, and to be honest, I continue to have doubts about the extent to which I have been able to meet it in this book. I have tried to make the theoretical perspectives that I introduce accountable in several ways: First, they must be made as accessible as possible. This, more generally, is a goal of this book, an attempt to make critical applied linguistics accessible. Second, I have tried not to present theory as a fixed body of immutable thought but rather as critical theory that is always prepared to turn a critical eye on itself. And third, this must be critical theory that can show its importance for political and educational practice. I endeavor throughout, therefore, to relate these ideas directly to issues in (critical) applied linguistics. But this has been hard work; moving across so many domains, trying to tie together so many varied approaches to critical work, and trying to locate ideas within different domains of practice have made it hard to maintain a good balance. I also ask, therefore, for the assistance of my readers to help with the ongoing project of making the ideas accessible, of continuing to turn a critical eye on the theory, and of relating the concerns to the many sites of practice with which critical applied linguistics is involved. Meanwhile, in the rest of this chapter, I discuss different configurations of knowledge, politics and language.

KNOWLEDGE OF POLITICS AND THE POLITICS OF KNOWLEDGE

A key term that reoccurs throughout this book is *politics*; indeed, I have even chosen to organize the book around themes such as the politics of language and the politics of pedagogy. This notion of politics has less to do with formal political domains (governments, elections, or state institutions) and more to do with the workings of power. Areas of interest such as *language policy* are sometimes taken to represent the political focus of applied linguistics because they have to do most often with governmental decisions about the use and status of languages. Yet I want to resist this view that politics has to do with policy making or with the more formal domain of politics or that language policy and planning is more political than other domains. Rather, the notion of politics I am using here takes as its central concern the notion of power and views power as operating through all domains of life. Power is at the heart of questions of discourse, disparity, and difference.

The crucial unexamined "given," then, is power. It is, generally speaking, some notion of power that underlies all critical or political analyses. But what is power? And, crucially, how do we relate it to language? The notion of power also sits at the heart of the term *empowerment*, and if we are to salvage anything useful for this bland and overused term, we need to know what version of power we are dealing with. One of the difficulties with the notion of power is that it is used so widely to mean so much (or so little). Consider, for example, some of its popular contemporary uses: power dressing, power to the people, money is power, the power of love. Power corrupts. There are the rich and powerful, the power behind the throne, and the vague "powers that be." Going beyond these general uses of the term, we might pursue the notion of power in the political domain. A liberal democratic view of politics tends to locate power in the government, and thus one political party is "in power" until a different party is voted into power. Most are aware, however, that behind the veneer of politics, there are many others that "hold power" or "wield power," and these may be anything from a general notion of the state to international capital, the aristocracy, or the media. Different political visions have different conceptions of how power can be shared, seized, or redistributed. Such general political domains start to give us some important metaphors for thinking about power: Does empowerment mean handing power over? Or does it mean helping others to seize, diffuse, share, consolidate, or redistribute power? These questions all imply different understandings of what power is, how it operates, and what strategies we should adopt in the face of power.

It is important, therefore, to distinguish between notions of power that focus on the individual and more sociological and critical versions of power. If we see power as something an individual has (a person has power over another; she or he is a powerful person), we miss the importance of understanding where power comes from, how it is socially constructed and maintained. But if we focus for too long on the broad structures of power, we may be left with an overdeterministic version of structural power. Critical applied linguistics needs ways of understanding how power operates on and through people in the ongoing tasks of teaching, learning languages, translating, talking to clients. If, for example, we acknowledge that men are powerful in relation to women, we need to ask how this operates, how it came to be, and what strategies should be adopted to oppose it. Different feminist approaches to language and gender may aim to seize power from men, to give greater power to women so that they are equal, to share power with men, or to diffuse the types of power that give men their ascendancy. And if we acknowledge an important role for language in the construction and maintenance of power relations, then we need to ask how power operates in and through language and what different versions of change we would then advocate. Do we need to change society first in order to change language? Is the issue one of giving people access to powerful forms of language? Can we change the way language is used in order to change how power is reproduced?

A key focus of critical applied linguistics, then, is to ask broad questions about language and power. Whether in John Honey's (1997) *Language is Power,* Norman Fairclough's (1989) *Language and Power,* Pierre Bourdieu's (1991) *Language and Symbolic Power,* Robyn Lakoff's (1990) *Talking power: The Politics of Language,* or Michel Foucault's (1980b)

Power/Knowledge, we need to know how language relates to power. This is a key theme throughout this book, and we return to a discussion of Foucault, Bourdieu, and others at various points. In the main part of this chapter, however, I want to explore different ways of understanding politics in relation to applied linguistics. The key questions here are: What different forms of politics (by which, as I suggested, we are really talking about understandings of power) can be allied with applied linguistics to form critical applied linguistics? And what understanding of knowledge do different conjunctions produce? For critical applied linguistics, then, the notion of politics needs to be seen as encompassing not just those areas that are more readily understood as social or political but, rather, all domains of life. How we understand relations between politics, knowledge, and language will greatly affect how we look at critical applied linguistics. I outline four different positions on the relation between politics and knowledge, all of which might in one way or another make a claim to have potential for critical applied linguistics (see Table 2.1). I do not deal at any length here with a potential fifth position, one that combines conservative politics and applied linguistics. Such a position might on some levels make a claim to being a form of critical applied linguistics (as a politicized form of applied linguistics that aims at critique), but since conservativism is an anathema for my vision of critical applied linguistics (e.g., in terms of its transformative vision), I do not dwell on this possibility.

Liberal Ostrichism

The first position, which is probably the most commonly held in applied linguistics, is what I call a centrist-autonomous (or liberal-ostrich) position. It espouses various forms of liberal or conservative politics but sees no particular connection between such politics and applied linguistic knowledge. Although this position may espouse any number of different approaches to research (from positivistic to more hermeneutic approaches), it takes such knowledge production to be an autonomous realm that is not connected to more general political views. Although it may not seem an obvious candidate for claims to be involved in critical applied linguistics, it is the apolitical orientation of critical thinking or literary criticism that has led proponents such as Widdowson (1999) to claim that this is what critical applied linguistics should really be. Arguing that applied linguistics should remain detached from political views, Widdowson suggests that it is the disinterested stance of rational inquiry rather than politicized orientations to applied linguistics ("hypocritical applied linguistics" in Widdowson's terms) that brings a true critical stance to applied linguistics. It may be useful, therefore, to explore a little further the background to a stance that tends to deny its own politics.

TABLE 2.1

Four Relations Between Knowledge and Politics

Framework	Epistemology & Politics	Relation to Language	Usefulness for Critical Applied Linguistics (CALx)
Liberal ostrichism	Liberalism and structuralism; critical as objective detachment; egalitarianism	Denies both its own politics and the politics of language	Mainstream applied linguistics: claims that the critical is nonpolitical; strongly opposed to CALx
Anarcho-autonomy	Anarcho-syndicalism and rationalism, realism, and positivism	Disconnects the political from the academic analysis of language	Opposed to CALx as confusing the political and the scientific
Emancipatory modernism	Scientific leftism: neo-Marxist politics and scientific analysis; macro structures of domination	Seeks to analyze relations between language and the social and political	Powerful critiques, limited by determinism, inflexibility, and belief in emancipation
Problematizing practices	Poststructuralism, postmodernism, postcolonialism, and other post positions	Views language as already political; analysis of the social through language	Constant questioning of applied linguistics; self reflexive; possible relativism and irrealism

Crucial in the formation of this view has been the conjunction between liberalism and structuralism. As a broad intellectual movement that emerged in the early to mid part of the 20th century principally in Europe and the United States, structuralism focuses on systems as entities in themselves, trying to establish how the structure of a system is made up of interrelated constituent parts. The work of the linguist Ferdinand de Saussure was the inspiration for much of this orientation. In his ground-breaking work, Saussure emphasized the importance of looking at language as a system, as a series of underlying structures. Thus, he suggested, the proper study of linguistics was not the surface features of everyday language or historical (diachronic) change in language but rather the (synchronic) underlying system; not the moves made in a chess game but the rules that define those moves. This view of structure was to influence many other areas of inquiry, including anthropology (where Claude Levi-Strauss stressed the importance of looking at areas such as myths in terms of their internal, relational structures), literary criticism, sociology, and more.

The most important characteristic of structuralism, then, is its focus on large-scale structures and their underlying principles. Because of the tendency to reduce the role of human agency in relation to structure, structuralism is often seen as somewhat antihumanist. Also highly significant was the connection between structuralism and positivism, or a belief in the investigation of the "human sciences" along lines similar to the natural sciences. The growth of structuralism as an intellectual movement was thus extremely important in challenging the elitism, evolutionism, and progressivism of earlier models of the social world. Structuralism as it developed in linguistics, sociology and anthropology helped move thinking away from a hierarchical view of values with primitive languages, cultures, and societies on the bottom and developed languages, cultures, and societies on the top. Instead, it urged us not to judge or evaluate from some external position but rather to describe from the inside. What mattered was how the internal structure of things worked, not their external relations. Not only were linguists then able to explore the complex inner workings of languages (showing indeed that so-called primitive languages were highly complex), but they were also able to argue that all languages were equal in that they served the needs of their speakers equally.

Such a view was anathema to more conservative, hierarchical views of difference. Here, for example, is Lincoln Burnett (1962) on what he saw as the damage done by structural linguistics:

> To almost everyone who cherishes the English language for its grace and beauty, its combination of precision and flexibility, the social philosophy of the Structural Linguists seems past comprehension—epitomizing indeed the "anti-intellectualism of the intellectual." Among all the forces of cultural vandalism at work in the country, their influence has been, perhaps, the most insidious. The vulgarities of advertising and mudflows of jargon can be shoveled aside. But the impact of the Structural Linguists is like that of slow atomic fallout: through their influence on teachers' colleges and teachers, hence on the schools and the pupils within them, they are incapacitating the coming generation. And the paradoxical aspect of their assault on the English language is that they claim to be motivated only by the purest democratic principles. (p. 221)

What Burnett and, more recently, Honey (1997), in his similar diatribe against the evils of linguistics, object to is the democratic egalitarianism of structural linguistics, which suggests that rather than prescriptive accounts of what should be, we need descriptive accounts of what is. Thus, it has become almost axiomatic in linguistics and sociolinguistics that all so-called dialects have grammars equal in all respects to those of so-called languages. Apparently *deviant* forms are explained in terms of their own structural consistencies. Thus, in anything from descriptions of Black English to descriptions of learners' interlanguages, there has been a strong tendency to accept and to describe, to look at supposed deviances in their own structural terms and to argue against any view that tries to relate such differences to a notion of deficit. Dialects, accents, language learners' language, and so on are all seen as different but logically coherent and in no way deficient. Similarly, work in literacy has sought to show that the home literacy practices of children from disadvantaged backgrounds are not so much deficient as different from those of middle-class homes and schools.

To the extent that structuralist egalitarianism has often successfully countered conservative calls for standards and denunciations of deviance, they have been politically significant. But there are several further points worth considering here. It is important to keep in mind the fact that structuralism in linguistics has grown up as a predominantly liberal defense against the more hawkish attitudes of the Right. Thus, it is not, as it might seem to many of us who have grown up with such structuralism as the standard received wisdom of applied linguistics, some neutral ground of scientific linguistics but is rather frequently tied to a distinct political position. Thus, as Milroy (1999) points out, linguists' views on the equality of languages are not "innocent linguistic pronouncements"; rather, they are "overtly and deliberately ideological, and it is disingenuous to pretend otherwise" (p. 20). Structuralism and liberalism are not inevitably linked—forms of structuralist analysis have also been closely tied to neo-Marxist sociology, for example—but they have become comfortable bedfellows, with structuralism supporting liberal pluralism (all structures are equal) and liberalism supporting structural isolation (if all structures are equal, why look elsewhere for inequality?).

Rampton (1995b) has suggested that we should be wary of spending too much time criticizing liberalism when it is conservativism that is most obviously opposed to a critical standpoint. But the problem with liberalism is that by appealing to a middle-of-the-road, commonsense, middle-class philosophy, it claims the constant middle ground of "reasonableness" and thus detracts from the possibility of more sustained critique. With its claims to scientificity (description) that obscure its underlying politics and a tendency always to deal with internal structures rather than external connections, this centrist-autonomous position mirrors Saussure's original distinction between *internal* and *external* linguistics. Thus, the structuralism of linguistics and sociolinguistics that commendably allows for the nonjudgmental view that all dialects are equal is also the view that has not allowed for an adequate understanding of how languages are complexly related to social and cultural factors, ignoring, therefore, profound questions of social difference, inequality, and conflict. Applied linguistics has been dominated by this bland egalitarianism that does not help us in framing questions of inequality, language and power. From my point of view, this denial of its own politics, this refusal to take into account broader social and political concerns, makes this an ostrich-like (head in the sand) approach to applied linguistics. Indeed, I would reverse Widdowson's (1999) labels and call this hypocritical applied linguistics (→ chap. 7).

Anarcho-Autonomy

While the liberal ostrichist position has laid claim to being a form of critical applied linguistics, it is generally opposed to the vision of critical applied linguistics I am trying to develop here. Another position that also is generally at odds with critical applied linguistics is what I call the anarcho-autonomous position, combining a more radical leftist politics with a view that this nevertheless has nothing to do with applied linguistics. The best known proponent of such a position in a related field is Noam Chomsky. It might appear that there is little point in discussing this position since its linguistic theory is of minimal relevance to applied domains and its view on knowledge and politics does not lend itself to adoption in critical applied linguistics. Nevertheless, there are important reasons for giving some space to these views: First, the political and epistemological frameworks I present in this chapter are common but not inherent conjunctions; thus, it is interesting to consider how and why they fit together but also important to see how they might not and what other possible conjunctions there may be (the same can be said of the liberal-structuralist position I outlined earlier). Second, Chomsky presents an interesting case of a public intellectual known both for his linguistic and for his political work. Third, although these two strands of his work seem separate, they do connect at certain levels and thus present an intriguing political and philosophical position with implications for understanding the politics of knowledge. And finally, there are well-known applied linguistic researchers, such as Mike Long, who share a similar orientation toward anarcho-syndicalist politics on the one hand (see Long, 1996) and rationalism and realism on the other.

The central question that arises from work such as Chomsky's is how his political work matches with his linguistic work. Politically, Chomsky defines himself as an anarcho-syndicalist or libertarian socialist, a radical tradition that draws on the thinking of Wilhelm von Humboldt, Mikhail Bakunin, John Dewey, Bertrand Russell, and Rudolf Rocker, among others. Current versions of this position tend to share a Marxist analysis of capitalism while eschewing Marxist analyses of state power and proletarian revolution in favor of "a federated, decentralized system of free associations, incorporating economic as well as other social institutions" (Chomsky, 1974, p. 169). The goals of this position, therefore, are to:

overcome the elements of repression and oppression and destruction and coercion that exist in any existing society ... [to oppose] centralised auto-cratic control of ... economic institutions ... either private capitalism or state totalitarianism or the various mixed forms of state capitalism ... [that] are all vestiges that have to be overthrown, eliminated in favor of direct par-ticipation in the form of workers' councils or other free associations that in-dividuals will constitute themselves for the purpose of their social existence and their productive labor. (p. 169)

Chomsky's political work has focused particularly on critiques of Ameri-can and international foreign policy in contexts such as Vietnam and East Timor and the role of transnational corporations and the media (Herman & Chomsky, 1988).

So how does this political position mesh with a linguistics that eschews external connections, real language use, context, or politics? There are two main things to consider here: first, the overall philosophical position of Chomsky and similar thinkers and, second, the underlying coherence between the positions. The aspects of Chomsky's worldview that are of in-terest here might be summarized as comprising rationalism, realism, mentalism, creativity, and freedom. This means he is committed to ratio-nalism, as opposed to empiricism, in research and rationality as the key guiding principle for thought. His realism means a belief that "the con-structs and entities he develops deal with real features of the world, just as the constructs of chemistry or biology do" (Smith, 1999, p. 137). Mentalism refers both to his emphasis on the innateness of linguistic (and other) competencies and to his attempt to "understand the workings of the human mind within the framework of the natural sciences" (Smith, 1999, p. 143). Finally, his libertarianism centers on his belief that hu-mans should be free from constraint.

The connection between these positions is not always evident. Accord-ing to Chomsky (1979):

> There is no very direct connection between my political activities, writing and others, and the work bearing on language structure, though in some measure they perhaps derive from certain assumptions and attitudes with regard to basic aspects of human nature. (p. 3)

Chomsky's politics and academic work do come together at one level, therefore—in his view of a universal human nature, of which the innate capacity for language is one aspect: "It is the humanistic conception of man that is advanced and given substance as we discover the rich systems of invariant structures and principles that underlie the most ordinary and humble of human accomplishments" (Chomsky, 1971, p. 46). As Newmeyer (1986) explains, although a view of innateness is often seen as politically suspect from a critical standpoint, Chomsky "sees such a con-ception in an entirely positive political light: our genetic inheritance—our human nature—prevents us from being plastic, infinitely malleable beings subjugable to the whims of outside forces" (p. 76). For Chomsky, he continues, "universal grammar unites all people, it does not divide them" (p. 77). Thus, for Chomsky, "there are two intellectual tasks." The first is to develop a "humanistic social theory" based on "some firm concept of the human essence or human nature." The second is to "understand very clearly the nature of power and oppression and terror and destruction in our own society" (Chomsky, 1974, p. 172).

Interesting as this position is, and potentially significant to critical applied linguistics as such anarchist politics may be, the particular political philosophy developed by Chomsky remains of little use for critical applied linguistics. It also puts into place a number of problematic propositions. First, the separation of the study of language from political questions places this position close to the liberal structuralism outlined earlier. What is significant here is the way in which a combination of a humanist belief in underlying similarity and a commitment to philosophical realism, scientific rationalism, and radical politics can lead to a position that once again disconnects the political from the theoretical. Second, Chomsky's divide between his linguistics and his political work means that the former is seen as conceptually difficult, while "the analysis of ideology" requires nothing but "a bit of open-mindedness, normal intelligence, and healthy skepticism" (Chomsky, 1979, p. 3). Chomsky draws a contrast between the linguistic challenge posed by "Plato's problem" (How can we know so much with such limited input?) and the political challenge posed by "Orwell's problem" (How can we remain so ignorant in the face of such contrary evidence? see Smith, 1999). His commitment to rationalism means he answers the first question not with empirical data but rather with attempts to theorize underlying mental structures, while the second question is answered via massive documentation of political, economic, and media self-interest. The problem here, then, is that by contrasting the inaccessibility of linguistic science with the accessibility of ideology critique, this position overestimates the complexity of problems of language and underestimates the need to understand ideology, politics, truth, and manipulation in more complex ways.

Third, the humanist or universalist position that underlies both the search for underlying human commonalities (from human nature to universal grammar) and the political critique focuses problematically on similarity rather than difference and locates freedom as an intrinsic property of being human. Although the emphasis on human similarities has been a useful strand in arguments against inherent deficit (some people are intrinsically less capable, or less valuable than others), this argument leads to a form of universalism that denies context and difference. It is against such claims that many postcolonial writers have struggled (➔ chap. 3), suggesting that claims to universality are always parochial claims for shared European or North American traits. As Foucault (1974) argued in his debate with Chomsky over the issue of human nature:

> You can't prevent me from believing that these notions of human nature, of justice, of the realisations of the essence of human beings, are all notions and concepts which have been formed within our civilization, within our type of knowledge and our form of philosophy, and that as a result form part of our class system. (p. 187)

To develop a viable philosophical and political background for critical applied linguistics, particularly because of the global and cultural challenges critical applied linguistics faces, such notions of universality and human nature must be rejected. (See Table 2.1.)

Emancipatory Modernism

The third position is the emancipatory modernist, or scientific leftist position. Unlike the autonomous-leftist view described earlier, which eschews connections between politics and language study, this nonautonomous leftist position aims specifically to relate language study to leftist politics. On the one hand, it tends to share a similar belief in rationality, realism, and scientific endeavor, including the old Marxist divide between science and ideology; on the other hand, it directly relates its political analysis to the study of language use. This position is one held by many of those who might typically be seen as falling within the rubric of critical applied linguistics. Phillipson (1992) explained the aim of his book *Linguistic Imperialism* (which is discussed further → chap. 3) as to develop a theory of linguistic imperialism, thereby "contributing to 'rational, scientifically-based discourse'" on the global spread of English, in the hope that "an adequate, theoretically explicit foundation for analysing the issues has been provided" (p. 75). From this point of view, language is deeply political, and the goals of one's work as a (critical) applied linguist are to uncover the operations by which the political nature of language is obscured and to reveal the political implications of language. Such an endeavor should be pursued from a "rational" and "scientific" point of view.

A similar view is held by a number of people working in critical discourse analysis (for more discussion, → chap. 4). Ruth Wodak (1996), for example, drawing on the framework of CDA developed by herself and Norman Fairclough, suggests that a key principle of CDA is that it is "a socially committed scientific paradigm. CDA is not less 'scientific' than other linguistic approaches" (p. 20). Summarizing work done in CDA, Kress (1990) also expresses this nervousness about it being a "proper" science, insisting that "while their activity is politically committed, it is nonetheless properly scientific, perhaps all the more so for being aware of its own political, ideological, and ethical stance" (p. 85). This view, then, although differing fundamentally from Chomsky's in terms of linking language study to politics, shares some similarities in terms of a view of scientific knowledge as its goal. Thus, while drawing on a neo-Marxist analysis of power and ideology and making awareness and emancipation its ulti-mate goals, it adheres to a hierarchy of knowledge production that places the scientific at the summit. Given the importance of this position to criti-cal applied linguistics, it is worth exploring these issues in greater depth.

A useful place to start is Mey's (1985) definition of critical sociolinguistics. In place of mainstream or traditional sociolinguistics, he offers "a *critical* sociolinguistics" that "seeks to recognize the political and economic distortions that our society imposes on us. It attempts to explain the differences between *oppressed* and *oppressor* language by pointing out that the different classes have unequal access to societal power" (p. 342). This critical version of sociolinguistics (which is discussed further → chap. 3) operates with very different assumptions from those of mainstream sociolinguistics. It clearly matches with a number of the criteria outlined in the last chapter (← chap. 1), with its focus on the role of language in repro-ducing inequitable social relations. But it also operates with a very particu-lar critical framework, with its talk of distortions, impositions, oppressed and oppressors, class, and access. Untangling some of the issues that under-lie critical work such as this is a major focus of this book. At this point, I want to point to the particularities of this neo-Marxist framework.

Mey (1985) goes on to explain that "sociolinguistics as a *critical* science bases itself on the assumption that the moving force of our society is capi-tal's need to accumulate profits" (p. 343). Here again, we have an empha-sis on science and on the primacy of capitalism as the driving force in society. Power is distributed to the dominant group/oppressors by the class system and ownership of the means of production. Power is owner-ship and wealth and the subsequent control of society through either co-ercive means (control via State apparatuses such as the police) or consensual means (through ideological control of schools, communica-tion, and so on). This type of analysis can also be seen in the work of criti-cal discourse analysts (→ chap. 4) such as of Norman Fairclough, who argues that "social order ... is the political objective of the dominant, 'he-gemonic,' sections of a society in the domain of language as in other do-mains" (Fairclough, 1992a, p. 48). Elsewhere, he explains that:

> The relationship between social classes starts in economic production, but extends to all parts of a society. The power of the capitalist class depends also on its ability to control the *state*: contrary to the view of the state as standing neutrally "above" classes, I shall assume that the state is the key el-ement in maintaining the dominance of the capitalist class, and controlling the working class. This political power is typically exercised not just by capi-talists, but by an alliance of capitalists and others who see their interests as tied to capital—many professional workers, for instance. We can refer to this alliance as the *dominant bloc*. (1989, p. 33)

Although Fairclough acknowledges other forms of power and inequality, such as gender or race, he regards "class relations as having a more fundamental status than others" (1989, p. 34). As a form of political analysis, then, this is a fairly traditional neo-Marxist position.

These versions of critical sociolinguistics or critical discourse analysis finally give us ways of relating analyses of language to broader social and political questions. Issues of power and inequality are linked to language both in terms of the material (infrastructural) questions of access to language use (Who gets to use what aspects of language?) and the less material (superstructural) questions of how power relations are maintained through ideological representations in language. But it is also just as important to see the particularity of this "mainstream critical" tradition as it is to understand the "mainstream uncritical" work in applied linguistics. Several important issues are worth looking at briefly here (these concerns will all be taken up at greater length elsewhere): power, ideology, science, and emancipation.

First of all, there are questions to be asked about the adequacy of the sociological framework supplied by neo-Marxist analysis, particularly the rather simple division between oppressed and oppressors, dominated and dominators, and the primacy given to capitalist accumulation as the primary source of power. As Giddens (1982) argues, "there are too many flaws and inadequacies in Marxist thought for it to supply an overall grounding for sociological analysis" (p. 167). Second, the version of ideology that operates here, with its suggestion that ideology is in the service of the "oppressors" and obscures the reality behind social relations, presents us with problems concerning truth and reality. According to Mey (1985), a goal of critical sociolinguistics is the "removal of the ideological spider's webs and assorted rubble that is cluttering the storehouse of our language" (p. 361). Having argued for the importance of a critical version of sociolinguistics that deals with conflict and inequality rather than consensuality, Williams (1992) takes issue with this version of ideology, "with meaning as the basis of sustaining domination, which has been at the center of most studies of language among contemporary Marxists, leading to what is referred to as critical sociolinguistics" (p. 243). This view tends to "treat ideology as conspiratorial, as the conscious production of an individual or group whose objective is the subversion of some other group" (p. 244). These issues will be taken up in much more depth later.

The third issue has to do with the claims to be involved in scientific analysis. Although this has been an important argument to claim equal status for critical work, it also leads to two problems: It continues to keep in play notions of objectivity and truth, and it fails to be reflexive about its own knowledge status. Mey's (1985) examples of nonobjective sociolinguistics, for example, tend to detract from the possibilities of making a broader critique. After his critique of the claims to objectivity and "clean" science made by many social scientists, he goes on to illustrate why such claims are untenable with examples of complicity between anthropologists and the CIA:

> The myth of "clean," objective, social science and research collapses irrevo-
> cably, when the results of ethnographic, anthropological or linguistic re-
> search are used in operations such as the massive concentration of whole
> native populations in government-controlled settlements (like the "strate-
> gic hamlets" of the Vietnam war, or current "relocation" policies in the
> Amazonas district of Brazil). (p. 345)

Such examples are of course immensely powerful illustrations of the complicity of social science with larger political motivations. Yet in their very powerfulness, by drawing connections between anthropology and military invasion, they detract from the possibility of the larger critique that *all* knowledge is linked to power and thus that the solution is not merely to critique social science in the service of the CIA but rather to critique all knowledge claims as interested. A similar point can be made about the typical examples used in critical sociolinguistics or critical discourse analysis, which often focus on newspaper reports of labor relations, strikes, big business, and so on. They make forceful reading, but they draw our attention back with too much insistence to the argument that the issue here has everything to do with class and capital and little to do with other micro relations.

Finally, there are difficult concerns here (as in all critical work) about what alternative vision or strategies for change we are left with. Two positions present themselves: either a strong return to neo-Marxist materialism, which suggests that to change relations in language we need to change social relations of power, or a focus on removing ideological obfuscation, leading to emancipation through awareness. Mey (1985) espouses the first of these positions and is fairly blunt in his dismissal of the possibility of change through teaching standard language to immigrant workers: "The immigrant worker who talks the language of his bosses may be able to obtain a personal advantage, such as a better position, but that doesn't solve any problems, either for himself or for the other immigrants" (p. 352). Thus, individual empowerment is fruitless since this only reproduces the same broader inequalities, which ultimately lie outside language. This is a very significant point because it counters the liberal humanist emphasis on individual empowerment by arguing that empowering individuals within inequitable social structures not only fails to deal with those inequalities but also reproduces them. But Mey's Marxist materialism ultimately leads him away from language as a potential site of action to a view that language (superstructure) merely reflects society (infrastructure): "In the final perspective, what we're dealing with, strictly speaking, is not linguistic oppression as such, but rather, *societal* oppression that manifests itself linguistically" (p. 352). This leaves us helpless as (critical) applied linguists.

The second alternative is more optimistic that change may come about in ways other than large-scale social change. From this point of view, by making people aware of forms of linguistic or ideological oppression, there are possibilities for forms of emancipation. Awareness, therefore, becomes a sort of political enlightenment that can lead to empowerment, which if turned into social action may become emancipation. As Clark (1992) suggests, discussing the notion of critical language awareness (CLA) and academic writing:

> A crucial aspect of CLA is to empower students by providing them with the opportunities to discover and critically examine the conventions of the academic discourse community and to enable them to emancipate themselves by developing alternatives to the dominant conventions. (p. 137)

Similarly, Janks and Ivanič (1992) suggest that CLA, as part of a more general process of consciousness raising, is the first step in the process of emancipation, a step "in which we come to understand that underdogs need liberation." The second step is *emancipatory discourse* or action based on this awareness, a step in which "we decide to act so as to contest subjection" (p. 307). Thus, as Clark and Ivanič (1997) suggest in the context of academic writing, "explicit discussion of the social origins of conventions for correctness and appropriacy" can on the one hand help students become aware of why they are often alienated by academic writing and its conventions and on the other hand

> provide the basis on which they can, when the risk is not too high, contribute to the ideological work of challenging and changing conventions that work to the detriment of values, beliefs and social groups and ideas with which they identify. (pp. 240–241).

And yet, while awareness and emancipation offer more hope than Mey's pessimism, they are also problematic categories (Price, 1999). First of all, this model of change can look very patronizing. In its worst form it can appear to suggest that people ("the people," "the masses," "women," "the working class," "minorities") are ideologically duped and need to have the veil of mystification lifted from them: "Underdogs need liberation." Second, it is rather less clear what in fact the reaction to such awareness might be. As Kearney (1988) argues,

> It is certainly unlikely that any amount of "knowledge" about the falsehood of our experience is going to help us think or act in a more effective or liberating way. A form of pedagogy, however accurate and scientific, which does no more than explain the intricate mechanisms of our enslavement offers little consolation (p. 386)

And third, by arguing that awareness can lead on to emancipation, this model of liberation operates with a problematic belief in its own righteousness and its ability to help others to see the light. This sort of emancipatory modernity suggests that there really is an enlightened state, an ideal speech situation that exists outside relations of power. At the very least, such a position lacks reflexivity about its own claims to truth:

> Discourses of emancipation—despite their emancipatory intent—are still bound up with the "will to power." Educators find it hard to accept that their emancipatory intentions, their desire to enlighten, may be implicated with the will to power and may, therefore, have oppressive consequences. (Usher & Edwards, 1994, p. 27)

These are again complex concerns to which I return.

I have been suggesting in this section that unlike the liberal approach to applied linguistics (which may make its own claims to be engaged in critical applied linguistics) or the anarcho-autonomous position, the emancipatory modernist framework provides an important basis for critical work. Nevertheless, this "mainstream critical work," which draws on neo-Marxist analyses of power, science, ideology, and awareness, has various limitations: while insisting on the importance of relating language to social and political concerns, it all too often presents a clumsy, material version of power located in class relations; it views ideology in a way that is opposed in too simple terms to a knowable reality; in unreflexive fashion, it suggests that scientific knowledge of reality can help us escape from the falsity of ideology; and thus, it offers us a rationalist model of emancipation that does not do enough to question the righteousness of its own assumptions.

Marxism has served crucial purposes, but it lacks a self-reflexivity: It has "enabled bourgeois men to analyse society from the point of view of the industrial proletariat but it has subsequently been shown to have occupied a position that was both masculinist in content and Eurocentric in context" (Barrett, 1991, p. 161). Although more recent Marxist-based thought has certainly moved on from and given a great deal of consideration to these concerns, it remains a problematic framework for analysis. This leaves me with what might appear to be a dilemma: In presenting an overview of work in critical applied linguistics, I necessarily have to draw on much of the work in critical sociolinguistics, critical discourse analysis, or critical language awareness while also being critical of many of the assumptions that underlie this work. But as I also suggested (← chap. 1), such a critical stance is part of how I see critical applied linguistics operating. This is not intended to be a model for critical work; rather, I hope this discussion will help illuminate significant concerns to do with power, ideology, language, and change. In the next section, I discuss the fourth possible conjunction of language, power and knowledge.

Critical Applied Linguistics as Problematizing Practice

My comments in the last section suggest a need to go beyond critical work as part of a modernist emancipatory framework in which power is held by the oppressors (the dominant bloc) and maintained by ideology, and in which emancipation can be brought about as a result of awareness of the operations of ideology. This type of emancipatory modernism is close to the project of Critical Theory as developed by Habermas (1972). Following on from a long line of critical thinkers (Horkheimer, Adorno, and Marcuse, among others; ← chap. 1), Habermas criticized the dominance of the "technical" domain of empirical analytic science and the resultant "conviction that we can no longer understand science as one form of possible knowledge, but rather must identify knowledge with science" (p. 4). He then seeks to open up the possibility of what he sees as the two other main types of human knowledge—a *practical* domain based on understanding through historical hermeneutic knowledge and an *emancipatory* domain based on forms of critical thought—and to develop a forum for rational emancipatory thought and communication (1984). But the failure to question the politics of *all* knowledge, including so-called emanci- patory knowledge, and the utopian modernist dream of an ideal space of rational communication leave such a notion incomplete. Patti Lather (1991), therefore, suggests we need to add a fourth category to Habermas' technical, practical, and emancipatory knowledge, a category that includes poststructural, postmodern, and "post-paradigmatic diaspora" approaches to knowledge.

This fourth position, then, although also viewing language as fundamentally bound up with politics, nevertheless articulates a profound skepticism about science, about truth claims, and about an emancipatory position outside ideology. This position, which we might call *critical applied linguistics as problematizing practice,* draws on poststructuralist, postmodernist, and postcolonial perspectives. Part of the focus of this book is to develop this position in greater detail. This *post* position views language as inherently political; understands power more in terms of its micro operations in relation to questions of class, race, gender, ethnicity, sexuality, and so on; and argues that we must also account for the politics of knowledge. Rather than continuing to see scientific endeavor as a means to further critical work, this view sees science—or claims to scientificity—as part of the problem. For many, claiming both a critical and a scientific stance would seem an obvious way to go about constituting a critical approach to academic work. But, while it should be acknowledged that a great deal of work in critical applied linguistics to date has been informed by this approach, I want to avoid the dogmatic assurity in both its politics and its science that can make such a position regrettably blind to other possibilities. Not only are questions about language always political but so are the answers.

Drawing particularly on the work of Michel Foucault (1980b; → chap. 4) and his understanding of power and knowledge as implying each other, this approach seeks alternative ways of understanding without recourse to discourses of science or humanism, with their underlying claims to fundamental or essential essences. Whereas, for example, in discussing the notion of justice, Chomsky (1974) argued for "some sort of absolute basis ... ultimately residing in fundamental human qualities, in terms of which a 'real' notion of justice is grounded" (p. 185), Foucault (1974) argued that

> the idea of justice in itself is an idea which in effect has been invented and put to work in different types of societies as an instrument of a certain political and economic power or as a weapon against that power. (pp. 184–185)

Rather than the prior belief in essential human categories, therefore I prefer to pursue with greater skepticism the ways in which concepts are mobilized. And crucially, this ties in with the notion of critical developed in the last chapter (← chap. 1), as a problematizing stance that is also "aware of the limits of knowing" (Spivak, 1993, p. 25). In this book, I argue for the importance of this problematizing practice position while also acknowledging the significance of work done within a more emancipatory framework. My argument, by contrast, is that all knowledge is political. This book and my understanding of critical applied linguistics are not "objective" or "scientific": They are political. And ultimately, as I argue later (→ chap. 5), they are grounded in an ethical vision. In the end, the question I would like to put on the table for debate is not about *whether* applied linguistics is political but about *how* it should be critical.

CONCLUSION: OUTFLANKING MARX FROM THE LEFT

In this chapter, I have sketched out four different positions on how knowledge, politics and language may be related. It might be useful to consider briefly how each might approach a similar question. Let us take, for example, an analysis of the language used by a second language speaker. The liberal-ostrichist position would be principally interested in showing that there is nothing wrong with the supposedly deviant forms of speech for they are part of the developing grammar (interlanguage) of the learner. All things being equal, the learner will go on developing to become a free and full-fledged member of the target speech community. For the anarcho-autonomist position, while there may be much to be said about the larger political context, the task here must be to demonstrate rigorously and scientifically how the development of the learner's language follows certain underlying and universal principles. By adhering to the tenets of realism, rationalism, and science, we can further our knowledge of language learning and move ever closer to a theory of how languages are learned. Such a position will be useful not only to learners, teachers, and applied linguists but also to a much wider community since it will have deduced scientific facts about the world that are no longer amenable to ideological manipulation.

For the emancipatory modernist, however, it is not so much the form of the learner's utterances that are of central interest but rather questions of access and content. All things are not equal. The learner may already be positioned within a classist division that relegates second language speakers to a secondary status. What access does this language user have to particular uses of language, how might they be positioned, how might they become more aware of the ways in which they are discriminated against, and how then could they find ways to struggle against an inequitable system? Similarly, from a problematizing practice perspective, the questions have to do with the social, cultural, and historical location of the speaker. But rather than assuming that the speaker is already marginalized as a member of the class of second language speakers and looking for signs of that marginalization in the speech, this approach seeks a broader understanding of how multiple discourses may be at play at the same time: What kinds of discursive positions does the speaker take up? How does the speaker position herself or himself, and how may they also be positioned at different moments according to gendered and cultured positionings?

It may be useful to look back at Table 1.2 (← chap. 1) to see how the various concerns of critical applied linguistics are taken up within the perspectives outlined earlier. It may also be a useful exercise to take other domains of applied linguistics, such as discourse analysis of a newspaper advertisement, a conversation between a doctor and a patient, or different translations of the same text, and to suggest ways in which different approaches to knowledge, politics, and language might lead to very different forms of analysis. And another useful thing to think about would be alternative conjunctions of knowledge and politics, alternative ways in which various approaches to knowledge domains may combine with different forms of politics to produce either more "noncritical" ways of doing applied linguistics or alternative forms of what I call critical applied linguistics.

Indeed, I have a number of concerns with the way I have constructed these arguments. By suggesting four different positions on politics and knowledge, I run the danger of suggesting that these are far more clear and discrete than I wish to. To compare, I have compartmentalized. As with the earlier example, these are as much caricatures as they are characterizations. As I suggested, these should not be taken as discrete configurations so much as convenient bedfellows. It may also seem that to argue for a critical standpoint that distances itself from mainstream critical theory may seem both a simplistic characterization of other critical work and a foolish marginalization of the directions I wish to follow here. My argument, however, is that on the one hand, we need to be able to be critical of critical work as much as any other and that on the other hand, too much mainstream critical work is not critical enough: It is too normative, too unquestioning of its assumptions. Following Giddens' (1982) discussion of the development of a critical sociology that avoids the reductionism of Marxism, perhaps what we need is to "outflank Marx from the left" (p. 169). Such an approach needs to incorporate understandings from the problematizing stance I started to outline earlier. And, it needs a view of language that is not merely a reflection of society or a tool of ideological manipulation but rather a means by which social relations are constructed. As does Williams (1992), I believe that to develop such a view of language, we need to take on board lessons from poststructuralist thinking about power and language, and we need to work toward a more contextual understanding of power relations. I will return to this argument (→ chap. 3).

The Politics of Language

Sociolinguistics and Power
  Liberal Sociolinguistics
Language Planning and Politics: The Global Spread of English
  Liberal Complementarity
  Language Ecology, Language Rights, and Linguistic
    Imperialism
Postcolonialism and Resistance
  Colonialism and Postcolonialism
  Resistance, Appropriation, and Third Spaces
Conclusion: Toward a Postcolonial Performative View
    of Language

In the last chapter (← chap. 2), I focused primarily on the relations between knowledge and politics as they related to language. Left hanging, however, was the issue of developing a political understanding of language. Since applied linguistics always has to do with language in some form, the development of a political vision of language must indeed form a backbone to critical applied linguistics. I have already alluded to a possible distinction between looking at the politics of language in terms of how forms of power affect language use and in terms of how power may operate ideologically through language. Although this may be a slightly crude dichotomy, it can serve to organize different domains of the politics of language. While the next chapter (→ chap. 4), therefore, is concerned with the analytical and pedagogical questions that emerge from a consideration of power and meaning within language—which I choose to call *the politics of texts*—this chapter deals primarily with issues to do with language use in different contexts—the politics of language. I focus on a number of principal concerns:

- Language and power within sociolinguistics;
- Language and power within different conceptions of language policy and planning, in particular, frameworks for understanding the global spread of English;
- Issues of resistance and appropriation raised by postcolonialism.

SOCIOLINGUISTICS AND POWER

Of course, some versions of language may disavow any connection to power: Language is language, and power is power, and ne'er the twain shall meet. But whatever view of language supports such a position, it is evidently not one that is concerned with language use, for even conservative views on language tend to draw connections between language and power. Indeed, the main title of Honey's (1997) conservative defense of standard English is *Language Is Power.* Such a title already points toward the arguments that underlie such a position: Particular forms of language (standard English) can convey social and economic power (language *is* power rather than Fairclough's language *and* power). It is worth looking very briefly at this position not only because it has had wide coverage at least within Britain and enjoys fairly considerable support in popular media (Cameron, 1995) but also because it is a position against which much liberal academic work reacts.

Honey's (1983, 1997) arguments about standard English have been massively critiqued elsewhere (Bex & Watts, 1999): They are contradictory; they rest on the "astonishing proposition, which seems to be the basis of all Honey's thinking on the subject" that standard English is "the English he himself uses" (Harris, 1997, p. 19); they repeat old myths about "speaking only a preliterate language with a tiny vocabulary" (Honey, 1997, p. 21); and they slide all too easily into a view of intellectual deficit as a result of speaking in a certain way when he asks:

> whether some languages (or, to some extent, some varieties of one language) might be less well equipped as vehicles of certain kinds of intellectual activity than others, with consequent intellectual disadvantage to those people who can handle effectively that one language or dialect, and not any other, less limiting form. (Honey, 1983, p. 9)

Nevertheless, it is worth looking briefly at part of his argument, which can be summed up through the following example:

> I believe that one of the most powerful factors contributing to the disadvantage of America's underclass—Blacks and other ethnic groups, and lower-class whites—is in reality capable of being changed: I refer to their ability to handle standard English. A properly funded and effective programme designed to add standard English to their repertoire of speaking and writing skills has the potential to transform the educational and occupational opportunities of members [of] these groups. (Honey, 1997, p. 240)

Putting aside for a moment the many inaccuracies in Honey's position and his claims that speakers of nonstandard forms of English suffer both communicative and cognitive disadvantage, the main point worth considering here is whether access to standard English is indeed as "empowering" as is claimed. The problem here is that first Honey presents us with an undifferentiated Other—people of different class, regional, and ethnic backgrounds who speak in different ways—and an unexamined notion of an inherently powerful standard version of the language, the learning of which can act as a panacea for all sorts of other social ills— poverty, racism, class bigotry, and so on. And second, this is coupled with a sociological naivete that learning a standard version of the language will bring about social and economic advantage. Honey's vision boils down to one in which difference will be effaced if everyone speaks like him. As Wiley and Lukes (1996) point out, following Wiggins (1976), "for all too many African Americans, the fact that mastery of the language does not ensure economic mobility or political access makes manifest the fallacy of standard English as the language of equal opportunity" (p. 530). The point here, of course, is not that learning standardized forms of English should be denied to students but rather that we need to understand in much greater depth how forms of language may be related to forms of power. On the one hand, the vision that access to standard forms will somehow be automatically empowering is inadequate; on the other hand, it is important not to fall into the trap of suggesting that power always lies outside language and that it is only with social change that different language forms may come to take on different roles.

Liberal Sociolinguistics

One of Honey's main points of attack is against one of the central orthodoxies of (socio)linguistics, that all varieties of language are "equal." As he suggests:

> To deny children the opportunity to learn to handle standard English, because of pseudo-scientific judgements about all varieties of language being "equal," is to set limits *in advance* to their ability to express themselves effectively outside their immediate subculture, and to slam the door on any real opportunity for social mobility. (Honey, 1983, pp. 24–25)

Honey's argument is problematic both because the pedagogical response to this stance has not been to deny access to standard English but to acknowledge alternatives and because once again he makes unwarranted claims about communication, subcultures, and social mobility. And yet, his critique resonates with more critical approaches to the question. As Giroux (1983) explains:

> Questions about the value of standard English as well as about the role of working-class culture in education become meaningful only if it is remembered that the skills , knowledge, and language practices that roughly characterize different classes and social formations are forged within social relations marked by the unequal distribution of power. Subordinate cultures are situated and recreated within relations of domination and resistance, and they bear the marks of both. To argue that working-class language practices are just as rule-governed as standard English usage and practice may be true, but to suggest at the same time that *all* cultures are equal is to forget that subordinate groups are often denied access to the power, knowledge, and resources that allow them to lead self-determined existences. (p. 229)

The problem here, then, is that while a conservative critique decries the liberal egalitarianism of (socio)linguistics, a more critical stance also finds fault with the liberal politics that wishes for equality where there is none. The liberal structuralism (← chap. 2) underlying the sociolinguistic argument—that we should deal with systems according to their own logics and eschew external evaluative positions—has been a highly significant one in promoting an antielitist stance on difference. It is worth looking in slightly greater depth at the problems with this liberal sociolinguistic vision of language and power.

It is important to acknowledge here that the work of sociolinguists such as William Labov was aimed directly to counter the sort of linguistic deficit arguments that Honey is still promoting (indeed, Labov is one of Honey's many antagonists). Labov took aim at what he called "verbal deprivation theorists," those who in the 1960s were arguing that nonstandard, particularly Black American, speech was illogical and malformed and that this showed an inability to think logically. For some (such as Arthur Jensen), this represented evidence of "the genetic inferiority of Negroes" (Labov, 1970, p. 181), while for others such verbal deprivation could be overcome through intervention programs such as Operation Head Start. Labov's (1970) argument was a crucial one in that he attempted to show how Black English vernacular (BEV) had its own rules and logic (and also that standard English has its own shortcomings). "Linguists," he suggested, "are in an excellent position to demonstrate the fallacies of the verbal deprivation theory. All linguists agree that nonstandard dialects are highly structured systems" (p. 184).

Although such arguments against the often blatant racism of theories that have connected nonstandard speech with cognitive difference—a po-

sition that reemerged all too quickly with the ebonics debates in the
United States (Perry & Delpit, 1998)—have been extremely important,
they have also led to shortcomings to the extent that they have been concerned principally with critiquing a conservative position and constructing a form of liberal structuralism in opposition. A key aspect, then, of the
attempt to relate power to language lies in how we understand relations
between language and society. As I suggested (← chap. 1), the issue here is
not only to relate language to broader social concerns but also to do so
within a critical model of society. This is one of the major concerns that a
domain of work such as (critical) applied linguistics faces: Any model of a
relation between language and society will only be as good as one's understanding of society. Unfortunately, the model of society in
sociolinguistics has tended to remain something of an unexamined given.
Sociolinguists, as Cameron (1995) points out, "have been content to
work with simple, commonsensical ideas about the social" (p. 15).

There are four principal concerns worth discussing in this context:

- The need for a critical social theory capable of dealing with the
  maintenance of inequality;
- The need for an approach to language that goes beyond description and moves toward critique;
- The need to understand the shortcomings of a model that emphasizes appropriacy;
- The need to view language as productive as well as reflective of social relations.

Williams (1992) critiques the sociolinguistic structural functionalist
view of society in which rational actors follow social norms for the general
good of society and their own social welfare. The understanding of society
is therefore a consensual one in which we all agree to act together for a mutual good. Society is described in limited terms (e.g., unexamined notions
of social class) with the focus ultimately being on the individual and her or
his linguistic behavior, rather than the complex workings of language
amid conflictual social contexts:

> Despite employing concepts such as social class, ethnicity or gender, which
> are explicitly related to domination and subordination, as independent vari-
> ables within the empirical framework, the conflict which is implicit in such
> dimensions is missing as a consequence of the structural functionalist orien-
> tation. The emphasis on normative consensus as the guiding force of indi-
> vidual speech results in the legitimisation of standard forms and the parallel
> marginalisation of non-standard forms. (p. 93)

Although as Giddens (1982) remarks, this consensual versus
conflictual dichotomy in sociology is not always helpful, it is nevertheless

clear that a critical sociolinguistics needs some model other than a bland consensual one in which all members of a society happily work together for collective gain. The liberal structuralism of sociolinguistics may have distanced itself from an elitist view of natural social hierarchies, but it still has little to say about how inequality is created, sustained, or overturned.

From a critical standpoint, furthermore, the sociolinguistic tendency to engage merely in description is problematic. As Cameron (1995) observes, the general tenet of linguistics and sociolinguistics that it is involved in description rather than prescription is untenable since "*both* prescriptivism *and* anti-prescriptivism invoke certain norms and circulate particular notions about how language ought to work." Thus, "'description' and 'prescription' turn out to be aspects of a single (and normative) activity: a struggle to control language by defining its nature" (p. 8). According to Harris (1981), the view of language sustained by linguistics is in many ways "no less rigid than the authoritarian recommendations of the old-fashioned grammarian pedagogue" (p. 46). Similarly, Parakrama (1995) points out that so-called descriptive work always focuses on certain forms of language at the expense of others. "This unequal emphasis," he goes on, "is not so much the fault of individual descriptivists as a problematic of description itself, which can never be a neutral activity. In other words, description is always a weak form of prescription" (p. 3). Thus, the claim that linguistic or sociolinguistic descriptions of language somehow are objective or value neutral goes against any more complex understanding of the politics of knowledge (← chap. 2).

The insistence on description rather than a more sustained critique of the conditions one is describing raises important questions about the politics of mainstream sociolinguistics. Jacob Mey (1985) has made this point forcefully in his argument that for "*traditional* sociolinguistics, the present organization of society's material production is the only natural one; so natural, in fact, that traditional sociolinguists, in their description of the language people use, totally disregard the existence of social classes" (p. 342). The notion of class that is employed in sociolinguistics (and against which linguistic phenomena are then correlated) tends "to refer to what might better be referred to as 'social strata'—groupings of people who are similar to one another in occupation, education or other standard sociological variables" (Fairclough, 1989, p. 8). A more critical view understands social class as bound up with inequality, struggle, and opposition. Thus, Mey (1985) suggests, by avoiding questions of social inequality in class terms and instead correlating language variation with superficial measures of social stratification, traditional sociolinguistics fails to "establish a connection between people's place in the societal hierarchy, and the linguistic and other kinds of oppression that they are subjected to at different levels" (p. 342).

Third, the framing of debates between either the conservative emphasis on standards or a more liberal model of diversity, in conjunction with a consensual view of society, leads to a problematic emphasis on "appropriacy." This last argument is the liberal compromise that suggests that we need to teach the appropriate forms at the appropriate times. But as Ivanič (1990) suggests, there are problems with this notion: "'Appropriacy' sounds more liberal and flexible than 'accuracy,' but I believe it is just as much of a straightjacket for the bilingual trying to add English to her repertoire" (p. 124). The problem here, according to Ivanič, is that "the dominant conventions of appropriacy are treated as natural and necessary" (p. 125). Thus, although the unquestioned concept of accuracy according to a "standard" version of the language can be criticized for its exclusionary linguistic stance, an emphasis on appropriacy may be equally criticized for its discussion of social appropriacy in normative terms. By contrast, "a critical view of language emphasizes the fact that prestigious social groups have established these conventions: they are not 'natural' or necessarily the way they are" (p. 126).

Fairclough (1992a) develops this critique further, arguing first that "models of language variation based upon the concept of appropriateness project a misleading and unsustainable image of sociolinguistic practice and how sociolinguistic orders are structured" (p. 47). He suggests that the appropriateness version of language variation, with its presuppositions that the distinction between appropriate and inappropriate is clear-cut, that such appropriacy is the same for all members of a community, and that there is a clear match between language variants and contexts of use, simply does not hold up under critical scrutiny. In many contexts—Fairclough provides the example of a professional woman talking to a senior male colleague—it is far less obvious what forms will be seen by the participants as appropriate. Secondly, Fairclough argues that the notion of appropriacy needs to be understood ideologically, that is in terms of the claims made to represent a social reality. Thus, he suggests, appropriateness models "derive from a confusion between sociolinguistic realities and political projects in the domain of language" (p. 48). The view that there is a static social order, as we saw in Williams' critique of sociolinguistics, needs to be seen as a very particular political view of language and society, "the political objective of the dominant, 'hegemonic,' sections of a society in the domain of language as in other domains" rather than "sociolinguistic reality" (Fairclough, 1992a, p. 48).

The sociolinguistic model of appropriacy underlies the widely promoted applied linguistic concept of sociolinguistic competence as an aspect of communicative competence (Canale & Swain, 1980). The resultant problem is that this view of communication has taken on board a notion of a static society with fixed social roles and hierarchies that are reflected linguistically, or as Fairclough (1992a) puts it, "imaginary representations of sociolinguistic reality which correspond to the perspective and partisan interests of one section of society or one section of a particular social institution—its dominant section" (p. 48). Peirce (1989) has argued that instead of adopting such models of social appropriacy, we need to consider language use in terms of political desirability, and thus instead of working with a model of communicative competence based on a static and unquestioned version of social order, we need to consider how our notion of communicative competence might also have a more transformative social agenda.

Finally, for much of sociolinguistics, both society and language remain rather static entities. From this point of view, language merely *reflects* society. As Williams (1992) explains, this leads to the tendency to treat the social as some sort of "independent variable," a static, given series of social relations, while language is treated as the "dependent variable," a static reflection of social relations (p. 39). This positivistic and behaviourist view of society, in which a stimulus (independent variable) produces a response (dependent variable), is, to say the least, a very limited view of the dynamics of social relations. Cameron (1990, 1995) similarly criticizes sociolinguistic research for its static labeling and the belief that "people's use of linguistic variables can be correlated with their demographic characteristics: their belonging to particular classes, races, genders, generations, local communities" (Cameron, 1995, p. 15). Thus, whether the view is one in which language use simply reflects society or one that allows for slightly more agency in this relation (so that language users actively "mark" their social identity), "it is implicitly assumed that the relevant categories and identities exist prior to language, and are simply 'marked' or 'reflected' when people come to use it" (Cameron, 1995, p. 15).

An alternative view, as Cameron suggests, sees language itself as *part of the social* and indeed an active element in its construction. As Cameron explains, "any encounter with recent social and critical theory" will cast doubt on a view that language reflects society:

> The categories sociolinguistics treats as fixed givens, such as "class," "gender" and even "identity," are treated in critical approaches as relatively unstable *constructs* which are therefore in need of explanation themselves. Furthermore, in critical theory language is treated as part of the explanation. Whereas sociolinguistics would say that the way I use language reflects or marks my identity as a particular kind of social subject ... the critical account suggests language is one of the things that *constitutes* my identity as a particular kind of subject. Sociolinguistics says that how you act depends on who you are; critical theory says that who you are (and are taken to be) depends on how you act. (1995, pp. 15–16)

This moves us toward the crucial insight that using, speaking, learning, teaching language is a form of social and cultural action; it is about producing and not just reflecting realities.

The overriding problem here, then, is that in debates around language, social class, and variety, there has been little critical understanding of how such questions are linked to issues of power. Thus, in debates on standard language, grammar and so on, the conservative arguments for traditional grammar and standard English (which, as Cameron, 1995, argues, serve as metaphors for greater social order, discipline, and authority) are countered only by a sociolinguistic liberalism. The same can be said of other domains of sociolinguistic interest such as language in the workplace and professional settings. Once again, while the principal goal of analyses of language in legal settings, doctor–patient interactions, or job interviews is usually to arrive at descriptive frameworks for generic forms of interaction, a second ostensible goal is to show how power may operate within such settings. Yet to the extent that such work operates with a model whereby personal and institutional power rests in the hands of doctors, lawyers, and interviewers and is reflected in language, it fails to illuminate sociologically how language operates in more complex ways.

In their study of language, discrimination, and disadvantage in British workplaces, by contrast, Roberts, Davies, and Jupp (1992) argue for an understanding of language that includes not just the local context but also

> an understanding of the wider context in which ethnic-minority workers live and work, an understanding of their experiences of racism and disadvantage and of the cultural knowledge which is part of their first language, and an understanding of how language in interaction creates a context which is particular to that interaction but which also reflects and helps to form social spheres and institutions. (p. 6)

Here we can see a more productive role for language, a more complex interweaving of social levels that goes beyond a simple micro/macro relation, and a diversity of forms of power operating through discrimination, social disadvantage, language, and cultural difference.

Similar interwoven layers of complexity emerge, for example, in Tara Goldstein's (1996) study of how social relations, language choice (Portuguese or English), and gender interact on the shop floor, or Crawford's (1999) study of communication in Cape Town (RSA) health services, where the relationship between patients, nurses, and doctors is interwoven with issues of power in language, culture, translation, race, and gender. But while some of this work on language in medical encounters, legal settings, and other workplaces attempts to relate the micro interactions of a conversation to complex institutional and social relations, far too much remains content with simplistic labels of power as simply reflected in the language of powerful individuals. Thus, although much of liberal structuralist sociolinguistics apparently has fairly emancipatory goals, it is frequently unable to do more than discuss differences and decry deficits, without being able to take on the relation between the two more critically. As Williams (1992) describes the problem, there is "evidence of an overriding desire to support the underdog, accompanied by a sociological perspective which reflects the power of the dominant" (p. 226). Liberal and critical approaches to sociolinguistics are compared in Table 3.1.

TABLE 3.1

Liberal and Critical Versions of Sociolinguistics

	Liberal Sociolinguistics	*Critical Sociolinguistics*
Theory of society	Consensual view of equitable society	Understanding of conflict and inequality
Goals	Description	Critique
View on use	Emphasis on appropriacy	Political desirablity
Language/ society relation	Language reflects society	Language produces social relations

LANGUAGE PLANNING AND POLITICS: THE GLOBAL SPREAD OF ENGLISH

Another domain of work often included under sociolinguistics is language policy and planning. As I suggested earlier, it is tempting to see such areas as inherently political and as therefore automatically making up part of the domain of work I call critical applied linguistics. Language policy and planning, however, needs to be subjected to the same sort of scrutiny as sociolinguistics more generally. As Luke, McHoul, and Mey (1990) explain, language planning as an academic area grew up at the same time as the more general social scientific orientation toward positivism, and thus its practitioners tended to work with the belief that questions of language policy could be solved by the application of scientific and technical models: "Many linguists and educational planners saw their task as an ideologically neutral one, entailing the description and formalization of language(s) (corpus planning) and the analysis and prescription of the sociocultural statuses and uses of languages(s) (status planning)" (p. 26). Thus, although maintaining a "veneer of scientific objectivity," language planning has "tended to avoid directly addressing larger social and political matters within which language change, use and development, and indeed language planning itself are embedded" (p. 27).

Luke et al. (1990) argue that what is omitted in most work on language planning is "an exploration of the complex theoretical relationship between language, discourse, ideology and social organization" (p. 28). Arguing that these areas are "precisely the central concerns of neo-Marxist social theorizing, post-structuralist discourse analysis and critical theory" (p. 28), they go on to show how an understanding of class, state, and power as they relate to language can give us a basis for a far more critical understanding of language planning. This critique, then, forcefully makes the point that language planning and policy , far from being some inherently critical or political enterprise, has often been just the opposite: an apolitical approach to language that serves very clearly to maintain the social and linguistic status quo. What language planning needs to make it critical is what all areas of applied linguistics need to make them critical: a critical view of language in relation to a critical view of society and a political and ethical vision of change.

Liberal Complementarity

To contextualize the discussion in this section, I look at different ways of understanding language policies in the context of the global spread of English (for a summary, see Table 3.2). I am therefore less concerned with the smaller-scale issues of corpus or status planning than with the broad questions of the political and ethical visions that support or oppose arguments for diversity. There are, of course, a number of conservative positions on the global spread of English that are akin to the conservative position on standard English discussed earlier: This view, which I have elsewhere (Pennycook, 1999b) termed a *colonial celebratory* position on English, has been well documented and critiqued (Bailey, 1991; Phillipson, 1992; Pennycook, 1994b, 1998a). Simply put, this is a position that trumpets the benefits of English over other languages, suggesting that English is superior to other languages in terms of both its intrinsic (the nature of the language) and extrinsic (the functions of the language) qualities. I use the term *colonial* in conjunction with *celebratory* here because I believe these celebrations of the spread of English, its qualities, and characteristics have a long and colonial history and form part of what I elsewhere called the *adherence of discourses* (1998a), the ways in which particular discourses adhere to English. Although I give this position short thrift here, it remains highly influential.

The more common line on English in academic circles, in a similar vein to sociolinguistics, espouses what I call a liberal laissez-faire attitude. The most recent example of this line of thinking is David Crystal's (1997) overmarketed book on the global spread of English. What Crystal tries to argue for is a complementarity between a support for the benefits of English as a global means of communication and the importance of multilingualism, a balance between the dual values of "international intelligibility" and "historical identity." On the one hand we have all the advantages created by the spread of English: ease of communication, global travel and communication, and so on, while on the other hand, we work to sustain local cultures and traditions. All we need in this way of thinking is to celebrate universalism while maintaining diversity. The Teachers of English to Speakers of Other Languages (TESOL) organization also reflects this naive liberal idealism in its mission statement on all its publications and communications "to strengthen the effective teaching and learning of English around the world while respecting individuals' language rights."

Unfortunately, the very seductiveness of this easy formulation makes its social and political naivete dangerous. Reviewing Crystal's book, for example, John Hanson (former director-general of the British Council) is able to view everything in terms of individual choice. For Hanson (1997), the spread of English is the result of

> countless millions of acts of choice, by students, teachers, employers and the employed who have no interest in the health, future, spread, or whatever of the English language. What "drives" them is a view of their job prospects, their relationship with the rest of the world, their excitement in youth culture, a wish to be insiders, to be in touch. (p. 22)

Such a view of individual agency and choice fails to account for social, cultural, political, and economic forces that compromise and indeed produce such choices. And such a view leads all too easily back to a colonial-celebratory mode:

> English speakers, relax: English is streets ahead and fast drawing away from the rest of the chasing pack .... On it still strides: we can argue what globalisation is until the cows come home—but that globalisation exists is beyond question, with English its accompanist. The accompanist is, of course, indispensable to the performance. (Hanson, 1997, p. 22)

Once again, these liberal laissez-faire views are inadequate because they fail to account for the power of English and thus the inequitable relation between English and local languages. A simplistic view of complementary language use—English will be used for international and some intranational uses, while local languages will be used for local uses—does not take into account the far more complex social and political context of language use. As Dua (1994) points out, looking at the context of India, such a view is quite inadequate:

> The complementarity of English with indigenous languages tends to go up in favour of English partly because it is dynamic and cumulative in nature and scope, partly because it is sustained by socioeconomic and market forces and partly because the educational system reproduced and legitimatizes the relations of power and knowledge implicated with English. (p. 132)

The dichotomy between "international intelligibility" and "historical identity" also leaves other languages as static markers of identity. This line of argument that promotes the global spread of English while supposedly supporting local languages also has a long history. Hogben's (1963) proposal for Essential World English, for example, develops a similar formulation to Crystal's in which English serves people around the world as a "medium of communication about what will matter to most of us in what we hope will be the One World of Tomorrow" (p. 7), a universal second language "for informative communication across their own frontiers about issues of common interest to themselves and others" (p. 20), while other languages are supported as "a home tongue for love-making, religion, verse-craft, back chat and inexact topics in general" (p. 20). Thus, Hogben claims that all language planners agree that we need a bilingual world

> in which one language has priority by common consent as the sole medium of informative communication between speech communities which properly prefer to retain their native habits of discourse for reasons which have little or no relevance to the exacting semantic demands of science (pp. 28–29)

As Dua (1994) cogently argues, such views immediately condemn other home languages to a less significant role. This view is already one nail in the coffin of other languages. In the context of the relation of English to Indian languages, he points out that

> It must be realized that language is basically involved with class, power and knowledge. Unless the newly emerging classes associated with the Indian languages organize themselves into counter-hegemonic struggle and fight for a different political, social and cultural arrangement of power and knowledge, they will not only fail in constraining the expanding and strengthening hold of English but also contribute to the marginalization of their languages and cultures. They will thus betray the cause of both the language and cultural renaissance and the destiny of [hu]mankind. (p. 133)

Phillipson (1999) argues that:

> Crystal's celebration of the growth of English fits squarely into what the Japanese scholar, Yukio Tsuda, terms the Diffusion of English Paradigm, an uncritical endorsement of capitalism, its science and technology, a modernization ideology, monolingualism as a norm, ideological globalization and internationalization, transnationalization, the Americanization and homogenization of world culture, linguistic, culture and media imperialism (Tsuda, 1994). (p. 274)

The problem here, then, is that once again the dominant liberalism of sociolinguistics can lead all too easily to a stance that slides back into celebratory conservativism. In the next section, I start to explore the alternatives, particularly issues of language ecology, language rights, and linguistic imperialism. Some of the different ways of conceptualizing the global spread of English are briefly summarized in Table 3.2.

TABLE 3.2

Frameworks for Understanding the Global Role of English

Framework for understanding the global role of English	Implications for English and language teaching	Politics, problems, and pitfalls
Colonial celebratory	English an inherently useful language; teach English as mission to the world	Arrogant appraisal of English and disdain for other languages; colonial politics
Laissez-faire liberalism	English a functional tool for pragmatic purposes; teach English to whoever wants it	Inadequate analysis of the global politics of English and of complementarity
Linguistic imperialism	Homogenization, destruction of other cultures and languages; teach English sparingly	Too powerful a model of structural power; strong on structure, weak on potential effects
Language ecology and language rights	English a threat to complex local ecologies; support other languages through language rights	Possible conservative form of conservation; identity too closely pinned to mother tongues
Linguistic hybridity	Languages and cultures change and adapt; world Englishes; teach multiple varieties	Blindness to threats posed by global forces; model of change as natural; weak theorization of hybridity
Postcolonial performativity	English as part of postcolonial problematic; cultural politics of resistance and appropriation	Complexity of relations between local and global contexts; potential romanticization of appropriation

Language Ecology, Language Rights, and Linguistic Imperialism

A number of approaches to language planning have developed more critical stances. Tollefson (1991) distinguishes between what he calls the *neoclassical approach* to language planning (perhaps not the best terminology for this), which he sees as a view of language planning as involving rational individual choice and individual factors such as motivation (compare Hanson's aforementioned views), and the *historical-structural* approach, which as its name suggests, deals with broader social factors affecting language policy. From this point of view, language policy is viewed as "one mechanism by which the interests of dominant sociopolitical groups are maintained and the seeds of transformation are developed" (p. 32). Thus, while the neoclassical approach looks at individual choice, the historical-structural approach tries to "discover the historical and structural pressures that lead to particular policies and plans and that constrain individual choice" (p. 32).

Tollefson's division, then, is akin to similar distinctions I point to elsewhere in critical applied linguistics between work that focuses on the individual, individual power, individual motivation, and rational choice and work that seeks to understand the broader social and political conditions in which any such action occurs and, indeed, questions the supposed autonomy, rationality, and choice of individual actors. Tollefson's (1991) ultimate interests in looking at language policy are to work toward a more equitable world:

> To understand the impact of language policy upon the organization and function of society, language policy must be interpreted within a framework which emphasizes power and competing interests. That is, policy must be seen within the context of its role in serving the interests of the state and the groups that dominate it. (p. 201)

Tollefson goes on to argue for the importance of an understanding of language rights. This means that we need to go beyond a general respect for diversity and instead view access to education and other domains of use of the mother tongue as a fundamental human right: "A commitment to democracy means that the use of the mother tongue at work and in school is a fundamental human right" (p. 211).

A similar perspective has also been developed by Robert Phillipson and Tove Skutnabb-Kangas. Drawing on Tsuda's (1994) distinction (see previous section) between a "diffusion-of-English paradigm" and an "Ecology-of-language paradigm," Phillipson and Skutnabb-Kangas (1996) argue that rather than accepting policies that promote the global spread of English, we should work toward the preservation of language ecologies. This notion of language ecology derives from Haugen (1972) and suggests the importance of "the cultivation and preservation of languages" (Phillipson & Skutnabb-Kangas, 1996, p. 441) in a way parallel to how we understand natural ecologies. Mühlhäusler (1996) has developed this idea considerably, arguing that the introduction of languages and literacy into particular language ecologies may have devastating effects on other languages and their uses. Taken alone, however, the language ecology metaphor is limited since it relies so heavily on a notion of what is "natural" and therefore on what may at times appear a conservative notion of preservation. Conservation may easily slide into conservativism. Similar to Mühlhäusler and Tsuda, therefore, Phillipson and Skutnabb-Kangas consider two components essential to this view of language ecology: the external threat posed by dominant languages such as English (linguistic imperialism) and the grounds for arguing for internal support for minority languages (language rights).

A term that Skutnabb-Kangas (1988, 1998) makes central to her view of the inequitable allocation of language rights is *linguicism*. Linguicism, she argues—akin to racism and ethnicism—is a sort of "linguistically argued racism" (1988, p. 13; 1998, p. 16), a process by which an unequal division of power is produced and maintained according to a division between groups on the basis of the language they speak. Phillipson has taken up this term and looked specifically at one form of such linguicism, namely what he calls "linguistic imperialism," and particularly English linguistic imperialism. It is important to view Phillipson's arguments on linguistic imperialism in this light for although his concerns about the global spread of English can be taken on their own, they are also deeply connected with this threat to linguistic human rights. What Phillipson tries to do is to show that there are significant relations between frameworks of global imperialism—that is to say, continuing relations of global inequality in terms, following Galtung (1980), of economic, political, military, communicative (communication and transport), cultural, and social imperialism—and the global spread of English. English linguistic imperialism Phillipson (1992) defines in the following way: "The dominance of English is asserted and maintained by the establishment and continuous reconstitution of structural and cultural inequalities between English and other languages" (p. 47). That is to say, the dominant role of English in the world today is maintained and promoted through a system both of material or institutional structures (e.g., through English maintaining its current position as the dominant language of the Internet) and of ideological positions (arguments that promote English as a superior language).

This framework has both strengths and weaknesses. Phillipson is reasonably convincing in his demonstration of how English has been promoted and supported by a range of institutions, particularly the British Council, or about the ideological underpinnings that construct English as a superior and beneficial language for all. But the crucial challenge must lie—as with all of these attempts to draw relations between language and the broader social and political domain—in both the ability to link the social to the linguistic and in the effectiveness of his theories of language and of power to contribute to critical analysis and to the demands of an understanding of human action. It is in these domains that Phillipson is less convincing. On the one hand, then, there is a model of politics based on a global theory of imperialism. Although Phillipson adds Galtung's other categories (see earlier list) to his model of imperialism, it remains first and foremost an economic model, with the nations at the *center* exploiting the nations in the *periphery*. The point here is that although wealthy countries do indeed continue to exploit poorer nations, their workers, and resources, it is reductive to view global relations in these terms, particularly when we are dealing with questions of language and culture. We are left, therefore, with the question as to how the support for English that Phillipson maps out so well does more than merely reflect such global relations. That is to say, if it is indeed the case that we live in a world of multiple imperialisms in which the *center* continually sucks the *periphery* dry, and if English is indeed promoted as a global language at the expense of other languages, how does this promotion of English produce or create the forms of imperialism rather than just reflect them?

The important point with Phillipson's (1992) view is to understand what it can and cannot do. As he suggests, the issue for him is "structural power" (p. 72), not intentions and not local effects. He is interested in "English linguistic hegemony," which can be understood as "the explicit and implicit beliefs, purposes, and activities which characterize the ELT (English Language Teaching) profession and which contribute to the maintenance of English as a dominant language" (p. 73). Thus, it is the ways that English is promoted through multiple agencies and to the exclusion of other languages that is the issue. What this, of course, lacks is a view of how English is taken up, how people use English, why people choose to use English. As we have seen, critical work often problematizes that notion of choice, arguing that choices are both materially and ideologically constrained. But Phillipson runs the danger of implying that choices to use English are nothing but an ideological reflex of linguistic imperialism. Such a position lacks a sense of agency, resistance, or appropriation (issues to which I return). What Phillipson shows, therefore, is how and for what purposes English is deliberately promoted and spread. What he does not show is the effects of that spread in terms of what people do with English.

Phillipson's work has been very important. Similar to Fairclough's (→ chap. 4), it has put into play political ways of understanding language that have had little discussion in more mainstream versions of applied linguistics. But also similar to Fairclough, he operates with a paradigm of both language and power that leaves us with several problems. Phillipson takes a static view of language and maps it onto a deterministic political framework, suggesting thereby that the promotion of English supports dominant capitalist and political interests. It is perhaps the very power of Phillipson's framework that is also its weakness. As Canagarajah (1999b) comments:

> In considering how social, economic, governmental, and cultural institutions effect inequality, his perspective becomes rather too impersonal and global. What is sorely missed is the individual, the particular. It is important

> to find out how linguistic hegemony is experienced in the day-to-day life of
> the people and communities in the periphery. How does English compete
> for dominance with other languages in the streets, markets, homes, schools,
> and villages of periphery communities? (pp. 41–42)

Thus, if a framework such as Phillipson's is used only to map out ways in
which English has been deliberately spread and to show how such policies
and practices are connected to larger global forces, it can be useful. But the
moment it slips into apparently implying effects of such promotion, it is
limited. As Canagarajah suggests, we then need to investigate the micro
politics of language use.

The main mode of opposition to this external threat posed by dominant languages is through a notion of language rights (Phillipson, 1998;
Phillipson & Skutnabb-Kangas, 1995; Skutnabb-Kangas, 1998;
Skutnabb-Kangas & Phillipson, 1994). Reviewing various documents on
human rights, they suggest that there is little provision for the positive
right to education in a mother tongue. Thus, Skutnabb-Kangas (1998) argues, "we are still living with linguistic wrongs" that are a product of the
belief ("monolingual reductionism") in the normality of monolingualism
and the dangers of multilingualism to the security of the nation state.
Both, she suggests, are dangerous myths. "Unless we work fast," she argues, "excising the cancer of monolingual reductionism may come too
late, when the patient, the linguistic (and cultural) diversity in the world,
is already beyond saving" (p. 12). What is proposed, then, is that the
"right to identify with, to maintain and to fully develop one's mother
tongue(s)" should be acknowledged as "a self-evident, fundamental *individual* linguistic human right" (p. 22).

> [These] universal linguistic human rights should be guaranteed for an *indi-
> vidual* in relation to the *mother tongue(s)*, in relation to an *official language* (and
> thus in relation to bilingualism), in relation to a possible *language shift*, and in
> relation to *drawing profit from education* as far as the medium of education is
> concerned (p. 22)

This, then, is a powerful argument in favor of the support for diversity in
terms of fundamental human rights. Where the liberal versions I discussed earlier considered support for diversity in terms of pluralism for its
own sake, diversity as a national resource, or language ecology as a natural
balance of languages, the language rights argument supplies a *moral* imperative to support minority languages (and access to majority languages). It is the strength of this position that gives weight to Tollefson's
(1991) demand that an applied linguist committed to democracy must
also show "a commitment to the struggle for language rights" (p. 211).

Powerful as such arguments are, there are also some concerns here.
First, there is at times a tendency to slip into simplistic dichotomizations:
Skutnabb-Kangas (1998), for example, talks of the way language perpetu-

ates the division between "the A-team, the elites of the world, and the B-team, the dominated, ordinary people" (p. 16). Such dichotomizing between the haves and have-nots can obscure social realities far more than they reveal them. Second, there is a related tendency to then suggest that those that have rights have full access to all aspects of language, while those without such rights do not:

> Linguistic majorities, speakers of a dominant language, usually enjoy all those linguistic human rights which can be seen as fundamental, regardless of how they are defined. Most linguistic minorities do not enjoy these rights. It is only a few hundred of the world's 6 - 7,000 languages that have any kind of official status, and it is only speakers of official languages who enjoy *all* linguistic human rights. (Phillipson, Rannut, & Skutnabb-Kangas, 1994, pp. 1–2)

My concern here is that while an important struggle is being fought here on one front, on another, there is a problem that the belief that speakers of "official languages" enjoy "*all* linguistic human rights" may overlook many other concerns to do with access and representation in language, concerns that are significant for speakers of both official and nonofficial languages (Pennycook, 1998b).

Other concerns have to do with the difficulties in translating broad appeals to language rights into legal definitions and in using the notion of human rights as a universal concept. Coulmas (1998), for example, draws attention to the problems involved in defining what a language and a speech community is (also see Pennycook, 1998b) and the problems in getting states to adhere to such necessarily vague definitions. "While general proclamations of linguistic human rights may not do much harm," he suggests, "it is doubtful that they can be translated into law" (p. 72). Rassool (1998) and I (1998b) have also pointed to the problem of human rights discourse as an unacceptably fundamentalist claim to morality in the contemporary world (for more discussion on fundamentalism, essentialism, and postmodernism, see later discussions). Rassool (1998) argues that the complex, interconnected nature of the modern world means we have to investigate other ways of looking at questions of language rights: "In the light of these dynamic changes taking place globally and nationally can the argument for a universalizing discourse on cultural and linguistic pluralism be sustained?" (p. 98). Finally, Coulmas (1998) also asks whether the notion that language shift is necessarily a catastrophe may be a passing ideological fashion, based as it is on a "nineteenth-century romantic idea that pegs human dignity as well as individual and collective identity to individual languages" (p. 71).

This discussion has raised some crucial questions. One of the great challenges for critical applied linguistics is to find ways of relating micro relations of language use to macro relations of social context. In the context of looking at implications of the global spread of English, such a relation is possibly at its most extreme, where the micro may be anything down to a conversation in English and the macro may be global capitalist relations. It is not surprising, then, given the scope of such a task, that it runs into a number of problems. I have suggested both that domains such as sociolinguistics and language planning need critical analyses of the social and political contexts of language use and that critical approaches should also be open to criticism for the reductive analyses of social relations that they at times produce. The frameworks I have discussed here clearly add some important dimensions to the discussion of language planning and policy by going beyond a vapid liberal argument for pluralism (everyone should be allowed to do what they want) and instead linking the support of diversity to broader questions of power, inequality, and racism. Thus, this support for linguistic diversity is not simply pluralism for its own sake but rather is pluralism as a necessary opposition to inequitable provisions based on linguistic hierarchies and also to the forces of homogenization, to linguistic and cultural genocide. It is also support for diversity grounded in a moral position based on a notion of human rights. As I argue later, to develop an adequate critical applied linguistics, we do indeed have to engage with questions of morals and ethics. And finally, the discussion here has pointed toward the need to understand contextually how broader social and political forces are felt; in what ways do people resist or appropriate what is being forced on them? This issue I now pursue further through a discussion of postcolonialism.

POSTCOLONIALISM AND RESISTANCE

As the earlier discussion suggested, a crucial aspect of critical theorizing needs to incorporate the notion of resistance, ways in which people are not mere respondents to the dictates of social structure and ideology but rather are social actors who also resist sites of oppression. Canagarajah (1999b) calls the first position—a deterministic argument in which the power of dominant groups is constantly reproduced and there is little chance for change (compare some of the frameworks discussed earlier and ← chap. 2; also see → chap. 5)—a *reproduction orientation* since it is centrally concerned with how power and inequality are reproduced. This he contrasts with a *resistance perspective,* which

> provides for the possibility that, in everyday life, the powerless in post-colonial communities may find ways to negotiate, alter and oppose political structures, and reconstruct their languages, cultures and identities to their advantage. The intention is not to *reject* English, but to *reconstitute* it in more inclusive, ethical and democratic terms. (p. 2)

Although resistance and appropriation are important in any context, they are central concerns of postcolonialism.

Colonialism and Postcolonialism

There have been many debates over the term *postcolonialism,* some seeing it as nothing but the historical period after colonialism, others viewing it as the intellectual movement that has revitalized English studies, and others viewing it as yet another Western elitist fabrication (Loomba, 1998). As McClintock (1994) warns, it is crucial at the very least to rescue the notion from the ahistorical and monolithic use that fails to differentiate between the many forms of colonialism and resistance. Just as the other *posts* of the triumvirate (postmodernism and poststructuralism) need to be understood in more complex terms than simply temporality (after structuralism, we have poststructuralism; after modernism, postmodernism), it is important to view postcolonialism not so much in terms of temporal progression but rather as a rewriting of colonialism, an oppositional stance to the continuing effects of colonialism, and an appropriation of colonial tools for postcolonial ends. Thus, in the same way that it is useful to distinguish between postmodernity and postmodernism (→ chap. 5), the former being a term used to describe a current condition—the state of life and thought in late capitalist society—while the latter is an intellectual and cultural movement that seeks to deconstruct givens of dominant modes of thought and to open a space for diversity, so it is useful to distinguish between postcoloniality and postcolonialism, the former being a material state after the end of colonialism and the latter a political and cultural movement that seeks to challenge the received histories and ideologies of former colonial nations and to open a space for insurgent knowledges to emerge.

To understand postcolonialism, then, we need some understanding of colonialism. I have written very extensively on these matters elsewhere (1998a) and here only sketch some important background understandings to establish the context of postcolonialism. From my point of view, in line with other arguments I make in this book about a move away from economic determinism, one of my central interests is in viewing colonialism in terms other than the purely economic. For some, such as Chrisman and Williams (1994), colonialism should be understood primarily as the local context of capitalist imperialism:

> [as] the conquest and direct control of other people's land ... a particular phase in the history of imperialism, which is now best understood as the globalisation of the capitalist mode of production, its penetration of previously non-capitalist regions of the world, and destruction of pre- or non-capitalist forms of social organization. (p. 2)

While acknowledging the significance of the history of colonialism as global capitalism, I also prefer to view colonialism in terms that go beyond economic determinism. As Nandy (1983) suggests, "It is becoming increasingly obvious that colonialism—as we have come to know it during the last two hundred years—cannot be identified with only economic gain and political power" (p. 1). For Nandy, colonialism is crucially a "state of mind in the colonizers and the colonized, a colonial consciousness which includes the sometimes unrealizable wish to make economic and political profits from the colonies, but other elements too" (pp. 1–2).

It is useful, therefore, to view colonialism as about far more than just economic and political exploitation; it was also a massive movement that both produced and in turn was produced by colonial cultures and ideologies. As Thomas (1994) puts it, "colonialism is not best understood primarily as a political or economic relationship that is legitimized or justified through ideologies of racism or progress. Rather, colonialism has always, equally importantly and deeply, been a cultural process" (p. 2). Such an argument, furthermore, is not merely aimed at switching the focus from economic exploitation to cultural imposition (colonialism was the site of both economic and cultural imperialism): Rather, it is concerned with how colonialism also *produced* European culture. Colonialism was the very context in which much of European culture and knowledge was developed. According to Fanon (1963):

> Europe undertook the leadership of the world with ardour, cynicism and violence .... That same Europe where they were never done talking of Man, and where they never stopped proclaiming that they were only anxious for the welfare of Man: today we know with what sufferings humanity has paid for every one of their triumphs of the mind. (p. 251)

As Young (1990) suggests, it is this relation between European enlightenment, with its "grand projects and universal truth-claims" (p. 9), and the history of European colonialism that Césaire and Fanon brought to light. And thus it becomes clear that:

> Humanism itself, often validated among the highest values of European civilization, was deeply complicit with the violent negativity of colonialism, and played a crucial part in its ideology. The formation of the ideas of human nature, humanity and the universal qualities of the human mind as the common good of an ethical civilization occurred at the same time as those particularly violent centuries in the history of the world now known as the era of Western colonialism. (p. 121)

This is, I believe, a crucial understanding since it makes of postcolonialism not just an attempt to rewrite colonial history or to allow voices from former colonies to be heard (as rather insipid versions of *postcolonial literature* would suggest) but rather a challenge to some of the "central" categories of Western thought. This argument about the development of European notions of "humanity," "human nature," and "human rights" suggests that they are far more problematic as tools for emancipatory purposes than many of their proponents would acknowledge. Whether used as a form of pedagogy, a search for underlying commonalities, or an argument for inalienable rights, such concepts have too long a history of Eurocentrism and collusion with colonialism to be either universal or innocent.

If we acknowledge too that colonial discourses have outlived the formal ending of colonial rule and are not merely dependent on continuing relations of neocolonialism, then postcolonialism becomes an ongoing challenge to the continuation of colonial discourses. As Singh (1996) asks

> Why is it that the colonial paradigm persists, and even acquires an urgent, *contemporary* validity? … Cultural, racial, and moral differences established by colonialism continue to have broad ramifications for the way in which marginal, subordinated races, cultures, economic groups, and sexualities are defined and figured as "others" in relation to dominant privileged categories. (p. 5)

It is in response to this question that postcolonialism is potentially the most significant of the *posts*: Its politics go to the very heart of treasured modes of European thought. It is postcolonialism that challenges claims to "rationality," "enlightenment," "logic," and so on, not merely because of their suspect epistemological status but because of the global horrors and inequities with which they are connected. An engagement with postcolonialism makes emancipatory critical modernism (← chap. 2) look most suspect since it is exactly the notions of enlightenment and rationality at the core of this view of change that are so profoundly complicit with, even in great measure products of, colonialism.

Resistance, Appropriation, and Third Spaces

Returning more explicitly to ways in which postcolonial perspectives help us to think about language and diversity, several new threads emerge:

- An historical understanding of language use,
- A nonessentialist stance emphasizing appropriation and hybridity,
- A focus on local contexts of language.

First is the need to develop an historical understanding. One of the abiding problems with applied linguistics is its lack of history. Apart from a few mentions in literature reviews of the historical formation of concepts such as *communicative competence,* there is little sense either of the larger historical formation of applied linguistics as a discipline or of the ways in which we exist as historical beings, how the words we use and the interactions we engage in are historically located, and as I have argued (1998a), how our words and discourses echo with historical relations. As Rampton (1995a) points out in his work on language use in school settings in England, there is a noticeable failure to address colonial and post-colonial language relationships in the countries where pupils have family ties. If one neglects historical and comparative sociolinguistic analysis, one loses a good deal of purchase on the ways in which British discourse about language, foreigners and education have been shaped within particular positions of power. (pp. 325–326)

As I argue later, a sense of the historical becomes a crucial element in locating critical work and moving toward the concept of situatedness that becomes a necessity once we accept postcolonial and postmodern challenges.

The critical histories of postcolonialism shed light on many areas such as translation. In light of the complicities between translation and Orientalism (Said, 1978) in the colonial context, Niranjana (1991), for example, argues that:

> Translation as a practice shapes, and takes shape within, the asymmetrical relations of power that operate under colonialism. What is at stake here is the representation of the colonized, who need to be produced in such a manner as to justify colonial domination. (p. 124)

As Niranjana shows, the practice of translation of Indian writing cannot be seen as some transparent project of representing Indian thought and history in translation. Rather, it was part of the whole colonial engagement with and construction of the "Other." Translation "reinforces hegemonic visions of the colonized" and helps to *fix* colonized cultures, "making them seem static and unchanging rather than historically constructed" (pp. 125–126). This historical hindsight, then, sheds light on more contemporary practices of translation as a process in "fixing the Other." As Venuti (1997) points out, the postwar translation of Japanese writing was dictated by the particular agenda of a conservative and nostalgic group of mainly North American academics, establishing "a canon of Japanese fiction in English that was not only unrepresentative, but based on a well-defined stereotype that has determined reader expectations for roughly forty years" (p. 72).

Second, Rampton's (1995a) focus on *language crossing*, "the use of language varieties associated with social or ethnic groups that the speaker does not normally 'belong' to" (p. 14), brings us to the issues raised by Canagarajah (1999b) of resistance and appropriation. Such a view of language use depends on a nonessentialist stance, a refusal of static categories of *ethnicity* and *belonging*, and an understanding of the possibilities of using language against the grain, of taking up and using a language that has been a tool of oppression, colonialism, or rigid identity and turning it against itself. It is to theorize the complexities of these relations that the notions of *hybridity* and *appropriation* have become so salient in postcolonial studies since a central part of the postcolonial is not only a critique of the metropolitan categories of knowledge and culture but also a taking over of and reuse of language, culture, and knowledge. This is most obvious in the use of English and other colonial languages in creative writing, in the ways "the empire writes back" (Ashcroft, Griffiths, & Tiffin, 1989), but it also extends to many forms of appropriation, from art to architecture, from cricket to music.

If we return for a moment to global theories of imperialism, a postcolonial perspective raises a number of different concerns. Phillipson and Skutnabb-Kangas (1996) argue that English goes hand in hand with processes of "ideological globalization ... transnationalization ... and Americanization and the homogenization of world culture ... spear-headed by films, pop culture, CNN, and fast-food chains" (p. 439). But globalization, especially if we are talking in cultural terms rather than mere economic terms (where culture is but a reflex of economic relations), needs a more complex vision than this. Appadurai (1990) suggests the "new global cultural economy has to be understood as a complex, overlapping, disjunctive order, which cannot any longer be understood in terms of existing center–periphery models" (p. 296). This position moves toward the

> conceptualization of global culture less in terms of alleged homogenizing processes (e.g., theories which present cultural imperialism, Americaniza-tion and mass consumer culture as a proto-universal culture riding on the back of Western economic and political domination) and more in terms of the diversity, variety and richness of popular and local discourses, codes and practices which resist and play-back systematicity and order. (Featherstone, 1990, p. 2)

This perspective, therefore, emphasizes the possibilities of change, resistance, and appropriation.

This perspective is to some extent reflected in the work on world Englishes (Kachru, 1996). Rajagopalan (1999) critiques the notion of linguistic imperialism and suggests that:

> The very charges being pressed against the hegemony of the English lan-guage and its putative imperialist pretensions themselves bear the imprint of a way of thinking about language moulded in an intellectual climate of ex-cessive nationalist fervour and organized marauding of the wealth of alien nations—an intellectual climate where identities were invariably thought of in all-or-nothing terms. (p. 201)

This point relates to the concern I raise in this book that emancipatory modernism bears too many of the hallmarks of its 19th-century European origins to continue to provide a framework for critical applied linguistics. In place of linguistic imperialism, Rajagopalan argues for a world Englishes perspective that focuses on how languages change and adapt.

As Canagarajah (1999a) warns, however, there are dangers with this position. Although he acknowledges the problems with the absolutism of the notion of linguistic imperialism (LI), he also takes the world Englishes linguistic hybridity (LH) position of Rajagopalan to task for its apolitical relativism:

> While LI is deterministic in perceiving these constructs as always pliable in the hands of dominant forces, LH is anti-nomian, in seeing them as perpetually unstable, and resisting control. While LI is activist in struggling against hegemonic discourses to reconstruct a more democratic order, LH leads to apathy (as languages are seen as deconstructing themselves, transcending domination) or even playfulness (as the provision of new meanings to these constructs is treated as subverting the status quo). (p. 207)

This, then, is an important final point: In avoiding the determinism of some critical stances, we need to be cautious not to slide into an apolitical relativism. We must be cautious not to lose sight of the very real forces of global capital and media while we also seek to understand the response to cultural spread and not assume its instant effects. Thus, as Claire Kramsch (1993) suggests, we need to start thinking here of what is produced in cultural encounters, not just homogeneity or heterogeneity or imperialism or resistance, but rather what *third cultures* or *third spaces* are constantly being created.

Finally, postcolonialism also demands that we work contextually. Thus, for example, Dua's (1994) analysis of the hegemony of English in India points to all the complex ways in which English operates in relation to indigenous languages, in education, language policy, mass media, and so on. And such local hegemonies contribute toward a larger position of hegemony. But such hegemonies are also filled with complex local contradictions, with the resistances and appropriations that are a crucial part of the postcolonial context. It is this understanding of global presence and local specificity that I (1994b) tried to capture in the concept of the *worldliness of English*. This is central to Canagarajah's (1999b) analysis of resistance in English language teaching. Thus, his work focuses on critical ethnographies of resistance, on the ways in which the Tamil community in Sri Lanka "appropriates English to dynamically negotiate meaning, identity, and status in contextually suitable and socially strategic ways, and in the process modifies the communicative and linguistic rules of English according to local cultural and ideological imperatives" (p. 76) If we start to pursue such questions in terms of local contexts of language, it becomes possible to consider using English not so much in terms of some inevitable commonality but rather in terms of what I have called *postcolonial performativity* (1999b).

CONCLUSION: TOWARD A POSTCOLONIAL PERFORMATIVE VIEW OF LANGUAGE

I suggested in this chapter that areas such as sociolinguistics and language policy and planning do not automatically constitute background theoretical domains for critical applied linguistics; indeed, they are in many respects deeply inadequate for such a task. Rather than the dominant liberal framework of politics that underlies much of the work in these areas, a more critical framework is called for. Here too we need to be cautious, however, since mainstream critical work often presents us with deterministic and materialist frameworks that map a static view of language onto a rigid model of politics. In general, I suggest:

- The need for a critical social theory capable of dealing with the maintenance of inequality,
- An approach to language that goes beyond description and moves toward critique,
- An understanding of the shortcomings of a model that emphasizes appropriacy,
- A view of language as productive as well as reflective of social relations.

In terms of the issues raised by postcolonial perspectives on the global spread of English, I also pointed to:

- The need for an historical understanding of language use,
- A view of culture, identity, and global politics that avoids essentialism and instead looks at forms of resistance and appropriation,
- A need always to work contextually.

This emphasis on appropriation and hybridity, however, needs to be viewed with caution lest it slide into an apolitical celebration of difference. Combining the insights of a postcolonial understanding of language as well as a nonessentialist view on language and identity (in terms of performativity → chaps. 4 and 6), the notion of postcolonial performativity may be a useful way forward here.

Two further key issues are worth considering. First, it may appear unproductive to devote as much space to a critique of both liberal and critical frameworks, especially when the latter includes powerful notions such as language rights and linguistic imperialism. Yet I believe it is important to do so. As I have been suggesting, my understanding of critical applied linguistics is that it should always be critical of itself. Thus, at the same time that I would include linguistic imperialism as an important part of critical applied linguistics, I also feel that it needs critical analysis. Here it is useful to recall Spivak's (1993) notion of "the strategic use of essentialism." As Spivak points out, the "critique of essentialism" should be understood not as an exposure of our or others' errors but as "an acknowledgment of the dangerousness of something one cannot not use"

(p. 5). Notions such as language rights and linguistic imperialism are very powerful and can be very effective for pointing out issues of tremendous moral and political concern. Putting such terms onto the applied linguistic agenda and into the applied linguistic vocabulary is of profound importance. Strategically used, they can be crucial tools in critical applied linguistic struggles, but we also need to acknowledge the dangerousness of these terms that we cannot not use. Using essentialism strategically is at least one way to do one's politics (see Fig. 3.1).

Second, then, although we do need a critical version of language and social relations, it needs to be one that can take us beyond deterministic and only pessimistic analyses: Critical applied linguistics needs forms of analysis that can lead to forms of action. Thus, in developing critical applied linguistics, we need not only large-scale theories of society but also ways of thinking about change, resistance, alternatives. Otherwise, both our analysis and our pedagogy are paralyzed. Mey's (1985) vision of language and power that I discussed in the last chapter (← chap. 2), whereby language only reflects social power, leaves us little chance for change. It is crucial that we develop useful, workable, and subtle analyses of language and power, and part of the process of developing critical applied linguistics has to be in the ways we work both with and against critical concepts such as class, patriarchy, or imperialism. I use this critique of overarching "structural" theories to point to the importance of dealing with contexts and the formation and tools of agency. As I argued earlier in this chapter, it is important to have a vision of language that not only reflects but also produces and therefore can alter social relations. As Cameron (1990) argues with respect to language and gender, a position that suggests that language merely reflects society suggests that the only domain for change must be social change: To change the way gender operates in and through language, we must change society first. But a great deal of feminist work on language has clearly operated from the belief that change in language may also produce change in society. And, as I argue more generally, we need a position in critical applied linguistics that suggests a complex interplay between language and social relations, that suggests that the work we do may have potential for change.

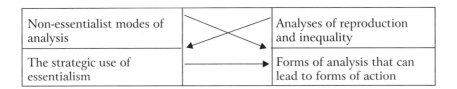

FIG. 3.1.   Analysis and action

The Politics of Text

Critical Literacy
    Literacies as Social Practices
Critical Discourse Analysis
Ideology, Discourse, Truth, and Power
    Knowledge Claims and Truth
    Order and Disorder
    The Nonmaterial Base of Discourse
    Production and Reception
Critical Language Awareness and the Genres of Power
Critical Literacy and Voice: The Word and the World
From Poststructuralism to Postlinguistics
    Toward a Postlinguistics
Conclusion: Toward an Applied Postlinguistics

The previous chapter (← chap. 3) looked at critical approaches to language that are concerned mainly with language use from an *external* perspective on how language operates socially: Who gets to use language(s)? How do we understand the social distribution of language? How is power conveyed and reproduced through language use? This chapter turns to the critical analysis of texts or discourses. Some of the questions are, on the one hand, quite similar: How do we relate a text to broader social and political contexts? How is power produced, conveyed, or diffused in acts of language use? How do particular understandings of power and ideology affect how

74

we look at texts? On the other hand, there is an important shift here to look at meaning and context: How is it that texts come to mean as they do? How can we understand the ways in which ideologies operate through texts? How do readers interpret texts, and what effects may this have?

I have chosen to call this chapter "The Politics of Text" to encompass the broad field of critical approaches to textual analysis, including critical literacy, critical discourse analysis, and critical language awareness. I try to show how different critical approaches to text fit together and how they approach the crucial questions of discourse, meaning and power in different ways. This discussion includes questions regarding:

- Understanding literacy as a social practice;
- Critical literacy as text analysis;
- Knowledge, ideology, and discourse;
- Critical literacy in terms of access and awareness;
- Critical literacy and voice.

Finally, I move on to discuss the possibilities and limitations posed by poststructuralism, the notion of *postlinguistics*—an amalgam of poststructuralist and linguistic approaches to textual analysis—and what an applied postlinguistics may need in terms of a critical approach to texts.

CRITICAL LITERACY

As Luke and Walton (1994) observe, critical literacy may take many forms. First of all, it is important to distinguish between concepts of the critical that relate more to literary criticism and those that might be seen as forms of *critical social literacy* and would therefore fall within the interests of this book (compare parallel arguments in ← chaps. 1, 2, and 3). According to Luke and Freebody (1997):

> Although critical literacy does not stand for a unitary approach, it marks out a coalition of educational interests committed to engaging with the possibilities that the technologies of writing and other modes of inscription offer for social change, cultural diversity, economic equity, and political enfranchisement. (p. 1)

Once again, the connections to my vision of critical applied linguistics are evident in the emphasis on relations between language and broader social and political concerns and on change, diversity, and enfranchisement. As Luke (1997a) suggests, although critical approaches to literacy share an orientation toward understanding literacy (or literacies) as social practices related to broader social and political concerns, there are a number of different orientations including text analytic approaches, Freirean-based critical pedagogy, and feminist and poststructuralist orientations.

Lankshear (1997) distinguishes between different objects of critique in critical literacy: a critical perspective on literacy (or literacies), a critical perspective on particular texts, and a critical perspective on wider social practices. Lee (1997) also draws a three-way distinction between critical literacy viewed in terms of access, in terms of textual meanings, and in terms of discourse critique. Putting Luke's, Lankshear's, and Lee's analyses together, we can distinguish the following approaches to critical literacy:

- A general critical view of what literacy is, which I discuss as literacy as social practice;
- Various approaches to critical textual analysis, which I discuss in terms of critical discourse analysis and critical language awareness;
- A focus on providing greater access to literacy, which I discuss under genre literacy;
- An emphasis on Freirean-based participatory literacies or critical pedagogical approaches to marginalization, which I discuss in terms of critical pedagogy and voice;
- Critical literacy as a form of poststructuralist practice that aims to explore the discursive construction of reality across different sites.

Literacies as Social Practices

The distinction between a critical view of literacy and a 'noncritical' view mirrors similar distinctions I already discussed in previous chapters (e.g., ← chap. 3) between, on the one hand, autonomous, cognitive, universalist accounts of language use as mental processes and on the other hand, socially grounded accounts of language use in context. It has been common to see literacy as a set of isolated skills: reading and writing, decoding and encoding texts. Within applied linguistics and TESOL, the tendency has been to view literacy for second language learners as solely to do with psycholinguistic processes, schema theory, or first language transfer. From this perspective, literacy is simply the ability to read and write, and these skills are seen as autonomous, asocial, and decontextualized cognitive processes, the second pair in the 'four skills' approach to second language education (listening, speaking, reading, writing).

In first language education this "autonomous" view of literacy is frequently tied to what has been termed the *literacy myth,* a view that ascribes to literacy many profound social, cultural, economic, and political effects. Indeed, literacy is often seen as one of the absolute dividers between "civilized" and "primitive," "literate" and "nonliterate." As Gee (1996) describes this view:

> Literacy leads to logical, analytical, critical, and rational thinking, general and abstract uses of language, skeptical and questioning attitudes, a distinction between myth and history, a recognition of the importance of time and space, complex and modern governments (with separation of church and state), political democracy and greater social equity, a lower crime rate, better citizens, economic development, wealth and productivity, political stability, urbanization, and a lower birth rate. (p. 26)

Such a view—that literacy is in and of itself beneficial—is very close to the views I discussed (← chap. 3) that learning "standard English" will somehow bestow all sorts of benefits on its users. As we saw in that context, not only is the notion of standard English something of a myth but so too is the idea that it can somehow bring automatic benefits to its users. The effects of learning a language or a variety of a language can only be understood within a broader context of social and cultural relations. So too with literacy.

An alternative view has suggested that literacy must be seen not so much as a monolithic entity but rather as a set of contextualized social practices. From this perspective, the notion that there is a "great divide" between literacy and oracy is called into question, and the focus is always on literacies (as plural and complex practices) in their social contexts as *literacy practices* (Baynham, 1995), *social literacies* (Gee, 1996; Lankshear, 1997; Street, 1995), or *multiliteracies* (Cope & Kalantzis, 2000; New London Group, 1996). Street (1995) argues that "literacy in itself does not promote cognitive advance, social mobility or progress: Literacy practices are specific to the political and ideological context and their consequences vary situationally" (p. 24). Crucial in the development of this perspective has been work such as Shirley Brice Heath's (1983) illustration of how people from different backgrounds had different ways of taking from texts and participated in different sorts of literacy events. This, she went on to show, had important implications for schooling since middle-class homes tended to mirror the literacy events of school more closely than did the literacy events of the different working-class homes she studied (→ also the discussion of Bourdieu and others in chap. 5). Heath's argument was not that homes should change to match school literacy practices but that schools should learn to accommodate different orientations toward texts.

Building on these perspectives, a great deal of work in critical literacy has shown how the significant issues for literacy are not so much how the brain deals with text but how literacy is related to its context. There are, however, a number of limitations with this work. While Street's autonomous/ideological dichotomy opened up a space for work on literacy practices, the ideological here remains ungrounded. Thus, there is only an injunction to contextualize but not to politicize in any direction toward social transformation. As Auerbach (1999) suggests, while a social practices approach to literacy may open up important dimensions ignored by either autonomous or cognitive approaches, it lacks a critique of power and a vision of change. Similarly, although Gee's (1996) work has been important in opening up understandings of literacy and of how and why children from different backgrounds may or may not succeed in school, his work suffers from a curious mixture of both under- and overdetermination. On the one hand, Gee's work rests on rather vague social and political views on class and *fast capitalism* (Gee, 2000) that have been used to underpin some of the New London Group's version of multiliteracies (see later). Again, there is no particular vision of social change here, only one that suggests that a working-class girl, whose language use he studies, may not be able to avoid traditional or service industry labor unless given access to multiple literacy skills. On the other hand, Gee (1996) relates his theory of primary and secondary discourse socialization to the work of Krashen, thus ending up by suggesting that primary discourses can be acquired but not learned. As Delpit (1995) remarks, "instead of being locked into 'your place' by your genes, you are now locked hopelessly into a lower-class status by your discourse" (p. 154). Often viewed as mainstream critical literacy work, then, this form of social practices literacy places literacy in context but fails to offer a political critique of those contexts or an adequate vision of change.

When tied to a more overt critical politics, however, the study of the social contexts of literacy has opened up many significant avenues for understanding how literacy is related to power, difference, and disparity, such as the critical study of workplace literacies (Lankshear, 1997), the role of early school and home reading materials in the socialization of children (Davies, 1989; Luke, 1988), the reading practices of teenage and adult women (Radway, 1984; Talbot, 1995; Walkerdine, 1990), or access and denial of access to literacy for women. Rockhill's (1994) study of Hispanic immigrant women in California, for example, points to the complex conflicts posed by the threat and desire of literacy:

> The politics of literacy are integral to the cultural genocide of a people, as well as the gendering of society .... Literacy is caught up in the material, racial and sexual oppression of women, *and* it embodies their hope for escape. For women, it is experienced as *both*, a threat and a desire—to learn English means to go to school—to enter a world that holds the promise of change, and because of this, threatens all that they know. (pp. 247–248)

Thus, while literacy is often "women's work but not women's right" (p. 248), their desire to "be somebody" by gaining literacy in English and the threat that such desires pose to the patriarchal structures of many family lives leaves many immigrant women in a conflictual and ambiguous situation.

CRITICAL DISCOURSE ANALYSIS

The notion of literacies as social practices links to the discussion (← chap. 3) of ways of viewing language use as part of a critical analysis of social contexts. As I suggested earlier, however, the focus of this chapter is more closely on texts themselves through a discussion of critical discourse analysis since this has become one of the most influential critical approaches to text in applied linguistics. Indeed, it sometimes seems that CDA is taken to be synonymous with a critical approach to applied linguistics.[1] Given the significance of CDA for critical applied linguistics, therefore, I devote considerable space here first to a general overview of CDA; second, to a discussion of some key concerns in CDA; and finally, to a consideration of how we can go beyond this important yet very particular orientation to critical textual work. A central point of my argument here is that although CDA has played a highly significant role in opening up the possibilities for doing critical work in applied linguistics, it has also become another form of "mainstream critical work" that also closes down the possibilities for thinking about critical text analysis in different ways.

Fairclough and Wodak (1996) discuss eight different approaches to CDA, including:

- The rather vaguely termed *French discourse analysis* (referring to the work of Foucault, Pêcheux, and others);
- *Critical linguistics,* particularly the work of Fowler, Kress, Hodge, and Trew (1979) and Kress and Hodge (1979), which uses the systemic functional linguistics of Michael Halliday (1978);
- The broader realization of this view in the *social semiotics* of Hodge and Kress (1988), who among other things, emphasize the need to move beyond looking merely at printed texts to explore how texts interrelate with other visual representations and how visual representations themselves operate as complex visual semiotic spaces (Kress & van Leeuwen, 1990);
- *Sociocultural change and change in discourse,* referring to Fairclough's interest in the ways in which changes in the broader social and cultural domain are reflected in changes in discursive practices;
- *Sociocognitive studies,* a category used by van Dijk to account cognitively for the relation between language use (discourse) and social relations;
- The *discourse-historical method* of Ruth Wodak and her colleagues, which has emerged particularly in their interdisciplinary work on anti-Semitic discourse in Austria (e.g., Wodak et al., 1999);
- The *reading analysis* (*Leseartenanalyse*) of Utz Maas, which combines Foucauldian and hermeneutic analysis and has looked particularly at the discourses of Nazism;

---

[1] There is a tendency, it seems, in applied linguistics today to sprinkle a few references to Norman Fairclough's work around and thereby to claim that this constitutes critical work.

- The *Duisburg School,* which refers to the Foucauldian-influenced work of Siegfred and Margret Jäger (Jäger & Jäger, 1993) that has focused particularly on the discourses of the new right in Germany.

Despite the useful broadening of scope here from the all too frequent inclusion only of work in and on English, it is also worth noting that this list remains narrowly Eurocentric and does not include, for example, forms of postcolonial discourse analysis (e.g., Said, 1978).

Drawing on Fairclough and Wodak (1996), Wodak (1996) lists the following eight principles of CDA:

1. "CDA addresses social problems"; thus, the interest is not in language use itself but rather in "the linguistic character of social and cultural processes and structures" (p. 17).
2. "Power relations are discursive" (p. 18); that is to say, the focus on discourse is also a focus on how power operates through language.
3. "Discourse constitutes society and culture," which suggests that, as we saw in the discussion of sociolinguistics, CDA operates with an understanding of language not merely as a reflection of social relations but also as part of them, as actually (re)producing them in a dialectical relation.
4. "Discourse does ideological work"; thus ideologies, which are "particular ways of representing and constructing society which reproduce unequal relations of domination and exploitation" (p. 18), are often produced through discourse.
5. "Discourse is historical," suggesting that we must always examine discourse in context, which must also include the intertextual level of how "discourses are always connected to other discourses which were produced earlier" (p. 19).
6. We need a "socio-cognitive approach" to explain how relations between texts and society are "mediated" in the process of production and comprehension (p. 19).
7. "Discourse analysis is interpretive and explanatory" (p. 19) and uses a "systematic methodology" to relate texts to their contexts. These levels of the descriptive, interpretive, and explanatory are explored in greater depth by Fairclough (1992b; and see following).
8. CDA is a "socially committed scientific paradigm" (p. 20) that actively attempts to intervene and change what is happening in particular contexts.

In broad terms, it is possible to distinguish two main types of analysis (see Table 4.1). The first has to do with ways in which unequal power rela-

TABLE 4.1

Two Different Domains of Critical Discourse Analysis (CDA)

Power and linguistic interactions	Power and meaning
Analysis of control over topics, interactions, turn-taking, etc.	Analysis of the linguistic realization of ideology

tionships between participants in conversations are reproduced. Thus, by analyzing interactions between participants in conversations, one can show, for example that "topics are introduced and changed only by the dominant participant" (Fairclough, 1992b, p. 155). This sort of analysis of how power may determine who gets to speak, about what, and for how long has also been a major focus of work on language and gender. The second focus is on the content rather than the structure of texts and has to do with ways in which ideologies are (re)produced through discourses. Fairclough's (1995) basic argument is this: The goal of critical discourse analysis is to denaturalize ideologies that have become naturalized. Ideologies, he explains, are particular representations of some aspect of the world (which could be alternatively represented) that can be associated with some particular "social base." Such ideologies have become naturalized, "dissociated ... from the particular social base" (p. 35). So what we assume to be background knowledge or common sense in fact are always ideological representations; that is to say, what we assume to be common everyday knowledge is in fact always the particular worldview (ideology) of a particular social group.

The goal of CDA is to make these ideological systems and representations transparent and to show how they are related to the broader social order. Critical discourse analysis, therefore, means investigating discourses "with an eye to their determination by, and their effects on, social structures" (Fairclough, 1995, p. 36). This can be done because Fairclough assumes, controversially (as he admits), "that there is a one-to-one relationship between ideological formations and discursive formations" (p. 40). Whereas a focus on control over conversations needs only a fairly rudimentary conception of power (and also often a fairly circular one—those with power control conversations/those controlling conversations have power), this second focus on ideology requires a much more complex chain of relations: Ideological positions can be uncovered in texts; ideologies are the (concealed) views of particular social groups; those groups that frequently manage to promote their ideological position to the extent that it becomes naturalized are able to do so because of their social power; and by reproducing their ideologies, they are therefore able to reproduce social relations of power.

Fairclough (1992b) discusses discourse, therefore, as a "mode of political and ideological practice":

> Discourse as a political practice establishes, sustains and changes power relations, and the collective entities (classes, blocs, communities, groups) between which power relations obtain. Discourse as an ideological practice constitutes, naturalizes, sustains and changes significations of the world from diverse positions in power relations. (p. 67)

In a series of books and articles, Fairclough (1989, 1992b, 1993, 1995) has developed and enlarged this view of CDA. Probably the best known element of his work is the development of what he calls his "three-dimensional" model of CDA (1995, p. 98), incorporating on one level the analytical procedures of description, interpretation, and explanation and on another level the different levels of text, text production and reception, and the larger sociopolitical context. As others who have employed this model (e.g., Janks, 1997) observe, using it flexibly (rather than in some linear fashion) allows for multiple points of entry into texts and their contexts.

A great deal of powerful and provocative work has now been done within CDA, from Fairclough's (1993, 1995) analysis of the marketization of public discourse and the changes to how courses and jobs are advertised in British universities, to Wodak's (1996) analyses of doctor–patient interviews and school committee meetings, or vanDijk's (1993) work on racism in political debates. The work of Fairclough, Wodak, van Dijk, and others has been very useful in opening up the possibility of more politicized analysis of texts. We finally have power fully on the agenda of an analysis of discourse. A number of these features, furthermore, clearly have a lot in common with the general picture I have been building of critical applied linguistics: a politicized view of language, a commitment to academic work that puts its politics foremost, an attempt to draw relations between micro relations of language and macro relations of society, and a belief that such work can bring about social change. At the same time, this work raises some key issues for critical applied linguistics concerning ways in which power, text, and meaning are related. To develop an understanding of these concerns I discuss them here in some detail (for a summary, see Table 4.2).

IDEOLOGY, DISCOURSE, TRUTH, AND POWER

Two of the central terms that have emerged in this discussion of CDA are *discourse* and *ideology*. Fairclough, Wodak, van Dijk, and others in CDA generally employ the term *discourse* in the common linguistic sense as language in use and *ideology* as a particular framework of knowledge that is tied to social power and may be manifested in language. Thus, the goal of the critical analyst is to look in discourse for manifestations of ideology. This approach makes sense for those coming from a linguistic back-

TABLE 4.2

Central Concerns in Critical Discourse Analysis (CDA)

Claims to Scientificity	Can CDA be concerned with distinguishing between truth and falsity in discourse (ideological or nonideological representations)?
Order and Disorder	Is discourse disordered by power or ordered by power? Is the goal of CDA to restore order or to destabilize order?
Material Base of Ideology	Is ideology (or discourse) the by-product of social and economic power? Is the goal of CDA to find prior relations of power in language?
Production and Reception	Are meanings in texts or only in their interpretation? What is the status of a CDA reading of a text?

ground, for whom language and discourse are elements that need to be related to larger concerns such as society and ideology. But for cultural and critical theorists more generally, a major point of debate has been not so much to relate discourse to ideology but rather to choose between the two as competing terms. As Mills (1997) suggests, "for all cultural and critical theorists there has been intense theoretical difficulty in deciding whether to draw on work which is based around the notion of ideology or work which refers to discourse" (p. 29). The issue here, as I suggested in an earlier attempt to deal with these issues (Pennycook, 1994c), is not merely one of terminology; rather, it raises key concerns about central questions of power, truth, and meaning.

The two positions (discourse *and* ideology as opposed to discourse *or* ideology) have not been sufficiently disambiguated in CDA, which often attempts an eclectic mix of different positions on discourse and ideology (see Wodak's, 1996, discussion of Habermas and Foucault). Yet since these different positions derive from very different positions on language, truth, and power, it is important to be able to differentiate between an understanding of discourse deriving from linguistics and an understanding developed in opposition to a concept of ideology. Foucault's notion of discourse is not a text or some grouping of signs but rather "something which produces something else (an utterance, a concept, an effect) rather than something which exists in and of itself and which can be analysed in isolation" (Mills, 1997, p. 17). Discourses are indelibly tied to power and knowledge and truth, but they do not either represent or obfuscate truth and knowledge in the interests of pregiven powers (as in the case of many versions of ideology); rather, they produce knowledge and truth (they have knowledge and truth effects). Foucault (1980b) explicitly rejected the use of ideology in favor of discourse. Indeed, as Mills points out, "much of Foucault's work on discourse has been an open discussion and dialogue with the term ideology, and in some sense the term discourse has been defined in dialogue with and in reaction to the definition of ideology" (p. 32).

Foucault's (1980b) first objection to the notion of ideology is that it "always stands in virtual opposition to something else which is supposed to count as truth" (p. 118). It is not so much that work in CDA is not aware of this problem of its truth claims but rather that by adhering to a traditional view of ideology, it seems to have few ways of escaping this dilemma. Thus, Wodak (1996), for example, suggests that ideologies are "often (though not necessarily) false or ungrounded constructions of society" (p. 18). As Patterson (1997) argues, it is in such claims that "critical discourse analysis occupies a somewhat contradictory position" because "if the positivist claim to grasping truth is to be discredited, it seems odd that as a critical analyst I should feel free to assume the truth about ideological operations is within my reach" (p. 426). But it is indeed precisely because most work in CDA sits within a modernist emancipatory model of knowledge and the world and thus continues to use positivist, rationalist, or enlightenment models of meaning that it has been unable to step out of this dilemma. I look at these problems next by examining first the CDA claim to scientificity; second, the possibility of an ideal *order* outside the *disorder* of discourse; third, the question of the material base of ideology; and finally, issues of production and reception of texts.

Knowledge Claims and Truth

The problem of truth and falsity has a long history in relation to the modernist discourses of Marxism, particularly in the claims made to being a *science*. A common way of framing this truth/falsity dichotomy is by invoking the old Marxist dogma of true science versus false nonscience. As I suggested (← chap. 2), one of the key issues we need to deal with in CALx is the way in which we deal with questions of knowledge. There are those who want to claim scientific status for applied linguistics and thereby remove it from the political domain. On the other hand, there are those, such as many practitioners of CDA, who wish to argue that taking a political line is no less scientific. Thus, many of these authors are committed to a rationalist and scientific enterprise. Wodak (1996) describes CDA as a "socially committed scientific paradigm" (p. 20) and Kress (1990) summarizes the view of CDA practitioners as insisting that "while their activity is politically committed, it is nonetheless properly scientific, perhaps all the more so for being aware of its own political, ideological, and ethical stance" (p. 85). This attempt to construct a scientific edifice around CDA also emerges in the modeling and systematizing that is particularly evident in Fairclough (1989, 1992b, 1995).

The problem I have with this is that it appears to lack an element of self-reflexivity and fails to problematize the status of scientific knowledge. Foucault's notion of discourse, by contrast, sees such a claim to science as exactly the sort of combination of power and knowledge that is part of the problem. Foucault was fundamentally interested not in truth, but in *truth claims,* in the effect of making claims to knowledge. The important point, Foucault (1980b) suggests, is not to try to construct a category of scientific knowledge that can then claim some monopoly on the truth but rather to see "historically how effects of truth are produced within discourses which in themselves are neither true nor false" (p. 118). Furthermore, Foucault (1980b) suggests, we need to ask: "What types of knowledge do you want to disqualify in the very instant of your demand: 'Is it a science'?" (p. 85). This position, then, takes seriously what we might call the politics of knowledge. It suggests we cannot simply try to construct a politically good science but rather must ask questions not only of our political view of society but also of our political view of knowledge. And, it suggests that Kress' assertion that CDA is all the more scientific because of its awareness of its own politics unfortunately tells only half the story since it is in its very claims to scientificity, and the claims to truth that go with that, that CDA shows a blindness to the politics of knowledge.

Order and Disorder

In the work of Fairclough and Wodak, an odd contradiction emerges that sheds some light on these concerns over truth and falsity, ideology and discourse. Wodak (1996) is centrally interested in showing how "disorders of discourse" occur. Drawing, she says, on Foucault's notion of orders of discourse—indeed the very title of her book, *Disorders of Discourse,* is a play on Foucault's term—she looks at how

> disorders in discourse result from gaps between distinct and insufficiently coincident cognitive worlds: the gulfs that separate insiders from outsiders, members of institutions from clients of those institutions, and elites from the normal citizen uninitiated in the arcana of bureaucratic language and life. (p. 2)

She is interested in how, "through an analysis of micro-discourses it is possible to indicate the extent to which participants in interactions approach or retreat from mutually comprehensible communication" (p. 7). Thus, for Wodak, the interest is in how disorders of discourse—ways in which language becomes opaque, ways in which people fail to understand each other—occur in various institutional settings. Critical discourse analysis, in this view, is the analysis of discourses "which are 'distorted' by power" (p. 17).

In Wodak's view, then, we have an ideal *order* that is distorted by power and becomes *disorder*. The goal of the critical analyst is to detect such disorders, to intervene, and to return interactions to their state of order. This general view that power distorts communication, providing a form of *disordered discourse,* is common in much of CDA. Kress (1990), for example, suggests that "one effect of power is a move away from relatively straightforward representation—power deforms communication" (p. 90). Thus, in this view, power is external to communication and causes what might otherwise be transparent to become murky and "deformed." Van Dijk (1993b) argues that CDA "implies a political critique of those responsible for its perversion in the reproduction of dominance and inequality" (p. 253). In this form, it becomes perversion. All these approaches therefore seem to share a belief in some form of truth, an ordered, properly formed (not deformed), nonperverted, normal discourse. This is doubtless a seductive notion since it allows for the idea not merely that CDA can show how a particular ideological formation is constructed but that it can help us return to normal, ordered, nonperverted discourse.

Turning to Fairclough's notion of orders of discourse, which he also relates explicitly to Foucault's formulation, it is clear that this means something quite different. The notion of orders of discourse is used as a higher order of constraints on discourse. An order of discourse "is really a social order looked at from a specifically discoursal perspective—in terms of those types of practice into which a social space is structured which happen to be discourse types" (Fairclough, 1989, p. 29). Orders of discourse are the discursive equivalent of the social order, and, therefore, just as the social order is a context of inequitable social relations, so orders of discourse are a context of the inequitable ordering of discourses. Thus:

> How discourses are structured in a given order of discourse, and how structurings change over time, are determined by changing relations of power at the level of the social institution or of the society. Power at these levels includes the capacity to control orders of discourse; one aspect of such control is ideological—ensuring that orders of discourse are ideologically harmonized internally or (at the societal level) with each other. (p. 30)

So what is considered *ordered* in discourse—whether in terms of interactions or in terms of background knowledge—may be understood as part of a higher system of "ideological positions and practices" (Fairclough, 1995, p. 35).

It is important to note, then, that for Fairclough, the issue is not one of disorder being the deviant state and order being the preferred one. For him, orders of discourse are part of what keep inequitable social structures in place. In fact, it seems that what Fairclough means by *orders of discourse* or *orderliness* of discourse (that is, the way in which discourse reproduces power through naturalized forms of interaction and through ideologies naturalized as common sense) Wodak calls *disorders of discourse.* For

Fairclough, the problem is the imposed orders of capitalist society; for Wodak, the problem is the institutional disordering of order. Fairclough's orders are Wodak's disorders. Both views, I believe, suggest conceptual problems, and the existence of such contradictory positions in apparently similar approaches to CDA is a product of a rather strange mixture of theoretical eclecticism and unreflexive modernism.

For Wodak (1996), the notion of the order of discourse appears to be a preferable state of affairs. Her book shows how disorders of discourse arise in institutional settings. Her goal is to critique these and to intervene so that such disorders can be put to right. In the introduction to her book, Wodak discusses both Foucault and Habermas as sources for her "discourse sociolinguistics." Habermas is heir to a particular line of critical theory deriving from the Frankfurt School (← chaps. 1 and 2) and may be seen as a traditional emancipatory modernist, arguing that systems of rational/technological thought have invaded (colonized) the "lifeworld," and that we should strive for a more truly rational "ideal speech situation." As McCarthy (1978) explains, Habermas' view is based on "rationally motivated consensus": "Universal-pragmatic analysis of the conditions of discourse and rational consensus show these to rest on the supposition of an 'ideal speech situation' characterized by an effective equality to assume dialogue roles" (p. 325). Habermas (1998) sees his form of critical philosophy as the "guardian of reason." His view rests on the possibility of "communicative rationality" that

> is expressed in the unifying force of speech oriented towards reaching understanding, which secures for the participating speakers an intersubjectively shared lifeworld, thereby securing at the same time the horizon within which everyone can refer to the same objective world. (p. 315)

This form of critical theory has been very useful as part of the critique of the problems with the ongoing development of social life under the banner of modernity, of positivism in the social sciences, and of the ways in which particular types of knowledge colonize others. But Habermas' belief that it is the distortion of modernity that is the problem, that we need to continue to believe in the possibilities of rationality, enlightenment, ideal speech situations, and positions outside ideology make his ideas difficult to use for the type of critical applied linguistics I am trying to develop here. His "post-Marxist masculine and modernist anxiety about order, arrangement and keeping everything in its assigned place—perhaps especially women" (Threadgold, 1997, p. 112) does not match well with the sort of problematizing practice I am advocating here. Nevertheless, Wodak (1996) follows Habermas' interests in overcoming "systematically distorted communication" (p. 28): Power distorts real communication or ordered discourse. Wodak is therefore interested in how the "distortion of discourse" leads to "disorders of discourse" (p. 15).

And, she is clear that since CDA "does not claim that all discourses are ideological" (pp. 18–19), there is an ideal space outside ideology:

> Undistorted communication thus arises out of the ability of each (communicatively competent) speaker to test vigorously the justifiability of each validity claim put forward by redeeming it discursively .... In contrast, systematically distorted communication occurs when the universal, pragmatic norms of the ideal speech situation become subordinated to privileged interests, producing asymmetrical power relationships and resulting in a false consensus about the validity claims made. (p. 30)

But this view that there is a place outside power, outside ideology, outside discourse that is somehow neutral or free, a place of ordered discourse and harmony—even if only posited as a utopian goal—is, I argue, part of the European rationalistic belief that its forms of thought present some form of "enlightenment."

My view, by contrast, is that there is no escape from questions of power, no escape from ideology or discourse. Some (e.g., both Fairclough and Wodak) see this as an impossibly pessimistic and relativistic outlook (there is no hope of change, we are all trapped in language games, there is no possibility of deciding the truth of a position): As Fairclough (1995) makes clear in the introduction to his book, he is adamant about the importance of opposing what he sees as poststructuralist relativism; instead, he urges that we "should not feel embarrassed about making judgements of truth" (p. 19). I believe, by contrast, that the more poststructuralist position presents not an impossible relativism but rather a more complex, subtle, and reflexive position. To claim otherwise is to claim for oneself a position of knowledge that is somehow able to decide for others what is true. And it is not a disempowering relativism to believe that there is no escape from ideology, discourse, or language. The struggle, then, has to go on within our cultures, discourses, or worldviews without claiming an objective truth outside them. As Allan Luke (1997b) puts it, "critical discourse analysis is a situated political practice: a machine for generating interpretations and for constructing readings, none of which is neutral or unsituated" (p. 349).

What of Fairclough's view of orders of discourse? Similar to Wodak, Fairclough (1989) tries an eclectic mix of views on discourse. There are times when his view of CDA seems to reflect a Habermasian notion of an ideal speech situation; in his distinction, for example, between *inculcation* ("the mechanism of power-holders who wish to preserve their power") and *communication* ("the mechanism of emancipation and the struggle against domination") (p. 75). His three-way distinction between description, interpretation, and explanation furthermore seems to echo Habermas' triparate view of knowledge as technical, interpretive, and emancipatory (← chap. 2). But more generally, Fairclough appears to be arguing not so much for a notion of ordered discourse as a goal but rather as ordered discourse as the linguistic manifestation of capitalist forms of power.

In borrowing Foucault's concept of orders of discourse (by which Foucault meant ways in which institutions guard against the threat of discourses by modes of exclusion) and using it to refer to discourse in the linguistic sense, Fairclough (1995) is watering down the power of Foucault's notion. He has tried at times to use both, suggesting that *discourse* as an abstract noun refers to "language use conceived as social practice" and that *discourse* as a count noun refers to "ways of signifying experience from a particular perspective" (p. 135). Gee (1996) has attempted a similar distinction between small *d* discourse and big *D* Discourse, the first akin to Fairclough's abstract noun discourse—language as social practice—and the second (big D) akin to Fairclough's count noun discourse (a particular worldview). But neither distinction is parsimonious. Second, and more importantly, by rendering orders of discourse as "determined by changing relations of power at the level of the social institution or of the society" (Fairclough, 1989, p. 30), Fairclough returns us to a materialist construction of power relations where the socioeconomic determines the discoursal. Thus, although we might suppose that by contrast with Wodak's call for ordered discourse to replace disordered discourse, Fairclough's goal must be to replace orders of discourse with disorders of discourse, what Fairclough must in the end be after is an *alternative order,* that is, a social order in which capital does not determine the order of discourse. Thus, whereas Wodak critiques disorder to show the way forward to order, Fairclough critiques how one order works to suggest how a preferable order might be. And at this point, we need to turn once again to questions of the relation between language, culture, and discourse and social and economic relations.

The Nonmaterial Base of Discourse

Foucault's (1980b) second objection to the notion of ideology is that "ideology stands in a secondary position relative to something which functions as its infrastructure, as its material, economic determinant" (p. 118). What he was objecting to, then, is the idea that ideology is the product of other social and economic factors. Of course, just as it does not have to be contrasted with the truth, the notion of ideology does not have to be used this way. But Foucault is arguing for a conceptual break away from this sort of thinking. I already discussed this issue (← chaps. 1, 2, and 3), arguing that to develop a more productive and dynamic version of critical applied linguistics, we need to escape from the holds of neo-Marxist structuralist determinism, by which I mean the tendency to look at large-scale systems of power as on the one hand based (only) in real-world relations of class inequality and on the other as determining language and ideology. As I suggested (← the end of chap. 3), this is also why I prefer to view colonialism and postcolonialsm in terms other than simply the economic and political.

There is a danger in some approaches to CDA or other critical discussions of education that power is simply linked to a notion of *dominant groups*. According to van Dijk (1993b), CDA deals with "the discourse dimensions of power abuse and the injustice and inequality that result from it" (p. 252). Thus, power for van Dijk "involves *control*, namely by (members of) one group over (those of) other groups" (p. 252). For van Dijk, this is where discourse links to power and cognition since control is an issue of "social cognition" and since "managing the mind of others is essentially a function of text and talk" (p. 254). But it is as important in CDA as it is in other areas of critical work that power is not merely assumed or mapped onto "dominant groups" or that "managing the mind of others" is taken to be a direct product of textually encoded ideologies of dominant groups.

For Fairclough (1989), the connection between language and power is drawn thus: "Ideologies are closely linked to power" because ideologies reproduce standard conventions that are already linked to power and because they legitimize "existing social relations and differences of power." Ideologies are also "closely linked to language, because using language is the commonest form of social behaviour" (p. 2). Thus, because ideologies are always (in his view) linked to the maintenance of inequitable relations of power and because ideologies are most commonly expressed in language, it is in language that we must search for the means by which power is maintained. The problem with this, as I already suggested, is that it locates power as an already given entity maintained through the ideological operations of language. Harland (1987) suggests that this attitude toward material relations, truth, and falsity is a particular facet of what he sees as pragmatic Anglo-Saxon scholarship prevalent particularly in Britain and the United States and often very much at odds with the *superstructural* orientations of scholarship in countries such as France.

Foucault's notion of power is very different. Power became the central aspect of Foucault's work, not as some undifferentiated whole that was linked to class, state, sovereign, or culture but as operating constantly on and through people. Perhaps most importantly, Foucault (1991) saw power not as a given totality that explains how things happen but rather as "that which must be explained" (p. 148). There are a number of dimensions to this view of power (see Table 4.3). First of all, power is not something owned or possessed but rather something that operates throughout society. For Foucault (1980a), power is not the institutional control of citizens within a state, or a mode of ideological control, or even "a general system of dominance exerted by one group over another" (p. 92); rather, power refers to the "multiplicity of force relations immanent in the sphere in which they operate" (p. 92). Thus, "power is not something that is acquired, seized, or shared, something that one holds on to or allows to slip away; power is exercised from innumerable points, in the interplay of

TABLE 4.3

Foucault and Power

Dimensions of Foucault's Vision of Power as "That Which Must Be Explained"

Power is not something owned or possessed but rather something that operates throughout society.

Power does not have some ultimate location or origin.

Relations of power are not outside other relations but are part of them.

There is no position outside power and no position from which one can arrive at the truth outside relations of power.

Power is always linked to resistance: Where there is power, there is resistance.

Power is not merely repressive but is also productive.

It is in discourse that power and knowledge are joined together.

---

nonegalitarian and mobile relations" (p. 94). Second, a related aspect of this view of power is that it does not have some ultimate location, it "must not be sought in the primary existence of a central point" (p. 93), whether social or economic relations, the power of a sovereign, or the power of a state. Power operates everywhere.

Third, relations of power are not outside other relations (e.g., knowledge or sex) but are part of them, "the immediate effects of the divisions, inequalities, and disequalibriums which occur" (p. 94) in all forms of relationship. Power, therefore, does not control from outside; it is not something linked only to coercion or repression but rather something that inhabits our interactions: "Power comes from below; that is there is no binary and all-encompassing opposition between rulers and ruled at the root of power relations" (p. 94). This connects to another crucial observation, namely that, fourth, there is no position outside power and no position from which one can arrive at the "truth" outside relations of power, for:

> Truth isn't outside power, or lacking in power .... Truth is a thing of this world: it is produced only by virtue of multiple forms of constraint. And it induces regular effects of power. Each society has its own regime of truth, its "general politics" of truth: that is, the types of discourse which it accepts and makes function as true. (Foucault, 1980b, p. 131)

And it also needs to be understood that, fifth, power is always linked to resistance: "Where there is power, there is resistance" (Foucault, 1980a, p. 95).

A sixth point is that power is not merely repressive but is also productive; it would be a "fragile thing if its only function were to repress": "Far from preventing knowledge, power produces it" (Foucault, 1980b, p. 59). And thus we link to the crucial seventh point, the connection between power and knowledge. But this point needs to be understood in the context of the conception of power already discussed: The issue is not that some people are powerful (have power) and are therefore able to control or manipulate knowledge (which is the version of power and knowledge that operates in rather crude versions of Marxism and ideology); rather, the point is that "power and knowledge directly imply each other" (Foucault, 1979, p. 27):

> We must cease once and for all to describe the effects of power in negative terms: it "excludes," it "represses," it "censors," it "abstracts," it "masks," it "conceals." In fact, power produces; it produces reality; it produces domains of objects and rituals of truth. (p. 194)

And finally, we come closer to the connection with language for "it is in discourse that power and knowledge are joined together" (Foucault, 1980a, p. 100).

It is not surprising that this version of power is not one that sits very comfortably with more traditional critical theorists. Habermas, following in the line of Critical Theory, sees in Foucault's work a dangerous and irrational relativism that goes against emancipatory possibilities. Clearly there is a major split here between the critical modernist view that sees emancipation in terms of a rational revelation of the truth obscured by ideology and a Foucauldian understanding of truth not as that which is obscured by power but that which is produced by power. Fairclough (1989, 1992b, 1995), as we have already seen (← chap. 2), turns to a fairly orthodox Marxist interpretation of power, a version of power grounded in a critique of capitalism: "The abuses and contradictions of capitalist society which gave rise to critical theory have not diminished, nor have the characteristics of discursive practice within capitalist society which give rise to critical discourse analysis" (1995, p. 16). He goes on to argue that "most analysis is with social relations of domination *within* a *social system* which is capitalist, and dominated by—but not reducible to—relations of class" (p. 18).

My concern here is not of course that Fairclough is concerned with class but that this is an a priori argument that capitalism and class form the major modes of oppression in our lives. It is this sort of structural materialism (by which I mean an emphasis on overarching structures of power that are produced in material conditions) that is opposed by a poststructuralist interest in culture and discourse. Rather than relying on a prior sociological analysis of power on which we can base an analysis of language and ideology, Foucault's view demands that power remains *that which is to be explained,* specifically, the analysis of power does not exist prior to the analysis of language. This, I think, is a crucial way of thinking about discourse analysis: If we take power as already sociologically defined (as held by dominant groups) and we see our task as using linguistic analysis of texts to show how that power is used, our task is never one of exploration, only of revelation. If, on the other hand, we are prepared to see power as that which is to be explained, then our analyses of discourse aim to explore how power may operate, rather than to demonstrate its existence.

Production and Reception

Finally, a crucial issue in critical text analysis concerns questions of text production and reception. Despite Fairclough's model including an analysis of the processes of production and reception of texts, he actually pays little attention to either of these processes in his work. In some of his most effective work, such as the analysis of changes in how universities advertise courses and jobs (1993, 1995, 1996, 2000), we are able to see how broader discursive shifts may affect localized text production and how these have changed over time. But all too often, the production of texts is left as a matter of institutional domination, and the reading of texts is the process of analysis conducted by the critical discourse analyst. Fairclough (1995) himself admits this in the introduction to his book *Critical Discourse Analysis*: "The principle that textual analysis should be combined with analysis of practices of production and consumption has not been adequately operationalized in the papers collected here" (p. 9). But given that these two domains form the crucial elements of the middle box of Fairclough's three-dimensional model (the *discourse practice* box between the *text* and *sociocultural practice* boxes), such an admission surely points to a major omission.

The crucial point here is that if indeed little attention is paid to either the production or reception of a text, then we are left with little more than a particular reading of a particular text. It may be a very interesting reading and one that makes very interesting connections between the text and the broader social context, but it is not able to tell us much about the social life of the text. It is interesting to observe in this context that van Dijk (1993b) points to the strategy of paying more attention to "top-down relations of dominance than to 'bottom-up' relations of resistance, compliance and acceptance" (p. 250). Thus, his critical approach focuses on "the elites and their discursive strategies for the maintenance of inequality" (p. 250). But although this can tell us something about particular discourses, it is not very illuminating in showing how these are taken up, understood, or resisted. We do not know how people read these texts. In terms of issues raised earlier about critical work in general, we fall here into the trap of structure over agency (what we are mapping is a supposed mode of domination, not the ways in which it happens). And, we are operating with a fixed concept of meaning.

It is important, therefore, to understand very clearly what this form of CDA is and is not able to do. Fairclough's work, which articulates a very particular form of critical theory, should perhaps not be taken as *the* way to do CDA but rather as a particular neo-Marxist, structuralist approach. As with my discussion (← chap. 3) of Phillipson's (1992) model of linguistic imperialism, in which he is able to show how the structure of imperialism may be put into place (the concerted effort to promote English) but not what effects this may have apart from the continued promotion of English, so this structuralist model of text analysis is able to show how certain meanings may be encoded in texts but not what the effects may be. As McCormick (1994) argues, Marxist-based views of texts provide "a problematic foundation on which to construct a theory and practice of reading" (p. 54) because of the predominant focus on production rather than reception, the "authoritarian strain that suspects the dissolution of historically produced, 'original' meanings into a myriad of 'subjective' ones" (p. 55), and the failure to problematize its own reading practices and thereby to realize that what is found in the text was not some pregiven textual or ideological reality but has been read into the text by particular reading practices. Thus, critical discourse analysis can show the possibility of reading ideologies in texts but not their interpretations. The way out of this difficulty, however, is not to move toward the sort of relativistic stance that texts can mean anything or are always open to interpretation, which is the direction that Widdowson (1998) moves in his critiques of CDA. Such a position slides back into a form of ungrounded liberalism and overlooks the cultural and social location of text producers, texts, and readers. In fact, as Price (1999) argues, both Widdowson and Fairclough remain stuck with a static vision of both discourse and the subject.

CRITICAL LANGUAGE AWARENESS AND THE GENRES OF POWER

CDA is generally viewed more as a research tool than as a form of pedagogical practice. Kress (1996) argues that CDA misses a pedagogical element, a means to operationalize the insights of CDA for educational purposes. He therefore suggests that "critical language projects" need to go beyond merely engaging in critical reading, analysis, and deconstructive activity to offer "accounts of alternative forms of social organization" (pp. 16–17). A more pedagogically focused version of CDA can be found in critical language awareness. Indeed, in some ways, CLA may be seen as the pedagogical wing of critical discourse analysis since its most visible exposition has emerged from the same context as the best known work in CDA, the work of Norman Fairclough and his colleagues. In his introduction to the key edited book, *Critical Language Awareness,* Fairclough (1992c) takes CLA to be an extension of more general work in Critical language study, more specifically, his work in CDA (Fairclough, 1989). The focus of critical language awareness, then, is to bring critical discourse analysis into the classroom as a pedagogical tool. As Fairclough (1992c) argues:

> People cannot be effective citizens in a democratic society if their education cuts them off from critical consciousness of key elements within their physical or social environment. If we are committed to education establishing resources for citizenship, critical awareness of the language practices of one's speech community is an entitlement. (p. 6)

It is useful, however, to look at CLA in a broader context and not specifically tied to a particular version of CDA. Various forms of CLA emerged as a response to the spread of liberal student-centered pedagogies in the 1970s and 1980s in many parts of the world. The move away from explicit grammar instruction and explicit pedagogies more generally that had evolved into the whole language approach in first language education and communicative language teaching in second language education came under critical scrutiny from a number of directions. While the conservative critique bewailed what it claimed to be falling standards, poor grammar, inability to spell, and poor reading and writing skills, a more critical orientation sought to divert this discussion away from a back-to-the-basics reactionism in favor of the development of critical literacy materials. The argument here is that liberal approaches to teaching, particularly as they evolved in student-centered or process pedagogies, eschewed explicit instruction and instead relied on an idealistic and romantic view (traceable back to the educational ideas of Rousseau) of the natural evolution of the child. Students are encouraged to express themselves, a process that will lead to individual development (and, of course, empowerment). As critics of this liberal idealism argue, however, it favors those children that already have access to the skills needed to succeed.

Thus Delpit (1995) takes issue with so-called student-centered expressive pedagogies, with their claims that a democratic approach to learning will empower learners as autonomous individuals. She suggests that this approach to education fails to give children from outside the mainstream culture of schooling (White, middle-class culture) access to the culture of power. Liberals, she suggests, "seem to act under the assumption that to make any rules or expectations explicit is to act against liberal principles, to limit the freedom and autonomy of those subjected to the explicitness" (p. 26). As I suggested (← chap. 2; Benson, 1997; Pennycook, 1997a), this liberal approach to autonomy avoids the whole social and cultural context in which autonomy is supposed to occur. This critical opposition to progressivist pedagogies took a number of forms. Fairclough and his colleagues developed the notion of CLA explicitly in reaction to what they saw as the inadequate approach to questions of language and power in the general language awareness materials. And in Australia, a similar dissatisfaction with whole language and other student-centered approaches led to the development of the genre-based literacy movement, based on the argument that the nonovert instruction of liberal progressivism disadvantaged children from minority backgrounds; in its place was proposed a form of critical literacy based on overt instruction of genres.[2]

Thus, although part of the genesis of critical language awareness was an attempt to apply principles of CDA to the classroom, it was also part of a larger movement to reintroduce an explicit and critical focus on language in classrooms. The work of Hilary Janks (1997) in South Africa, for example, bridges some of the Lancaster CDA and Australian genre approaches (see following). And the work presented in *Critical Language Awareness* is in fact more diverse than an application of CDA to educational contexts. A number of articles, such as Catherine Wallace's (1992) "Critical Literacy in the EFL Classroom" or Mary Talbot's (1992) "The Construction of Gender in a Teenage Magazine," draw on the more general domain of critical literacy and are concerned with the social context of literacy practices. Bhatt and Martin-Jones (1992) deal not so much with reading or writing as with the need for minority community languages and antiracist education, a need they feel has been overshadowed by a bland focus on language awareness. Others, such as Janks and Ivanič (1992) and Clark (1992), are more concerned with developing critical language awareness in the context of writing programs. As Clark (1992) puts it:

> A crucial aspect of CLA is to empower students by providing them with the opportunities to discover and critically examine the conventions of the academic discourse community and to enable them to emancipate themselves by developing alternatives to the dominant conventions. (p. 137)

A parallel critique of liberal pedagogies emerged in North America through the work of Lisa Delpit (1988, 1995), who argues forcefully for the importance of explicitly teaching the languages of power to Black and other minority children. From Delpit's point of view, what minority children need is explicit instruction in the "culture of power": "If you are not already a participant in the culture of power, being told explicitly the rules of that culture makes acquiring power easier" (1995, p. 25). She goes on to argue:

> To act as if power does not exist is to ensure the power status quo remains the same .... I prefer to be honest with my students. I tell them that their language and cultural style is unique and wonderful but that there is a political power game that is also being played, and if they want to be in on that game there are certain games that they too must play. (pp. 39–40)

And thus, "students must be *taught* the codes needed to participate fully in the mainstream of American life" (p. 45).

---

[2]The development of this movement is interestingly documented in Cope et al. (1993).

A similar line of argument occurs in Australia in what Cope and Kalantzis (1993) call an "explicit pedagogy for inclusion and access" (p. 64). Following Delpit's views and also the arguments of Bernstein (via the work of Michael Halliday and his followers in Australia), they argue that disadvantaged students need explicit education (formal teaching) in the powerful forms of language. This is not, however, an argument for simply teaching the standard language but a more carefully worked out version of teaching particular genres of language. If teaching "is to provide students with equitable social access" (p. 67) it needs to link the social purposes of language to predictable patterns of language (genres). On the face of it, this can look a little like the conservative argument for teaching standard English, but it differs significantly in that it is a much more contextual view in terms of identifying particular forms of powerful language rather than assuming that something called *standard language* is powerful, and it sees such power as culturally and historically contingent rather than inherent. This view can clearly be seen in Delpit's aforementioned argument that students need to learn how to play "particular political power games." Thus, the focus is not on some monolithic structure called *standard English* but rather on particular strategies and language uses. In the case of the Cope and Kalantzis argument, this is a focus on genres, or particular forms of text that students need to know.

Perhaps most importantly, then, this argument is based on an explicit and critical political position that looks at access to powerful forms of language. It is therefore based on a view that children from nonmainstream backgrounds lack access to certain forms of language; it does not, by contrast, have much to say about language and ideology. As Kress (1993) explains, the work on genre literacy sought to "bring about greater possibilities of access to the resources and the technology of literacy, and, through greater access, to bring about some of the conditions for a redistribution of power in society" (p. 28). He goes on to argue that this view is "based on the assumption that freedom of choice in cultural, social, political and ethical areas depends on access to the most powerful forms of writing, the most powerful genres in one's own society" (p. 29). And, as Kress and Cope and Kalantzis also point out, this should not be a transmission version of teaching whereby these powerful genres are simply taught to students; rather, it should always be a critical form of teaching that points not to the intrinsic power of these genres but to their socially produced power:

> An explicit pedagogy for inclusion and access does not involve unproblematically telling students how to use genres for prescribed social purposes. It operates with a degree of critical distance so that, simultaneous with analysing the linguistic technology of genre, students relate the form of the text critically to its purpose—its culture and the human interests it serves. (Cope & Kalantzis, 1993, p. 86)

There are, however, a number of concerns about such a position. First, Allan Luke (1996) has suggested that it is not based on an adequate theory of language and power. What tends to happen is that the power of systemic-functional linguistics (which underlies this particular version of genre) and what it can reveal about language is mistaken for discoveries about the social operations of language. The problem is that it is not clear how genres are supposed to be powerful. "In critical sociological terms, it is impossible to theorise or study empirically the social or intellectual 'function' of texts independent of the complex ideological forces, powers and struggles implicated in the social formation and organization of technology and knowledge" (p. 310). As Luke goes on to argue, one of the central errors is the tendency to believe that genres in themselves have power.

There are, Luke (1996) suggests, too many jumps in the argument of genre theory:

> The justification for genre approaches is based on a movement from those linguistic "truths" yielded by systemic text analyses; to sociological "truths" about how schools and social structures work to structure and produce unequal outcomes; to psychological and developmental "descriptions" of the cognitive and intellectual effects of writing, literacy and particular genres; to pedagogical "truths" about how pedagogies and classrooms work; to political imperatives about what should be done. (p. 316)

This problem is closely linked to the technicist claims of systemics, allowing for an equation between textual analysis and right action. "Scientific mastery and knowledge—the ethos of *technical control* which is aspired to in systemic linguistics qua science—becomes the teleological principle of genre-based pedagogy, and indeed, its principle of power" (pp. 319–320). Thus, asks Luke, does such textual description "necessarily lead to the conclusion that text and that metalanguage are ethically, politically and culturally worthy of transmission?" (p. 320). What Luke is pointing to here, then, is that although the argument for access to powerful language may make political sense, we need much more careful analyses of what actually *is* powerful. And such an argument can never come from an internal analysis of texts; rather, it must be a sensitive sociological analysis of texts in context.

The second concern has to do with the extent to which tools for text analysis can be seen as merely tools and to what extent they need to be seen as part of grammatical models of the world. Lee's (1996) critical reading of this tradition points to its "fetishization of technicism and a celebration of a masculinist mode of knowledge production" (p. 198). As Corson (1997) warns:

> I am not convinced that the conceptual boundaries surrounding systemic linguistics are desirable ones. There is a political agenda at work in systemic linguistics, but I suspect that it may not be the liberal one that its initiates

expect .... This makes me wonder if there is an unwitting conservativism in systemic linguistics that makes it politically reactionary at the applied level, because it is tied to such a singular view of the world, a view rather removed from the influence of other accounts. (p. 175)

Similarly, as Watkins (1999) argues, social theory in systemic functional grammar "bears the hallmark of structuralism; namely it is conceptualised as an objectified phenomenon whose lifeforce has been sapped" (p. 122). Fowler (1996) also asks whether "the structural characteristics of the systemic-functional model of grammar have not unduly constrained the range of statements made about ideology in critical linguistics up to now" (p. 11). The problem here, then, is that systemic functional grammar, as a form of structuralist linguistics that is linked to a form of social theory, presents a static social analysis that may easily slide into conservativism.

Third, as Lee (1997) argues, by making its central focus one of access, genre-based literacy "is at base a liberal politics, specifically a liberal-democratic politics of equality" (p. 411). Thus, while access to literacy remains a basic sociological issue—women around the world, for example, continue to have lower rates of literacy than men—an argument for critical literacy based on access to genres of power remains questionable in terms both of its politics and its model of language and power. The more recent reworking of these arguments via the notion of *multiliteracies* (Cope & Kalantzis, 2000; New London Group,[3] 1996) is in many ways a continuation of the earlier argument about access to literacy but now with a more complex understanding of access by multiple means to a more complex world of multiple literacy skills. Although interesting, therefore, the New London Group's work on multiliteracies also presents us with several problems.

First, I have elsewhere (1996b) characterized this work as a form of neomodernism, based as it is on a notion of real changes in the economic and social infrastructure. The core argument here is that communication and the workplace are becoming more complex and we therefore need to ensure that students have access to multiple forms of literacy. To a large extent, the notion of multiliteracies seems little more than access to literacy in a changing era of fast capitalism, and thus it may still be answerable to Lee's (1997) suggestion that critical literacy that focuses so centrally on issues of access remains tied to a liberal democratic politics of equality. Second, this view is based on a rather inadequate theorization of changing social and cultural relations that hinges on an assumed tension between

---

[3]The New London Group brings together not only the Australian explicit pedagogy arguments of Cope and Kalantzis but also CDA through Fairclough, social semiotics through Kress, and the North American version of social literacies through James Gee. Other members of this group are Allan Luke, Carmen Luke, Martin Nakata, Sarah Michaels, and Courtney Cazden. More recently (Cope & Kalantzis, 2000), Joe Lo Bianco has been invited to join the group.

globalization and an increasing emphasis on local diversity. Third, as Auerbach (n.d.) has pointed out, the multiliteracies framework is something of an eclectic hodgepodge. There are serious and unexplored tensions, she suggests, between an emphasis on access and an emphasis on critical engagement. You cannot ultimately try to sit in both camps, and since the ideological backgrounds to the different positions they adopt are not made explicit, we are left with a range of contradictory positions that try to cover everything. The point, then, is not that they are wrong about the need for metalanguage, overt pedagogy, critical engagement, situated practice, and so on but rather that if you throw these all in together without being explicit about what sort of metalanguage or critical engagement, when, where, and to whom, this is little other than a bag of handy but incommensurable tricks.

Finally, we come back to questions about the effects of overt pedagogy and awareness. Prain (1997) points to a number of problems with the New London Group (NLG) view of multiliteracies, including the notion that explicit instruction can indeed bring about social change. I already discussed problems with the notion of awareness and emancipation (← chap. 2), so it is worth here only raising this question again: In what ways are awareness or explicit instruction supposed to bring about change? And even if we are able to provide adequate answers to such a question in terms of knowledge and access, we also have to address the question of whether by trying to develop awareness through one form of analysis we may be either assuming or indeed constructing a unitary form of awareness. The danger here, which signals a warning to all domains of critical applied linguistics, is that if we attempt critical work through one methodological or analytic lens, we can end up all too quickly with a hollow term. Critical work must always be on the move.

CRITICAL LITERACY AND VOICE: THE WORD AND THE WORLD

Another approach to critical literacy emerges predominantly from the North American context and is based on critical pedagogy. Whereas critical language awareness focuses on critical readings of texts and ways of questioning academic norms in writing, and critical genre literacy makes access to literacy through overt teaching of powerful genres its central focus, North American critical literacy is most centrally concerned with the *voices* of marginalized students, arguing that the dominant curricula and teaching practices of mainstream schools silence the ideas, cultures, languages, and voices of students from other backgrounds. Thus, although genre literacy, as Lee (1997) observes, is something of a "pedagogy of deferral" (students are not literate until they have mastered key genres), this form of critical literacy might be seen as more of a pedagogy of inclusion (it is the students' own languages and lives that form the stuff of critical literacy). The focus of this approach, then, is on a notion of voice, the opening up of a space for the marginalized to speak, write, or read (*voice* does not refer necessarily to oral language) so that the voicing of their lives may transform both their lives and the social system that excludes them. As Giroux (1988) argues, voice "constitutes the focal point" for a critical theory of education: "The concept of voice represents the unique instances of self-expression through which students affirm their own class, cultural, racial, and gender identities" (p. 199). It refers to our own articulation of agency against the exclusions of structure and thus is supposed to be not so much a liberal humanist celebration of free will (← chap. 2) but a struggle for the power to express oneself when those forms of expression are discounted by mainstream forms of culture and knowledge.

Paulo Freire is often taken to be the key figure in the development of this line of critical literacy. It is worth, therefore, looking briefly at his work and some of the more direct descendants of Freirean pedagogy. It is also important to separate his work from the particular direction critical pedagogy has taken in North America. One of Freire's most often quoted statements is this:

> Reading the world always precedes reading the word, and reading the word implies continually reading the world .... In a way, however, we can go further and say that reading the word is not preceded merely by reading the world, but by a certain form of *writing* it or *rewriting* it, that is of transforming it by means of conscious, practical work. For me, this dynamic movement is central to the literacy process. (Freire & Macedo, 1987, p. 35)

For Freire, as he developed literacy programs among the poor in Brazil—and later elsewhere—literacy pedagogy was always about learning to read the world; it was always political, either domesticating or liberating. Freire argued that standard literacy programs with their readers and meaningless exercises served only as a form of banking education, a transmission of received knowledge from teachers to students. What was needed, by contrast, was a liberatory education—a pedagogy for the oppressed as his best known book (Freiere, 1970) was called—that started with the local conditions and concerns of people. From these, a list of generative words was produced (e.g., *tijolo*, brick; *favela*, slum) that then served as the basis for the literacy course. Freire saw literacy education as a form of *conscientização*—conscientization—that would bring people to understand that the conditions they lived in were not natural but were rather something against which they could take cultural action.

Bee (1993) discusses a program she developed for immigrant women based around Freirean principles. For her:

> The point of taking a critical approach to women's literacy is to use reading and writing as a means for enabling women who have been conditioned to accept second-class status to affirm their aspirations as valid and their

knowledge and views of life as genuine contributions to the net stock of human understanding. (p. 106)

She then shows how developing a Freirean-style pedagogy for immigrant women in Australia helped them both in their literacy and in their awareness of the oppressive gendered structures of their lives. As she argues:

> Literacy programs which merely address immediate practical and functional problems of women, important though these are, neglect to take up questions concerning their structured subordination and control, and tacitly encourage women to locate the source of their problems within their personal selves and not to interrogate those socially structured processes, practices, and ideologies that impede women in realizing their potential. (p. 122)

Here, then, we have a form of critical literacy intended to help women both read the word (gain in literacy) and the world (understand the nature of gendered oppression).

Similarly, working with migrant farm workers in Colorado, Graman (1988) reports his frustrations with the initial materials he had for teaching English, materials with sentences such as "Miss Meek lives on Fifth street" (for short and long vowel contrasts). After reading Freire's (1970) *Pedagogy of the Oppressed*, however, Graman saw a different way forward: Working with generative themes and words such as *bonus* and *short-hoe* (two issues of great significance to these farm workers), he sought to develop an ESL pedagogy that again linked the word and the world together critically. Graman argues that "what is needed in the field of second language pedagogy is an approach that addresses the existential, political, and axiological questions touching the lives of both students and teachers" (p. 441). At the very least, such lessons should teach us the importance of starting ESL and literacy classes with a critical exploration of student contexts rather than an a priori concept of what they need to know.

Broader developments of a Freirean perspective can also be seen in work such as Elsa Auerbach's emphasis on *participatory* education. For Auerbach, despite the problems and complexities of developing participatory approaches to literacy (2000), the involvement and centrality of learners and their communities in the educational process nevertheless remain a cornerstone of critical literacy. Her work thus draws on a Freirean perspective by emphasizing forms of research and pedagogy that start with the learners' real concerns and emphasize a critical process of exploration so that these students are then able to develop their language skills through this process of exploration. As she explains:

> The classroom becomes a context in which students analyze their reality for the purpose of participating in its transformation. They address social problems by sharing and comparing experiences, analyzing root causes, and exploring strategies for change. Knowledge, rather than being transmitted

from teacher to student, is collaboratively constructed, involving the trans-formation of traditional teacher–student roles. (Auerbach, 1995, p. 12)

Similar approaches can be found in Rivera (1999) and Frye (1999). The emphasis in all of this work on connecting the outside world to the world of the classroom also emerges in Walsh's (1991) use of "sociodrama" with Puerto Rican students to help them reflect on and start to articulate the difficulties they face. Her attempt to "include the experiences, percep-tions, and voices that have been traditionally shut out" (p. 126) she sees as part of the development of critical bilingualism:

> the ability to not just speak two languages, but to be conscious of the sociocultural, political, and ideological contexts in which the languages (and therefore the speakers) are positioned and function, and of the multiple meanings that are fostered in each. (pp. 126–127)

Whereas the version of critical literacy discussed in the previous sec-tion focused predominantly on questions of access to powerful forms of language, this version of critical literacy focuses on the opposite side of ac-cess, namely the possibility for participation, the possibility for different languages and cultures and forms of knowledge to be allowed a pedagogi-cal role. Freire's work has been criticized over the years on many grounds, including a reductive view of oppressed and oppressors, an inability to see women's literacy as more than an addition to economic oppression, and a tendency to be overoptimistic about the effects of conscientization. Ac-cording to Weiler (1992):

> While Freire's work is based on a deep respect for students and teachers as readers of the world, the conscientization he describes takes place in a rela-tively unproblematic relationship between an unidentified liberatory teacher and the equally abstracted oppressed. The tensions of the lived subjectivities of teachers and students located in a particular society and de-fined by existing meanings of race, gender, sexual orientation, class, and other social identities are not addressed by Freire. (p. 325)

It is also unfortunate that Freire has been taken up and coopted by ver-sions of North American critical literacy, thus aligning his work for many with the notion of voice that remains a cornerstone of North American critical pedagogy and literacy. Although this sense of voice is intended to be a critical and political version of language use, a view that acknowl-edges the struggle to make oneself heard, it has received fairly strong criti-cism in Australia (Cope & Kalantzis, 1993; Luke, 1996) for what is seen as an inability to escape a North American individualistic idealism. Thus, although on the one hand we might ask how it is that access to or aware-ness of powerful forms of language is indeed supposed to change social re-lations, we might equally ask here how the possibility of using one's voice is supposed to be related to change. The problem, then, as far as Luke (1996) is concerned, is that neither of these two dominant models of critical literacy have adequate models of how power relates to language and literacy. The problem for genre versions of critical literacy is that "without a sociological theory of power, conflict and difference, such models fail to provide an account for why and how some discourses, knowledges and texts 'count' more than others" (p. 312). Meanwhile, North American interpretations of a Freirean-style critical literacy tend to romanticize voice as the writing/speaking of marginalized people:

> Each model is based on broad assumptions about the sociological effects and consequences of literacy. The Freirean model theorises "empowerment" as the opening of pedagogical spaces for marginalised peoples to articulate their interests and develop an analysis of the world; there power is vested phonocentrically in the "dangerous memories" of individual and collective voice. By contrast, genre-based pedagogies tend to begin from the logocentric assumption that mastery of powerful text types can lead to intellectual and cognitive development, educational achievement and credentials, and enhanced social access and mobility. However, both models tend to presuppose what we might call a "hypodermic effect" of literacy: that their preferred literate practices directly inculcate "power." (p. 315)

Thus, Luke (1996) suggests, neither genre-based literacy pedagogy nor Freirean-type critical literacy come to grips "with their assumptions about the relationship between literacy and social power" (p. 309). Rather, he suggests, we need to look at how power is produced, maintained, and resisted in relation to different language forms. I attempt to pull these concerns together at the end of this chapter (also see Table 4.4). First, however, I want to move on to look briefly at poststructuralism.

FROM POSTSTRUCTURALISM TO POSTLINGUISTICS

As I suggested earlier (← chap. 2), linguistics has been broadly dominated by structuralism for much of this century. While this has enabled a great deal of linguistic work, it has also had major limiting effects by narrowing the scope of linguistics largely to the internal workings of language. One of the problems with CDA has been its tendency to operate with a fairly standard form of traditional linguistic thought and to graft on to this a political dimension. Thus, although taking linguistics to task for not having a political dimension, it does not do much to challenge the linguistic understandings of language. As Poynton (1993a) argues, "no linguistics that does not and cannot engage with central issues of feminist and poststructuralist theory concerning questions of subject production through discursive positioning can be taken seriously as a theory of language" (p. 2).

Harland (1987) argues that structuralism and poststructuralism can be grouped together as two aspects of what he calls *superstructuralism,* a term

TABLE 4.4

Approaches to Critical Literacy

Approaches to Critical Literacy	Features	Criticisms
Social practices	Ideological vs autonomous; social context of literacy	Ungrounded notion of ideology; limited to studies in context; no transformative element
Critical textual readings	Approaches to textual analysis (critical discourse analysis and critical language awarenenss)	Static models of textual meaning; limited view of power and ideology
Access/genre	Overt instruction in genres or other powerful texts	Static model of context; transmissive pedagogy; pedagogy of deferral
Multiliteracies	Changing context of literacies; global/local; multimodality	Neomodernist, reactive stance; stressing access rather than changes; eclectic hodgepodge
Freirean pedagogy	Relating the word to the world; diaologic pedagogy; participatory	Limited oppresed/oppressor relation; limited model of language
Critical pedagogy/voice	Opening space for diversity; letting other voices be heard	Pluralist model of inclusion; relation between inclusion and change unclear
Discursive mapping	Poststructuralist attention to discourses across sites	Weak textual analysis; overdetermined view of subjectivity

he uses both as an umbrella term for structuralism and poststructuralism and as an indication that both emphasize superstructure over infrastructure. By this, he means that superstructuralism has tended to invert the materialism of Marxism in which the "real" social and economic conditions of society (base or infrastructure) determine and produce the cultural or ideological superstructure. As we saw earlier, it is various forms of this materialism that often still dominate mainstream critical work. Superstructuralism, by contrast, tends to focus more on the cultural or ideological domain as relatively autonomous. To focus on this commonality between structuralism and poststructuralism, however, obscures the major rift between the two. Applied linguistics has, broadly speaking, tended to operate with the same structuralist view of language handed down by linguistics and thus in many ways uses a version of language that poststructuralism views itself as *post*. As Poynton (1993a) explains:

> From the poststructuralist side, linguistics as a profoundly structuralist enterprise has been trenchantly critiqued or marginalised as of no conceivable interest. In significant respects, linguistics as the founding structuralist enterprise has come to signify what poststructuralism is "post" in its radical critique of the structuralist project. Conversely, linguistics itself ... has been so seduced by its standing as senior technicist discipline within structuralist conceptions of the humanities and social sciences as to fail to register that the "linguistic turn" of the last twenty or so years within these areas was not only asking different kinds of questions about language as a social phenomenon but was calling into question the premises of established ways of "knowing about language" within disciplinary linguistics itself. (pp. 3–4)

Thus, as Parakrama (1995) suggests:

> Much of the most exciting work in post-structuralism has gone unnoticed [in linguistics because of] the conceptual framework of linguistics as a *science* which still remains in place even with the subdisciplines of sociolinguistics and applied linguistics; and the historical complicities between linguistics and colonialism (both "internal" and "external") which still pervade its "neutral" systems of classification and nomenclature. (p. 3)

Poststructuralism, then, tends to take a very different view on issues such as science, objectivity, and truth, categories that remain relatively unproblematic for structuralism. Poststructuralism also takes far more seriously the potential of a superstructuralist stance (which structuralism rarely engaged with seriously) by making the cultural and ideological, or rather the discursive, as not merely a secondary by-product of material relations, or even as relatively autonomous, but rather as primary.

One central feature of poststructuralism, then, is that it locates a notion of reality not in the material world (reality is out there in the objects of the real world) or in the individual (reality is only what each individual perceives) but rather as something produced by social and cultural organization. This does not make things less real, but it does mean that we have no unmediated access to the real. It is more useful, therefore, not to make claims to objectivity and a real world (hence the problems with claims to being scientific) but to investigate the ways in which our real worlds are constructed. The central emphases are on systems of meaning before reality, so that any notion of reality is viewed as a product of a sign system, and on systems of meaning before individuals, so that individual subjectivity is also a product of sign systems. For poststructuralism, therefore, language, culture, and discourse become central categories. It is these that construct our worlds and our sense of selves (subjectivities), and it is these that are amenable to analysis.

Poststructuralism (and postmodernism → chap. 5) becomes a skepticism about common assumptions, a questioning of givens, and here, of course, we return to one of the modus operandi of critical applied linguistics (← chap. 1), the restive problematization of the given. One strategy by which this is sometimes achieved is through pluralization: Knowledge becomes knowledges, subjectivity becomes subjectivities. Beyond the often obscure discussion of the sign, subjectivity, and discourse, poststructural- ism becomes a way of thinking, a tendency always to question given categories (human nature, universalism, the individual, culture, language, knowledge) and to try to explore how these categories are not so much real qualities of the world but are products of particular cultural and historical ways of thinking.

This leads to another crucial aspect of poststructuralism, an antiessentialist stance (compare the discussion of postcolonialism ← chap. 3). By this is meant a constant questioning of any pregiven categories, especially those that seem to suggest some underlying essence. Thus, feminist poststructuralism has sought to undo the categories that define what it is to be a *woman* or a *man*. Indeed, in the work of Judith Butler (1990), we see a profound questioning of any pregiven notions of gender and sexuality. As I suggested (← end of chap. 3), this position then allows us to think in terms of the ongoing performance of identity rather than identity as the manifestation of some inner essence. I return to this (→ chap. 6). The usefulness of poststructuralism, then, is as a way of thinking that constantly leads to the questioning of assumed categories. Once you have lived poststructuralism long enough, the issue no longer is one of theorizing the sign or engaging in deconstructionist abstractions but rather of listening to those alarm bells that go off in your head every time you hear another dichotomy or essentialist category: man, woman, dominance, difference, language, culture, knowledge, nature, nurture.

Clearly, poststructuralism presents some very interesting challenges for applied linguistics. On one level, it asks how different constructs are produced and maintained. What are the discourses that produce structuralist binaries such as native speaker–nonnative speaker, first language–second language, qualitative–quantitative, integrative–instrumental, acquisition–learning? On another, it opens up many received categories for questioning. If gender or ethnicity are not so much pregiven but constructed in and performed through discourse, how do we start to understand the ongoing production of such identities in and through language? And the politicized and contextual end of poststructuralism that interests me brings back all those aspects of language that Saussure set aside as external (language and politics, language and colonialism, etc.), not so much as language add-ons (language and power, language and culture, language and politics) but as part and parcel of language (the politics of language, the politics of text). Language is always already political.

Toward a Postlinguistics

Poststructuralism, therefore, opens up a space for a view of language and discourse that goes beyond some of the limitations of a combination of linguistics and ideology critique. As Mills (1997) explains, the turn away from ideology toward discourse reflects a desire to "develop an intellectual practice concerned to analyse the determinants of thinking and behaviour in a more complex way than is possible when using terms like ideology" (p. 29). The benefits of the move away from a more Marxian framework toward a more Foucauldian one is that it allows for more complex and subtle analyses. The Marxist model of ideology "implied a simplistic and negative process whereby individuals were duped into using conceptual systems which were not in their own interests" (Mills, 1997, p. 30). A poststructuralist approach to critical discourse analysis allows for a move away from the frequent clumsiness of a model that works with ideologies produced by dominant groups. It sees discourses as having multiple and complex origins rather than a basis in some form of social reality. It avoids the problems of claiming to reveal the truth by unmasking the obfuscatory workings of ideology. It gets away from a view that meaning resides in texts and can be extracted from them. As Patterson (1997) points out, "the idea that something resides in texts awaiting extraction, or revelation, by the application of the correct means of interpretation is precisely the assumption that poststructuralism set out to problematise" (p. 427). Instead, it points to the importance of intertextual and situated meanings. And it puts into play a notion of the subject, which, although still requiring some caution to escape a form of discourse-determinism (our subjectivities are merely the products of discourses), does start to point to ways in which we take up positions in discourses and live in fragmented ways.

Nevertheless, a poststructuralist position on discourse leaves various issues hanging for the development of a critical applied linguistic approach to text. Poststructuralism may be criticized on a number of grounds including its inability to deal with "the real," its tendency to slide back into forms of determinism (we are all products of discourse), and its apparent relativism. Of particular relevance to the discussion here are its sometimes ephemeral politics and its lack of a means to deal closely with texts. As Mills (1997) suggests, a discourse model, "because of its lack of alliance to a clear political agenda, offered a way of thinking about hegemony—people's compliance in their own oppression—without assuming that individuals are necessarily simply passive victims of thought" (p. 30). But this very lack of alliance to an a priori political agenda is also part of its problem, leading some critical theorists to reject it as apolitical. Nevertheless, as Barrett (1991) argues:

> Foucault's work provides us ... with an approach to discourse and power in society and history that matches Marxism in its sweep and scope, draws attention away from some overplayed themes and focuses it on to topics of great, but neglected significance. His emphasis on the body was timely and has been highly influential; his arguments about knowledge and truth were not so much relativist, as highly politicised. (pp. 160–161)

And it is when poststructuralism is allied with a politics such as feminism, antiracism or postcolonialism—as in the work of Mills (1997), Weedon (1987), Poynton (1993a), Lee (1996), Kumaravadivelu (1999), and many others—that discourse analysis moves forward in a productive way.

Another critique that has been leveled at poststructuralist discourse theory from CDA practitioners is that it lacks an approach to dealing with texts in a more detailed fashion. Thus, Fairclough (1992b) criticizes Foucault's discourse analysis because it "does not include discursive and linguistic analysis of real texts" (p. 56). Now it is clearly not the case that Foucault does not deal with "real texts": The account of Damiens, the regicide, being hung drawn and quartered as reported in the *Gazette d'Amsterdam* of April, 1757, (Foucault, 1979) is surely a real text. But the point that this type of approach to text lacks the tools for detailed textual analysis is a significant one: Poststructuralist discourse analysis makes often very large claims about the effects of language and discourse without the tools to analyze the microactions of language. This does not seem to be a good reason for abandoning poststructuralism, however; rather, it presents us with the crucial challenge of combining poststructuralist discourse theory with detailed analysis of text. How indeed do we relate discourse (language acts) to discourse (power/knowledge)?

This challenge has been taken up in interesting ways by Lee (1996), Poynton (1993a, 1996), and Threadgold (1997), who have argued for the possibilities of doing feminist poststructuralist work while using linguistic tools, particularly from systemic functionalist linguistics. According to Poynton (1993a), there is:

> a need for the recuperation within poststructuralist theory of certain kinds of linguistic knowledge, considered as technologies for understanding how the representations constituting discourses are actually constructed and the linguistic means by which subjects come to be constituted in terms of specific power/knowledge relations. (p. 2)

Similarly, Lee (1996) argues for the use of linguistic analysis as a way of "engaging with the density and specificity of texts" (p. 5). And Threadgold (1997) argues that the tendency in poststructuralist thinking to reject metalanguage means that a useful resource may get overlooked since "there are things the metalanguage of linguistics will allow you to say about ... the relations between the micro-processes of texts and the macro-processes of cultural and social difference—that the other feminist and poststructuralist discourses cannot address" (p. 14). The argument for using systemic functional analysis is based on the one hand on a simple pragmatics—this is the tradition that all three are most familiar with—and on the other hand an acknowledgment that it at least has a more social and functional framework than other forms of linguistic analysis. This is, then, a form of political pragmatism that argues for the politics and the poststructuralism first and the linguistic tools second.

Poynton's (1996) and Lee's (1996) proposal for a "feminist (post)linguistics" (Lee, 1996, p. 5) that combines feminism, poststructuralism, and text analysis presents us with a useful way forward. Poststructuralism and feminism in combination on the one hand give a needed political focus to discourse theory and on the other hand challenge the essentialism that may underlie other forms of political action. Two notes of caution are worth sounding, however: The first has to do with the continuing necessity to look at text reception. However good our combinations of textual and theoretical tools may become, we should be wary of letting them seduce us into a belief that we can derive meanings from texts or that we can assume that our reading of a text can tell us how "subjects" are "positioned." And second, feminism should not of course claim the only mode of politics here: Other work such as postcolonialism (← chap. 3) can also combine effectively here. And indeed, it is the work that argues that all these political struggles are indelibly connected that makes for the most potent and the most convincing combination: postcolonial/feminist/antiracist/antihomophobic postlinguistics.

CONCLUSION: TOWARD AN APPLIED POSTLINGUISTICS

It is evident, I think, that critical applied linguistics needs sophisticated approaches to critical text analysis. In this chapter, I have presented and critiqued some of the main ways in which critical literacy is understood. In focusing on CDA as commonly understood and practiced, I tried to show the particularity of this mainstream critical work in order to raise central concerns for the development of a critical view of texts. This is not to deny that a great deal of highly significant work has been produced from this perspective and that it has provided useful tools for people in related fields. The use of insights from CDA to shed light on aspects of translating and interpreting, for example, has helped to "provide evidence of the ideological consequences of translators' choices and to show the linguistic minutiae of text-worlds in transition" (Hatim & Mason, 1997, p. 143). CDA has played an important role in drawing to applied linguists' attention the importance of the political and in drawing to other political analysts' attention the importance of the linguistic (e.g., Foley, 1999).

The position I have been developing in this chapter seeks to draw on many of the insights from critical literacy, critical language awareness, and critical discourse analysis while at the same time trying to establish critical literacy as a form of poststructuralist practice that aims to explore the discursive construction of reality across different sites. Such a view has a number of features. First, it starts with an understanding of literacy as always political. Second, it operates with a view of texts and literacy practices as always embedded in social contexts. Such contexts, however, are highly complex. They are not limited to the immediate surroundings, the participants, or the textual features but include the historical (pretextual) and discursive (subtextual) location of texts and readers. It is in part the historical context of texts and interpretation that leads Threadgold to adopt a notion of poetics rather than CDA:

> It is important for me to understand the historical context in which my individual snapshots occur. That's what I was trying to do ... and that's why I called it poetics, *poiesis,* not critical discourse analysis—because I was trying to "perform a rewriting," critically, and at the same time to stop the process every so often to do the critical discourse analysis. (Threadgold & Kamler, 1997, p. 444)

For a summary of applied postlinguistic approaches to text, see Table 4.5.

Third, any position on texts must be able to take into account processes of production and, most significantly, reception: Texts do not mean until they are interpreted. But such a position needs also to be understood in terms of contextual, subtextual, and pretextual constraints and possibilities. Not only do texts suggest the likelihood of certain readings, but the readers themselves are bound by particular discourses and come to any text with a history of interpretation. Thus, what we need is an understanding of texts that avoids both an overdetermination by social structure (of which CDA is at times guilty) and an underdetermination that suggests that texts are simply open to all interpretations (one of the pitfalls of Widdowson's, 1998, attempted critique of CDA). There are "preferred meanings" (Hall, 1994, p. 207) of texts—within any society or culture, there are dominant or preferred meanings or interpretations—and readers, listeners, or viewers may interpret texts in line with, in negotiation with, or in opposition to such preferred readings. But, perhaps most obviously, what we need to do is actually investigate how texts are read, to engage with the production and reception of texts. This does not, of course, provide some kind of answer to the meaning of texts, but it allows us to start to map out different formations of meaning (discourses).

Fourth, the approach I am developing here focuses not so much on looking for evidence of prior social analysis within texts as on mapping across texts how discourses are constructed through intertextual relations. The elision of discourse/ideology implied by this intertextual view means that this is not a search for linguistic manifestations of social real-

TABLE 4.5

Applied Postlinguistic Approaches to Text

Aspects of an Applied Postlinguistic Approach to Text	Features
Language and literacy as always political	There is no context in which language, text, or literacy can be outside political relations
Texts and literacy practices as always embedded in social contexts	Texts and readers are located historically (pretextually) and discursively (subtextually)
Focus on the production and reception of texts	Contextual, subtextual, and pretextual constraints on and possibilities of textual meaning
Power as that which must be explained; textual analysis as social analysis	Discursive mapping across texts as social analysis; intertextual meanings in relation across texts
Pedagogical and analytic praxis	Developing ways in which students can resist and change the discourses that construct their lives

ity, but rather, this is the search for the production of social reality itself; this is social analysis. Rather than the social being open to prior analysis and the critical linguist then looking at language to understand how social relations are reproduced in language, this view takes the social as produced in language. And thus, the focus is no longer one that assumes power to be located in some given social or economic structure—or even in some fixed structure of patriarchy or racism—and the task of critical textual analysis is no longer to uncover the workings of ideologies that support such structures as they operate in texts. Rather, following Foucault, power is that which needs to be explained. Critical approaches to text become situated political practices (Luke, 1997b) that search for the political/discursive (subtextual), social/historical (pretextual), and local/contingent (contextual) ways in which texts and readers produce (intertextual) meanings in relation across texts.

Finally, a critical applied linguistic approach to texts needs some form of pedagogical action that looks at ways in which students can move to resist and change the discourses that construct their lives. Critical literacy as outlined earlier starts with an understanding of literacy as always located within complex cultural and political sites. But rather than focusing primarily on critical readings of texts, access to genres of power, or the inclusivity of voice, it takes up the need for broad discursive analyses.[4] As McCormick (1994) suggests:

> If students are to learn how to read the world critically, they must be given access to discourses that can allow them to analyse that world, discourses that can enable them to explore the ways in which their own reading acts, as well as the texts of their culture, are embedded in complex social and historical relations. (p. 49)

This, then, is a major task for a critical applied postlinguistics.

---

[4]One final point in this overly long chapter is worth making: It is important to understand, particularly from a poststructuralist perspective, that my critique of others' work here is not about people but about ideas. Throughout these chapters I make a number of clumsy categorizations of different approaches to (critical) applied linguistics. I employ these categorizations to highlight various distinctions and I maintain that these represent various possible positions. But by linking these positions to other people's work and names (Fairclough, Wodak, Giroux, etc.), I run the danger of suggesting that they represent these views or that they blindly adhere to them. By contrast, I suggest that many of these writers hold far more complex and even contradictory views than this allows and that my critique is not of them but of particular articulations of particular positions.

The Politics of Pedagogy

Classrooms in Context
Structure, Agency, Determinism, and Resistance
Social and Cultural Reproduction in Schooling
    Bourdieu and Forms of Capital
    Resistance and Change
Critical Pedagogy
Education, Postmodernism, and Ethics
    Postmodernism and Ethics
Toward a Postcritical Pedagogy

One of the key challenges for critical applied linguistics is to find ways of mapping micro and macro relations, ways of understanding a relation between critical views of the world—theories of society, ideology, global capitalism, colonialism, education, and so on—and the world of applied linguistics—classrooms, translations, conversations, interviews, and texts. Whether it is critical applied linguistics as a critique of mainstream applied linguistics, as a form of critical text analysis, as an approach to understanding the politics of translation, or as an attempt to understand implications of the global spread of English, a central issue always concerns how the classroom, text, or conversation is related to broader social, cultural, and political relations. As the discussion in previous chapters also suggested, however, the task is not merely to map micro and macro relations but to understand in much more subtle ways how power circulates at multiple levels. Indeed, we might do well to dis-

114

pense with the micro–macro dichotomy and instead talk of detailed understandings of the contextual workings of power.

This chapter explores these issues further by looking at the context of language education. To some (Widdowson, 1999), language education—or the mediation between language teachers and linguistic theory—is the true domain of applied linguistics. My understanding of (critical) applied linguistics is rather different (← see chap. 1), including many more domains and avoiding this notion of the applied linguist as intermediary. Nevertheless, it cannot be denied that language education, in particular second language education and even more particularly the teaching of English as a second language, plays an important role in applied linguistics. From the discussion in previous chapters, a number of critical concerns might already be identified: struggles over which languages and which versions of language are to be taught in schools, questions about developing critical language awareness, or the role of translation in classrooms not so much in methodological as ideological terms. The focus of this chapter, however, is principally on classrooms and pedagogy. The discussion includes questions of reproduction and resistance, critical pedagogy and postmodernism.

CLASSROOMS IN CONTEXT

Whereas classrooms in much of applied linguistics are construed as fairly neutral sites of pedagogical transaction, where teachers are engaged in imparting their knowledge of language to students or setting up the conditions for students to learn, Elsa Auerbach (1995) suggests that we must understand the social and ideological relations within the classroom and their relation to a larger world outside. According to Auerbach (1995): "Pedagogical choices about curriculum development, content, materials, classroom processes, and language use, although appearing to be informed by apolitical professional considerations, are, in fact, inherently ideological in nature, with significant implications for learners' socioeconomic roles" (p. 9). From this point of view, "the classroom functions as a kind of microcosm of the broader social order" (p. 9), that is to say, the political relations in the world outside the classroom are reproduced within the classroom. Auerbach (1995) goes on to suggest that:

> Once we begin looking at classrooms through an ideological lens, dynamics of power and inequality show up in every aspect of classroom life, from physical setting to needs assessment, participant structures, curriculum development, lesson content, materials, instructional processes, discourse patterns, language use, and evaluation. We are forced to ask questions about the most natural-seeming practices: Where is the class located? Where does the teacher stand or sit? Who asks questions? What kinds of questions are asked? Who chooses the learning materials? How is progress evaluated? Who evaluates it? (p. 12).

From this perspective, then, everything we do in the classroom can be understood socially and politically. It is important to understand once again that this connection to politics is not just a connection between classrooms and those areas that are more readily understood as social or political—such as language policy—but rather a view that sees politics as addressing relations of power in everything we do and say. Developing what he calls a political orientation to learner autonomy, Phil Benson (1997) outlines this distinction clearly:

> We are inclined to think of the politics of language teaching in terms of language planning and educational policy while neglecting the political content of everyday language and language learning practices. In proposing a political orientation for learner autonomy, therefore, we need a considerably expanded notion of the political which would embrace issues such as the societal context in which learning takes place, roles and relationships in the classroom and outside, kinds of learning tasks, and the content of the language that is learned. (p. 32)

It is this political understanding of the language classroom that is the primary focus of this chapter.

There are a number of concerns that need to be thought through, however. If we view the classroom as a "microcosm of the social order," does this mean that social relations in classrooms merely reflect those of the broader social world (a position akin to the language-reflects-reality argument critiqued in ← chap. 3)? Or, if we acknowledge that classrooms also operate in a more dynamic way than this, how can we conceptualize ways in which what happens in classrooms may be related to broader social and political domains? These are concerns that Suresh Canagarajah (1993) raises in his critical ethnography of his own English classroom. To contextualize the discussion here, it may be useful to look at this study in closer detail. The class consisted of 22 first-year students doing a mandatory English class at the University of Jaffna in Sri Lanka. They are using *American Kernel Lessons: Intermediate* as a core text. The 13 female and 9 male Tamil students are mainly from rural communities and the poorest economic groups, and few of their parents have much education. English has "limited currency" in their lives outside the class and the university. The university had only opened belatedly for the academic year because "renewed hostilities between the Sinhala government and Tamil nationalists had brought life to a standstill in the Tamil region" (p. 612). These tensions continued to provide a backdrop to the classes, with government planes bombing the vicinity of the university during placement tests.

Given the extreme circumstances of his classroom, one might have expected Canagarajah to see everything inside as determined by what is going on outside. Whereas some might be happy to believe that classrooms are autonomous islands of language learning, unaffected by the world outside, we might nevertheless acknowledge that with government jets screaming overhead, the outside world sometimes cannot be ignored. But Canagarajah is interested in a more complex story: Despite such loud and urgent claims to see what happens in this classroom as determined by the outside world, he goes on to argue for an understanding of the *relative autonomy* of classrooms, suggesting both that they are social and cultural domains unto themselves and that they are interlinked with the world outside. In his critical ethnography of this class, he shows how anything from student annotations in textbooks to preferred learning styles and resistance to his own preferred teaching approaches are connected in complex ways to the social and cultural worlds both inside and outside the classroom. Through looking at these many dimensions—teaching style, textbooks, language, cultural background—he shows how we need to steer a careful path between an overdetermined notion of the classroom as a mere reflection of the outside world and an underdetermined vision of classrooms as islands unto themselves. The different understandings of classrooms are outlined in Table 5.1.

STRUCTURE, AGENCY, DETERMINISM, AND RESISTANCE

The issues of structure, agency, determinism, and resistance have already been raised at various points in this book (← chaps. 3 and 4). Their salience in the context of education, however, requires a slightly longer treatment at this point. The comments by Auerbach and Benson suggested that we view all aspects of classrooms in political terms, but to do so, we need to be able to establish how classrooms are related to social, cultural, political, and ideological concerns. This requires understanding, but also going beyond, two dichotomous relations: macro and micro; structure and agency. On the one hand, we have the macro structures of

TABLE 5.1
Alternative Conceptions of School and Society

	Standard View of Classrooms	Reproductive Standpoint	Resistance Standpoint
Knowledge and curriculum	Knowledge as neutral	Knowledge reflects dominant interests	All knowledge as political
Social role of schools	Equal opportunities for everyone	Reproducing social inequality	Classroom as site of social struggle
Social relations in schools	Classroom as educational, not social, space	Classroom reflects external social roles	Classroom as site of cultural struggle

the larger social and political order; on the other, the micro politics and individual actions in classroom contexts. This chapter is largely about finding useful ways of understanding such contexts without reducing them
either to a mere reflection of the social order or to a place of entirely
free-willed activity.

In establishing his position on the relative autonomy of classrooms,
Canagarajah (1993) critiques two earlier articles on critical approaches to
TESOL by myself (Pennycook, 1989) and Peirce (1989). My article on
methods in language teaching suggested in part that the concept of *method*
was a product of Western academic thinking and was exported to periphery classrooms around the world as part of a global export of Western
knowledge and culture. Peirce's article had focused on the emergence of
"People's English" in South Africa, suggesting that this use of English represented a new form of possibility for Black South Africans. Canagarajah
chides my "delineation of ideological domination through TESOL" for
being "overdetermined and pessimistic," while Peirce's "characterization
of the possibilities of pedagogical resistance" is criticized for being "too
volitionist and romantic" (p. 602). Arguing that both of us need to attend
to the complexities of classrooms themselves rather than the "politics of
TESOL-related macro-structures" (p. 603), Canagarajah argues that we
need to understand the relative autonomy of classrooms, Peirce needing
to focus more on the adjective (*relative*) and myself more on the noun (*autonomy*). He himself then goes on to "interrogate the range of behaviors
students display in the face of domination" (p. 603).

This debate captures several basic issues that critical applied linguistics
needs to deal with. First of all, we can see the tension between the macro
and the micro; the difficulty in looking at broad social and political concerns while also trying to take into account more specific local concerns.
One part of Canagarajah's (1993) critique, then, points to the problem
that Peirce and I were both dealing with broad macro issues in TESOL
without adequately attending to the micro issues of how they actually get
played out in classrooms. But his critique points not only to our failure to
deal with the local but also with overdeterministic (me) or overvolitionist
(Peirce) implications for how such local conditions may be affected. What
he is suggesting is that my view of the imposition of methods implies too
great a possibility of imposition without resistance, too simple an acquies-
cence to power, hence his argument that I need to understand in particular the relative *autonomy* of the classroom. Peirce, on the other hand,
implies too ready a series of possibilities, too easy a resistance to power,
hence Canagarajah's argument that she needs to address the *relative* autonomy of the classroom.

As I already discussed in previous chapters (← chaps. 3 and 4), a great
deal of macro critical work seeks to identify the social and ideological
structures that limit our possibilities as humans. The issue, then, is not

THE POLITICS OF PEDAGOGY

how free-thinking individuals act in relation to social structure but rather how that social structure may also profoundly affect how people think. Thus, various strands of critical theory take aim at the individualistic, humanist version of the free-willed subject. This view of autonomous and free-willed human beings appears to be a product of a particular historical and cultural period: the so-called European Enlightenment. It should be acknowledged that such an understanding of the individual was a very significant shift, allowing for a rejection of prior static images of individuals as subjects of autocratic regimes, cogs in a given social order, or beings in eternal obeisance to God. Instead, humans were free individuals, the center of their own universes, free-willed subjects giving meaning to the word and the world through their own thought. But as it has come down to us in a legacy of Euro-American thought, tinged today with additional discourses of individualism, liberalism, and capitalism, this version of free individuals misses an understanding of how society, culture, and ideology make us anything but free. It is important to view this form of individualism, particularly as it has developed in areas such as "learner-centered" pedagogy, as a very particular cultural and historical development.

Various critical stances, therefore, have suggested that we need a far more skeptical view of human freedom. In Marxist, structuralist, and poststructuralist analyses of social and political power, the individual almost disappears from view. Instead of free-willed subjects deciding what they want to do, we have relations of power, classically produced in a Marxist framework through class relations (and access to and ownership of the means of production) in which individuals are pawns within larger class struggles. Indeed, in the strongest versions of this form of social analysis, people are victims of *false consciousness* produced by ideologies that are in turn produced by the dominant class. That is to say, our very existence (material) and how we think about it (cultural, psychological) are determined by ideologies that are a product of class relations. As I suggested in the discussions of notions such as linguistic imperialism or various approaches to CDA (← chaps. 3 and 4), some critical approaches to applied linguistics have failed at times to avoid the reductionism and determinism of such models. Thus, it is important to avoid not only locating power fundamentally in material relations but also viewing it as an all-controlling dimension of patriarchy, center–periphery relations, or heterosexism.

As Giddens (1979) points out, a great deal of work in sociology has tended to look at structure (macro) at the expense of agency (micro). He uses the term *structuration* to capture the relation and the mutual interdependence of structure and agency. In this view, there is a constant reciprocal structuring, with social structures both the medium and the product of social action. Thus, what we do, think, say as humans is always affected by larger questions of social power and to some extent reproduces those same relations, which then reaffect what we do, think, or say. As we shall see, this view underlies many critical understandings of classrooms as social contexts, language as social action, implications of the global spread of English, and so on. Drawing on insights from poststructuralism (← chap. 4), I prefer to see this relation as one of *poststructuration,* through which we can see the ways in which discourse and subjectivity (also see → chap. 6) reciprocally reproduce and change each other. This position also sheds light on why even the smallest words and deeds may have major implications, why a classroom utterance, textbook illustration, favoring of a particular version of a translation, arrangement of seats, or choice of language may have major effects. Thus, once we have started to work out how structure may limit or produce (rather than absolutely determine) human agency and how agency may work in fairly complex oppositional ways (but never outside some domain of power), we can then start to work toward a more multilayered model in which the issue is not merely one of a dialectical relation between macro structure and micro agency but rather a poststructuration of constant recycling of different forms of power through our everyday words and actions.

A major task for critical applied linguistics, therefore, is to find ways to meet the challenge of working across multiple levels, of looking at contextual issues of second language acquisition, for example, while also accounting for layers of institutional influence (see → chap. 6) and relations of ethnicity, gender, or social class; or of conducting large-scale analyses of social and political factors affecting TESOL without imputing necessary effects on the micro level. The challenge is to find a way to theorize human agency within structures of power and to theorize ways in which we may think, act, and behave that on the one hand acknowledge our locations within social, cultural, economic, ideological, discursive frameworks but on the other hand allow us at least some possibility of freedom of action and change. The difficulty, simply put, is getting the balance right. Canagarajah (1993) suggests my view of Western teaching methods being imposed on teachers around the world has too much structure in it, is too deterministic, allows for too little agency and resistance (this is a very similar critique to the one I made ← in chap. 3 of work such as Phillipson's). Peirce's discussion of a "pedagogy of possibility" (a notion she borrows from Roger Simon, 1992), on the other hand, has too much agency, allows for too easy a form of opposition, is too autonomous. To pursue this challenge, we need complex ways of thinking about social class, gender, ideology, power, resistance, human agency. It is not adequate to talk in terms of people as either ideological dupes or autonomous subjects; it is not sufficient to assume on the one hand that reading a text will lead us to believe the ideological messages in that text or on the other hand that anyone can read a text as they choose; it will not be enough to try to deal with power relations in the classroom just by aiming for student autonomy (Benson, 1997; Pennycook, 1997a).

SOCIAL AND CULTURAL REPRODUCTION IN SCHOOLING

To understand language classrooms within a wider context, I look briefly in this section at the broader context of education and the notions of social and cultural *reproduction* through schooling. By contrast with an optimistic liberal view of education that it provides opportunity for all (anyone can go to school, receive equal treatment, and come out at the end as whatever they want), more critical analyses have pointed out that schools are far greater agents of social reproduction than of social change. What we need, therefore, is an understanding of how schools operate within the larger field of social relations, how, as a key social institution, they ultimately serve to maintain the social, economic, cultural, and political status quo rather than upset it. From Althusser's (1971) observation that schools were the most significant part of the *ideological state apparatus* (as opposed to the *repressive state apparatus* of police, army, courts, and prisons) and were crucial for the ideological subjugation of the workforce, to Bowles and Gintis' (1976) illustration of how schools operate to reproduce the labor relations necessary for the functioning of capitalism, this focus on the roles of schools in the reproduction of social inequality has been an important focus of critical sociology of education.

Given the severe lack of critical sociologies of language classrooms, it is important to be able to understand how, for example, ESL classrooms may operate within this broader social field. As Tollefson (1989, 1991) and Auerbach (1995) argue, education for Indochinese refugees, either in resettlement camps in Southeast Asia or in ESL classrooms in the United States, need to be understood as part of a larger social and economic policy. According to Tollefson (1991):

> Refugees are educated for work as janitors, waiters in restaurants, assemblers in electronic plants, and other low-paying jobs offering little opportunity for advancement, regardless of whether the refugees have skills ... suitable for higher paying jobs. Thus refugee ESL classes emphasize language competencies considered appropriate for minimum-wage work: following orders, asking questions, confirming understanding, and apologizing for mistakes. (p. 108)

Similarly, Auerbach (1995) points out that:

> Work-oriented content often is geared, on the one hand, toward specific job-related vocabulary and literacy tasks (reading time cards or pay stubs) and, on the other, toward "appropriate" attitudes and behaviors and their concomitant language functions or competencies (learning how to call in sick, request clarification of job instructions, make small talk, follow safety regulations). (p. 17)

Thus, we can see ESL in its many contexts as linked to various social and economic forces. As Benson (1997) observes, teachers of English "are more often than not engaged in political processes of a distinctive kind" since the "acceptance of English as a second language very often implies the acceptance of the global economic and political order for which English serves as the 'international language'" (p. 27). In the broadest context of understanding English teaching in an international context, then, we need to be able to understand how English is connected to other global forces (← chap. 3). Indeed, in the international context, it is quite possible to view English language teaching as a major player in the production of an international class of English speakers. And since "learning foreign languages (and again English in particular) is more often than not premised upon inequalities between learner and target communities" (p. 27), the development of this class of international speakers of English is set against the use of other languages. Indeed, one might suggest that Teaching English to Speakers of Other*ed* Languages might more accurately describe the implications of TESOL.

As Giroux (1983) points out, however, arguments about social reproduction through schooling leave us with large-scale social analysis rather than an understanding of either how such reproduction takes place or how it may be resisted. Theories of cultural reproduction take up where theories of social reproduction leave off: they focus much more closely on the actual means by which schooling reproduces social relations. One version of cultural reproduction can be found in the work of Basil Bernstein (1972), for whom a central concern was the relation between social class, language, education, and the "social distribution of knowledge" (p. 163). Bernstein set out to investigate how "the class system has affected the distribution of knowledge" so that "only a tiny percentage of the population has been socialized into knowledge at the level of the meta-languages of control and innovation, whereas the mass of the population has been socialized into knowledge at the level of context-tied operations" (p. 163). What Bernstein was claiming, therefore, was that social classes were tied to forms of language-based socialization perpetuated through schools that gave only a very limited social class access to forms of knowledge.

Bernstein's views have been critiqued from many directions. Sociolinguists such as William Labov have dismissed Bernstein as another deficit theorist because of his arguments that different social classes use different linguistic codes. Although on the one hand it is true that Bernstein's use of the terms *elaborated* and *restricted* code left him open to such critiques, it is also important to understand on the other hand that part of this critique is based on an inability to grasp the implications of a more critical sociology of education than that offered by mainstream sociolinguistics (see ← chap. 3). As Glyn Williams (1992) suggests, "whatever its limitations, the work of Bernstein and his associates ... has served to demonstrate the role of the education system in producing and reproducing the written standard" (p. 143). From different standpoints, however, it has been suggested that Bernstein's view remains a deterministic view of reproduction (Giroux, 1983) and that his "fetishizing of the legitimate language" fails to relate "this social product to the social conditions of its production and reproduction" (Bourdieu, 1991, p. 53). Nevertheless, Bernstein's views have been quite influential, particularly for genre-based versions of critical literacy (← chap. 4), where the questions he raises of differential access to powerful forms of language have led to the strong orientation toward overt pedagogy in this form of critical literacy (Christie, 1998; Williams, 1998).

Bourdieu and Forms of Capital

A more significant version of cultural reproduction can be found, however, in the work of Pierre Bourdieu, and since notions such as *cultural capital* have started to enter the vocabulary of applied linguistics, it is worth giving his views and their uptake in studies of language education a more extended space here. Exploring different ways of understanding language and power, Luke (1996) suggests that the almost metaphysical definition of power in Foucault's ideas (← chap. 4) renders it hard to analyse the actual workings of power in particular social contexts:

> Without classificatory categories of power, the danger is that the Foucauldian model falls into situational relativism (i.e., every site deploys power differently and there are no shared characteristics) or a globalisation of the principle that defies empirical analysis (i.e. that everything, everywhere, is power, differentiated only by site. (p. 326)

Thus, although Foucault's concept of power takes us usefully beyond critical modernism, it may not necessarily lend itself readily to contextual analysis of power. Luke suggests that the work of Bourdieu provides a more useful way of looking at how power operates in particular contexts. Bourdieu describes power in terms of the forms of capital people have access to, use and produce in different cultural fields. As Thompson (1991) explains, Bourdieu "views the world as a multi-dimensional space, differentiated into relatively autonomous fields; and within each of these fields, individuals occupy positions determined by the quantities of different types of capital they possess" (p. 29). Crucially, such capital is not simply something one has but something that has different value in different contexts, mediated by the relations of power and knowledge in different social fields.

In his discussion of the forms of capital, Bourdieu (1986) defines three forms of capital (economic, social, cultural) and adds that symbolic capital is also crucial for any of them to operate (see Table 5.2). In later work (1991), symbolic and linguistic capital take on a greater role. Unlike standard materialist views of political economy, therefore, Bourdieu sees economic capital as only one among the different forms of capital. Thus, one's ability to use differential access to material goods only relates to power to the extent that it is combined with cultural, linguistic, social, and symbolic capital. The notion of cultural capital, Bourdieu (1986) explains, was first developed

> as a theoretical hypothesis which made it possible to explain the unequal scholastic achievement of children originating from the different social classes by relating academic success, i.e., the specific profits which children from the different classes and class fractions can obtain in the academic market, the distribution of cultural capital between the classes and class fractions (p. 243)

This notion of cultural capital as the differential value given to different cultural (and linguistic) forms in education can be related to other work such as Shirley Brice Heath's (1983) ethnography of how different communities in the Carolinas in the United States socialize their children into different ways of *taking from books*—different types of *literacy events*—and how the language and literacy skills of these children are differently valued in school (← chap. 4).

Cultural capital takes three forms: Embodied cultural capital is the part of the *habitus* we internalize through socialization and education.

TABLE 5.2

An Overview of Bourdieu's Forms of Capital

Forms of capital		Operating in social fields	Examples in the field of Teaching English to Speakers of Other Languages (TESOL)
Economic	All must have	Monetary power that can be exchanged for other forms of capital	Money to pay for English classes; money received as a native speaker
Social	**symbolic capital**	Social connections and group memberships that provide access to other forms of capital	Social connections within the field; access to certain people
Cultural (and linguistic)	(be recognized as having value within a particular field)	Embodied (habitus) Objectified Institutionalized forms of cultural capital	Ways of speaking, reading, behaving Textbooks, materials TOEFL scores, teaching certificates

Bourdieu's notion of *habitus* is, as Jenkins (1992) points out, a bridge between structure and agency, a notion of embodied habits, dispositions, attitudes, and behaviors that become written onto our bodies. Importantly, then, what we learn at home and at school are not merely cognitive skills but rather are embodied practices. Objectified cultural capital takes the form of material cultural goods that can be transferred from one person to another. Institutionalized cultural capital takes the form of various credentials or certificates. It is often the case that whatever one may have gained in terms of embodied capital is of little significance without the sanctification of institutionalized capital. Cultural capital, furthermore, is of little value unless it can be used in specific social contexts, access to which is provided by one's social capital. Social capital, then, has to do with group membership, one's ability to participate in different social contexts and thus to use and gain other forms of capital. One might, for example, have the embodied and objectified cultural capital to enter certain domains (business, academic communities, etc.), yet one may still be excluded on social terms (through issues of gender, ethnicity, race, sexual orientation, etc.). Finally, in Bourdieu's account, none of these forms of capital matter unless they are accorded symbolic capital; that is to say, unless what they represent is acknowledged as having legitimacy, they will not be usable as capital.

Such a framework may give us quite productive means for analyzing, say, the global position of English in terms of the problems posed by the global symbolic capital of English, the effects of the embodied linguistic/cultural capital of the native speaker, the power of the institutional linguistic/cultural capital of the TOEFL, and the draw of English because of the social and economic capital it promises. Native speakers of English have linguistic capital that can be turned into economic capital (access to jobs), and because of the symbolic capital accorded to this linguistic capital, native speakers often claim social and cultural capital of other sorts (Brutt-Griffler & Samimy, 1999). Lin's (1999) analysis of four classrooms in Hong Kong, which takes as a starting point a "concern with exploring ways of doing TESOL that do not participate in the reproduction of student disadvantage" (p. 394), looks at how different approaches to teaching may have different implications for the reproduction or transformation of student lives. For the middle-class students (Classroom A), the cultural capital or habitus they brought to the school was compatible with the forms of schooling they were exposed to, and thus "doing-English-lessons in Classroom A reproduced and reinforced the students' cultural capital" (p. 407). Meanwhile, the incompatibility between schooling and the habitus of working-class students in Classrooms B and C also led to student opposition and further reproduction of disadvantage. But in Classroom D, she found potential for change as the incompatible habitus of the students was "being transformed through the creative, discursive agency and efforts of their teacher" (p. 409).

As Lin (1999) shows, Bourdieu certainly gives us some useful tools and terms for thinking about reproduction and transformation in schooling. And as Luke (1996) argues, his view of the operation of power within different fields has strong potential for contextualized and localized sociologies of language and schooling. Nevertheless, there are a number of limitations here (see Table 5.3). First, it remains hard to see how, despite Lin's analysis, Bourdieu's framework avoids being a deterministic process of reproduction: We can trade forms of capital, but as Jenkins (1992) observes, Bourdieu fails to show how actors can actually intervene to change how things happen. Bourdieu "vociferously rejects determinism while persistently producing deterministic models of social process" (p. 175). Second, although his use of different versions of capital (social, cultural symbolic) is supposed to take us beyond economic determinism, the capital, trade, and marketplace metaphors he uses still seem to leave us with an economic view of the world that suggests a rational model of capital accumulation: Bourdieu appears to "maintain a rationalist perspective on practice whereby it is ultimately reducible to the accumulation of cultural capital, i.e., of power," which is "tantamount to economism and fails to take into account the non-rational constitution of desire" (Friedman 1990, p. 313; see → chap. 6 for further discussion).

Finally, as Butler (1997) argues, Bourdieu's view of language and power is premised on the prior existence of forms of power that underlie the power of certain uses of language: "If one argues that language itself can only act to the extent that it is 'backed' by existing social power, then one needs to supply a theory of how it is that social power 'backs' language in this way" (p. 158). As I suggested in previous chapters, one aspect of the sort of critical applied linguistics I am trying to develop here needs a more poststructuralist notion of performativity whereby power in language is not always dependent on prior sociological notions of power but can have power in its utterance and performance (← chap. 3 and → chap. 6). According to Butler, by viewing power in language as dependent on prior social power, "Bourdieu inadvertently forecloses the possibility of an agency that emerges from the margins of power" (p. 156). It is to issues of resistance and change, therefore, that I now turn.

Resistance and Change

These critical understandings of social and cultural reproduction in education take us usefully beyond a view of education as an autonomous or neutral activity. Instead, they locate schooling in the context of social class and inequality, showing how schools are precisely part of society, indeed a key social institution, and must be seen as both reflecting and reproducing social relations. Yet, as Giroux (1983) and Canagarajah (1993, 1999b) argue, there is a danger here that this view of reproduction allows no understanding of opposition and resistance, of the complex ways in

TABLE 5.3

Strengths and Weaknesses of Bourdieu

Strengths of Bourdieu's Framework	*Potential Weaknesses*
Contextualized sociologies of power: not pregiven but in context	Reproductive model of social relations
Relational view of power: power dependent on social field	Economic and rational model of accumulation
Habitus as embodied forms of socialized power	Power as outside language rather than potentially within

which students and teachers act within the context of schooling. What is needed, then, is a way of understanding resistance and change. This is important not only because we need better understandings of what actually goes on in classrooms but also because as educators we need a sense that we can actually do something. A problem with broad critical analysis is that it is often fundamentally pessimistic: We live in a patriarchal, homophobic, racist world increasingly governed by the interests of multinational business. This is a useful understanding of the world, but we also need to be able to believe in some alternative.

This, then, is one of the central issues in developing a usable critical theory for critical applied linguistics. As I already argued in the context of critical theories of language and text (← chaps. 3 and 4), we need to escape overdeterministic, overtotalizing critical analyses to be able to show how critical applied linguistics may make a difference. It is for these reasons that Giroux (1988) talks of the need to develop a language of both critique and hope in critical educational theory and why Roger Simon (1992) talks of a pedagogy of possibility. But, as we saw in Canagarajah's critique of Peirce's use of this notion of a pedagogy of possibility, such a notion of possibility must also always occur within a critical framework in which the limitations on possibilities have been adequately dealt with. From this perspective, we are now able to look at how different possibilities are struggled over in educational (or other) contexts. And, we are able to argue that all such struggles are part of, but not completely determined by, larger social and cultural struggles. Both micro and macro (and all the levels in between, for these labels are but convenient fictions) produce each other.

Such a vision of the struggle between alternative worlds is the domain of cultural politics. Rather than the deterministic view of culture common in applied linguistics (in which cultures are static constructs that determine our behavior; see → chap. 6), and rather than the deterministic view of culture that suggests that it is merely a representation of social difference and therefore a means by which social inequality is reproduced, we can now start to develop a notion of cultural difference and struggle. The students who came to Canagarajah's classroom were not defined by some simple cultural Tamil-ness, by Tamil learning styles or food preferences, but were part of a complex world that they brought to the classroom, a world in which culture and ethnicity is bound up with other political domains such as social class, gender and age. And it is important to observe here that such cultural preferences can't be mapped simply onto cultural bodies: Canagarajah is, like his students, a Tamil Lankan; but he is also a "young (in my early 30s), male, 'progressive', Christian, culturally Westernized, middle class, native Tamil, bilingual, director of English language teaching at the university" (1993, p. 620).

This notion of cultural politics, then, gives us another, but more open, way of getting at questions to do with the politics of classrooms. Cultural politics have to do with whose versions of reality gain legitimacy, whose representations of the world gain sway over others (Jordan & Weedon, 1995). From this perspective, classrooms become sites of cultural struggle, contexts in which different versions of the world are battled over. In this context it is also possible to see how students and teachers operate in accordance with or in opposition to different cultural possibilities. As Canagarajah (1993) describes what happened in his class: "On the one hand, they oppose the alien discourses behind the language and textbook. On the other hand, they oppose a process-oriented pedagogy and desire a product-oriented one" (p. 617). From this point of view, the cultural struggle in classrooms is not reducible to one between ideologies of the dominant and dominated but rather to a whole circulation of different ideas, cultural forms, ways of thinking, being, and speaking.

As Canagarajah (1993) observes, therefore, although his classroom is bound up with everything happening outside, it is also a context in which students resist and appropriate what is happening. They resist his more Westernized teaching approach and opt instead for an approach to learning with which they were more familiar. They annotated the textbooks with anything from "Tamilization" of the characters or the addition of phrases (in English) such as "I love you darling" to dialogues to the inclusion of references to the struggle for Tamil independence. Students in this class also struggled with the textbook and its meanings. According to Dendrinos (1992):

> the language of the EFL textbook is not merely an instrument for constructing learners as subjects of the educational institution but for positioning them as particular social subjects, by involving them in the creation of social meanings through the presentation of particular social realities arbitrarily selected. (p. 152)

As she goes on to show through a critical analysis of EFL texts, however, although the content is in one sense *random* (in that it is chosen as illustrative material for linguistic forms), it nevertheless presents very particular views of the world. Many EFL textbooks, she suggests, "portray a reality of the will and freedom of individuals who are alone in shaping their life in any way they choose" (p. 159); and texts "contribute to the construction of a specific social reality concerning the family institution, concerning gender, ethnicity, race and class" (p. 177). All teaching materials carry cultural and ideological messages. The pictures, the lifestyles, the stories, the dialogues are all full of cultural content, and all may potentially be in disaccord with the cultural worlds of the students. Everything we use in class is laden with meanings from outside and interpretations from inside. And these meanings and interpretations occur amid the complex cultural politics of the classroom.

Once we open up this perspective of the cultural politics of classrooms, we can start to see how everything that goes on in classrooms is related to broader concerns. And the relation I am trying to emphasize here is a reciprocal one: This is not one where the classroom is determined by the outside world, a mere reflection of what happens elsewhere; it is one where the classroom is part of the world, both affected by what happens outside its walls and affecting what happens there. Classrooms, from this perspective, are also sites where identities are produced and changed (see → chap. 6). The language we teach, the materials we use, the way we run our classrooms, the things students do and say, all these can be seen in social and cultural terms, and thus, from a critical perspective as social political and cultural political questions. Assumptions about "active" and "passive" students, about the use of groupwork and pairwork, about self-interest as a key to motivation ("tell us about yourself"), about memorization being an outmoded learning strategy, about oral communication as the goal and means of instruction, about an informal atmosphere in the class being most conducive to language learning, about learning activities being fun, about games being an appropriate way of teaching and learning—all these, despite the claims by some researchers that they are empirically preferable, are *cultural preferences.*

The classroom thus becomes a site of cultural struggle over preferred modes of learning and teaching. Students resist teachers' pedagogies, and teachers resist students' practices. What may appear to be lack of ability or lack of preparation may in fact be resistance, as Kumaravadivelu (1999) observed when students' "unwillingness to prepare for the class and to participate in class discussions appeared to me to be a form of passive resistance" (p. 454). And all these forms of resistance are connected in complex ways to the world beyond the classroom. As Canagarajah (1999b) suggests:

> It is important to understand the extent to which classroom resistance may play a significant role in larger transformations in the social sphere. To say that signs of critical thinking, writing, or reading mean that students are as-

sured of political and material empowerment is to exaggerate matters. To think that such signs are indications of imminent political transformation and social reconstruction is to simplify such processes. Although the school has an obvious connection in the reproduction of power structures, material and ideological realities have a life of relative autonomy that needs to be tackled in its own right. (p. 196)

CRITICAL PEDAGOGY

Although the earlier discussion helps illuminate the background to a critical theory of education, there is also a need for a form of critical praxis in response. One candidate here is critical pedagogy as identified with the writings of Henry Giroux (1988), Peter McLaren (1989), Barry Kanpol (1994, 1997), and others. Put simply, they have developed a critique of formal education that suggests that it "always represents an introduction to, preparation for, and legitimation of particular forms of social life" (McLaren, 1989, p. 160). Once one acknowledges the cultural politics of schooling, the fact that curricula represent not so much timeless truths and knowledge but rather very particular ways of understanding the world, then one can start to develop a critical form of pedagogy that addresses the marginalizations and exclusions of schooling by encouraging students to develop their own voice (see ← chap. 4). Voice in this context is understood as far more than just speaking; rather, it is a broader understanding of developing the possibilities to articulate alternative realities. And since it has to do with gaining the agency to express one's life, it is less about the medium of voice (speaking, writing, etc.) and more about finding possibilities of articulation. The ultimate goal of critical pedagogy, as Kanpol (1994, 1997) describes it, remains tied to a vision of more inclusive social democracy. It is a pedagogy of inclusion.

One of the critiques leveled at critical pedagogy has been its tendency to remain at the level of grand theorizing rather than pedagogical practice. As with the discussion of critical literacy (← chap. 4), we may also see critical pedagogy as operating in two domains, one a research- or theory-oriented critical discussion of schooling, the other a critical practice of teaching. As Gore (1993) has observed, however, critical pedagogy is often something of a misnomer since most of what is discussed as critical pedagogy in fact falls into the former category of critical theory. She takes Giroux and McLaren to task for their "grand theorizing," which she suggests is ultimately prescriptive: "A major danger of this strand of critical pedagogy lies in the juxtaposition of its abstract metatheoretical analysis of schooling with its abstract dictates and declarations for what teachers should do" (pp. 110–111). Similarly, Usher and Edwards (1994) point to the "curious silence on concrete educational practices" (p. 218). Johnston (1999), relating critical pedagogy to TESOL contexts, mounts a similar critique, suggesting that the abstractions and political posturing of critical pedagogy can be alienating.

If we take critical pedagogy to include Freirean-based approaches to education, however, it is worth noting that there are in fact a number of quite detailed accounts available of critical praxis in EFL/ESL (also see the discussion ← in chap. 4 of Freirean approaches to literacy). Rivera's (1999) account of a popular education program in New York focuses on the use of a bilingual curriculum (also see Auerbach, 1993), the involvement of current and former participants as popular teachers, and the use of video technology as a tool for exploring a range of critical concerns in the community. Through this program the participants "learned how to read and write in two languages by engaging in projects through which they collected and analyzed data about issues affecting their lives" (p. 497). A similar participatory approach is described in Frye's (1999) account of an ESL class for Latina women in Washington, D.C. She reports that her "critical, participatory approach" led to "the development of solidarity among participants, an increased sense of identity, the exploration of women-centered issues, and the emergence of and focus on different learning styles" (p. 507). From a slightly different perspective, Benesch (1999) demonstrates how "dialogic critical thinking" can play a role in "expanding students' understanding beyond what they may have already considered to promote tolerance and social justice" (p. 573). Meanwhile, Morgan's (1998) use of critical pedagogy in community ESL classes in Toronto (which will be discussed further in → chap. 6) shows how a constant focus on broader critical concerns (community policing, the Gulf War) may be interwoven with standard elements of ESL pedagogy (intonation, grammar).

Despite these interesting developments in critical pedagogical approaches to TESOL, mainstream critical pedagogy remains problematic. As Usher and Edwards (1994) point out, throughout all this work "the principal issue is the introduction of heterogeneity and the recognition of difference into educational practices" (p. 215). As I discussed in the previous chapter, the version of voice used in critical pedagogy has been criticized, particularly in Australia (Cope & Kalantzis, 1993; Luke, 1996), for what is seen as an inability to escape a North American individualistic idealism. From this perspective, critical pedagogy seems more concerned with just letting everyone "have a voice," and it is unclear how this enunciation of marginality can actually bring about social change. Furthermore, as Simon (1992) points out, both the notion of voice and the notion of dialogue (the engagement with voice) are often treated trivially:

> The concept of a dialogic pedagogy is perhaps one of the most confused and misdeveloped ideas in the literature on critical teaching. At a simplistic level it has been taken as a process within which a student "voice" is "taken seriously" and in this respect is counterposed to a transmission pedagogy. But this is both a vague and trivial statement. (p. 96)

Critical pedagogy, Gore (1993) suggests, has failed to problematize its own status as, in Foucault's terminology, a *regime of truth*. One of the most significant critiques, however, has come from Ellsworth (1989), who takes critical pedagogy to task for being tied to a rationalist view of education in which students are supposed to arrive logically at the understanding that they have a right to freedom from oppression, for employing a simplistic version of empowerment and dialogue that obscures power relationships between students and teachers, for failing to develop an adequate understanding of how giving people voice can bring about their empowerment (compare the critique by Luke and others), and for working with too simple an understanding of the multiplicities of oppression so that it is too easily assumed that students will side with the "oppressed" and against the "oppressors." These critiques point to very real problems with critical pedagogy as expounded in the work of Giroux, McLaren, and Kanpol, problems that, as Lather (1995) points out, have not been adequately addressed by these writers (see Table 5.4).

Some of the criticisms here also reflect earlier criticisms of emancipatory modernism. Indeed, although critical pedagogy often claims to take on postmodern, poststructuralist, and postcolonial insights, it might be argued that it has tended ultimately to stay firmly grounded in a modernist discourse. This point can be seen in some of Ellsworth's critiques of its rationalist and monolithic assumptions. It has also been addressed by Gore (1993), who argues that whereas the critical pedagogues pay lip service to questions raised by postmodernism, their pedagogy remains firmly modernist: "The pedagogy of the argument remains a directive one. The goal remains a universal, rather than partial and contradictory, one of empowerment" (p. 39). It might not at first seem obvious to suggest that critical pedagogy remains wedded to a modernist dream given the current critical pedagogical tendency to embrace postmodernism and postcolonialism, but this generally operates by borrowing some critical

TABLE 5.4

Features and Critiques of Critical Pedagogy

Features of Mainstream Critical Pedagogy	Critiques and Weaknesses
Political understanding of schooling	Grand theorizing rather than pedagogical practice
Emphasis on inclusion and voice	Tied to narrow vision of inclusion; voice as individualistic; dialogism as trivial
Transformative vision of education	Rationalist and modernist notion of change and empowerment

tools from postmodernism while staying firmly grounded in modernism (Kanpol, 1990; Pennycook, 1990, 1991).

Usher and Edwards (1994) make a similar point, suggesting that critical pedagogy continues to operate with universalist discourses of modernism, a simplistic belief in the shared goals of democracy. Thus, they argue, "many criticalist texts seem curiously unreflexive as they do not subject themselves to the forms of critical engagement to which they subject others" (p. 220). Ultimately, critical pedagogy "continues the modern project of emancipation through the adoption of certain postmodern ideas" (p. 221). As Johnston (1999) remarks:

> Critical pedagogy has given me insights into and understandings of the educational process that I would not otherwise have had ... but it is not enough to capture the complex essence of teaching, especially of ESL/EFL teaching in the postmodern world. (p. 564)

How an understanding of education and postmodernism may illuminate this debate is therefore the topic of the next section.

EDUCATION, POSTMODERNISM, AND ETHICS

It is not my purpose here to expound at any length on postmodernism or postmodernism and education (see Usher & Edwards, 1994, for an extended discussion). Rather, my concern here is to tie in the discussions (← chaps. 3 and 4) of postcolonialism and poststructuralism with a brief overview of postmodern considerations of education as well as the significant ethical questions that such a position raises. The earlier discussion of critical pedagogy pointed once again to the need to be suspicious about modernist narratives of education, empowerment, and emancipation and to engage with the challenges presented by poststructuralism, postmod- ernism, and postcolonialism. The failure of mainstream critical pedagogy to escape its modernist dream of the shared goals of democracy, like the failure of critical literacy theorists such as Cope and Kalantzis (1993) to engage in any substantive way with the postmodern challenge—they dismiss it as another form of liberal progressivism, while Kress (1993) dismisses poststructuralism as a form of "(neo-)romanticism" (p. 30)—and the failure of other critical work to go beyond a belief in emancipatory awareness limit the possibilities of all these approaches to critical pedagogy and literacy.

Postmodernism can be taken to mean many different things. A useful distinction to start with is between postmodernism and postmodernity, the latter referring to the state of the world as we enter the new millennium, the former to a crisis in the project of modernism. Postmodernity, then, appears to be what Johnston (1999) is discussing when he refers to "the complex essence of teaching, especially of ESL/EFL teaching in the postmodern world" (p. 564), that is to say, a real state of affairs brought about by increased complexity in our lives. Postmodernism, by contrast, is more of a philosophical questioning of many of the foundational concepts of received canons of knowledge: It is antiessentialist and antifoundationalist and opposed to grand narratives. Thus, it calls into question any claims to overarching truths such as human nature, enlightenment, or emancipation; it makes us skeptical about talk of reality, truth, or universality. Postmodernism rejects unity, totalization, transcendental concepts, or a belief in disinterested knowledge. And it is this sort of skepticism, this attempt to understand things in more local terms rather than in terms of grand theories or utopian dreams of equality, that makes it hard to believe in notions such as emancipation. Thus, as Lather (1992) explains, "postmodern theories of language, subjectivity and power profoundly challenge the discourse of emancipation on several fronts" (p. 98).

Amid the many discourses on postmodernism, there are some central issues that I wish to take up. First, I am more interested here in considering it as a way of thinking. In this sense, postmodernism refers "more to a state of mind, a critical posture and style, a different way of seeing and working, than to a fixed position, however oppositional, or to an unchanging set of critical techniques" (Usher & Edwards, 1994, p. 17). In this context, it is worth recalling some of the defining elements of critical applied linguistics that I suggested earlier. This view of postmodernism as a shifting, critical way of thinking is reflected in Foucault's point that the goal of our thinking is to find new politicizations rather than to adopt an established position. And another of the guiding frames of my thinking on critical applied linguistics—the restive problematization of the given—is proposed by Dean (1994) as a way of understanding postmodernism. As I argue later (→ chap. 7), my goal in this book is to outline a way of thinking, a different way of seeing and working, rather than a model, a canon of thought, or a set of techniques. Second, it is important to consider postmodernism in relation to postcolonialism. As Young (1990) suggests, "postmodernism can best be defined as European culture's awareness that it is no longer the unquestioned and dominant centre of the world" (p. 19). Such a view of postmodernism links it specifically to a politics that seeks to question the canons of Eurocentric knowledge, a stance of great significance in the context of applied linguistics, particularly when linked to its global role in relation to the teaching of major languages such as English.

Third, it is important to understand that despite the resistance to large-scale theories and the insistence on complexity and localized forms of knowledge, postmodernism cannot be simply dismissed as a form of relativism. As Lather (1992) argues, following Haraway (1988), relativism and universalism sit as complementary poles within a modernist frame of knowledge. If challenges are made to objectivist or universalist frameworks of knowledge, the counterargument simply involves accusations of relativism or nihilism, which, Lather (1992) suggests are "an implosion of Western, white male, class-privileged arrogance—if we cannot know everything, then we can know nothing" (p. 100). This is not to say, of course, that there are not all sorts of difficulties involved with working with a postmodern view of knowledge; rather, the point is that to dismiss postmodernism as relativist is to fail to engage with the complexity of postmodern approaches to knowledge. A useful postmodernism, by contrast, works with a notion of *situated knowledges* (Haraway, 1988) that should not be equated with relativism: "The relativism of modernity needs to be distinguished from the partiality and particularity of the postmodern moment" (Usher & Edwards, 1994, p. 223). Postmodernism, then, questions the whole polarity between universalism and relativism, suggesting instead that knowledge, action and value are always specifically located.

Giroux and McLaren's heavy-handed responses to Ellsworth's critique of critical pedagogy suggest, among other things, that her arguments about the multiplicities of oppression and the complexities of competing student and teacher positions leave us with nothing but postmodern nihilism. Lather (1995) suggests, however, that Giroux and McLaren's worries "about the nihilism assumed to undergird postmodernism's suspicion of claims to truth, the will to knowledge and the primacy of reason" (p. 176) fail to engage adequately with postmodernism. Ellsworth's project, she suggests, "belies the spectre of nihilism" since it "demonstrates how postmodernism has much to offer those of us who do our work in the name of emancipation to construct the material for struggle present in the stuff of our daily lives to which we all have access" (p. 177). The postmodern moment, she suggests, is "an open-ended construction that is contested, incessantly perspectival and multiply-sited" (p. 177). This theme relates to my earlier discussion (and ← chaps. 3 and 4) of the importance of localized and contextualized work in critical applied linguistics.

Finally, I argue for a postmodernism of engagement (compare a pedagogy of engagement → chap. 6). Taking certain approaches to postmodernism to task for being "unwilling to engage at other than the textual level," McGee (1995, p. 206) argues for a form of postmodernism as "critical analysis which flows from concerns about issues such as gender inequality, social injustice, racism, and poverty" (p. 206). There are times, of course, when such a postmodernism of engagement is hard to achieve given the shaky ground on which postmodernism and poststructuralism leave us. They present not just an antirealist stance but a position that reality is produced through representations and that such representations are never neutral, are always constructed in particular ways and with particular complicities with power. Essential categories such as men, women, class, race, awareness, emancipation, language, power are seen as contingent, shifting, and produced in the particular. My vision of critical applied linguistics is based on this view: It is not intended to be a method, a canon of texts, a series of techniques but rather a shifting and critical way of thinking about questions to do with language. After 10 years of trying to engage with a notion of critical applied linguistics, I feel that it is better to live with the slipperiness and contradictions of postmodernism than the emancipatory claims of modernism. But to ground a notion of engagement, a postmodern critical applied linguistics needs a way of dealing with ethics.

Postmodernism and Ethics

One of the problems with postmodernism is that once we have shaken knowledge claims to their foundations, there seems little place from which to ground a critical project. As I discussed earlier, a postmodern position is highly skeptical of the alluring yet problematic modernist discourses of emancipation. One way forward here is to reground one's critical project in ethics. As Kearney (1988) describes this moment, although postmodernism may call this into question

> *epistemological* limits (in so far as it undermines every attempt to establish a decidable relationship between image and reality), it must recognize *ethical* limits. We reach a point in the endless spiral of undecidability where each one of us is obliged to make an ethical decision, to say: *here I stand*. (Or, at the level of collective responsibility, *here we stand*). Here and now, in the face of the postmodern logic of interminable deferment and infinite regress, of floating signifiers and vanishing signifieds, here and now I face an *other* who demands of me an ethical response. (p. 361)

In his article, "Postmodernism and Literacies," Gee (1993) arrives at a similar point. When one comes to the end of the questioning, he suggests, we need some form of ethical principles on which we can ground our work: If there is no way of establishing reality or truth outside a particular sign system, how then can we still make judgments about preferable outcomes? Gee suggests that the only way forward at this point is to consider the *effects* on other people of what we do and say. At the end of our questioning, at the end of our search for stable ground, Gee suggests we come against "two conceptual principles that serve as the basis of *ethical human discourse* (talk and interaction)" (p. 292): "That something would *harm* someone else ... is *always* a good reason (though perhaps not a sufficient reason) *not* to do it" (p. 292), and "One always has the ethical obligation to explicate ... any social practice that there is reason to believe advantages oneself or one's group over other people or groups" (p. 293).

Corson (1997) notes that very little attention has been paid to questions of ethics in applied linguistics, apart from a rather superficial view of ethics in research. Indeed, discussions of ethics in applied linguistics have failed to go beyond issues of "professional conduct," whether in discussions of research or of "ethicality" in language testing. Corson goes on to argue that it must ultimately be on ethical grounds that we make epistemological choices. He suggests three basic ethical principles drawn from moral philosophy: the principle of equal treatment (compare Gee's second principle), the principle of respect for persons (compare Gee's first principle), and the principle of benefit maximization (a more utilitarian concern with the consequences of actions). Taking issue with the tendencies toward foundational or hegemonic theory construction (also see → chap. 6), Corson argues that:

> Only an inclusive epistemology is ethically acceptable once we have decided that the reasons and the accounts of stakeholders are ontologically basic to our actions as researchers and practitioners in applied linguistics. This is because only an inclusive epistemology is consistent with all three ethical principles at the same time. In other words, applied linguistics needs to open its windows to other disciplines and to other points of view, especially to the points of view of its informants, clientele, and potential victims. (p. 183)

Here, then, the turn toward plurality and situated knowledge obliges us to confront some of the hardest questions. No longer can applied linguistics at this point continue to believe arrogantly in its methods, canon of knowledge, or research. At this point we have to deal with the raw edge of basic ethical decisions. And in this postmodern framework, there are no moral assurances to fall back on: This is not a normative morality, a fixed body of codes to follow; there are no religious or objective morals to speak of, only confrontation with the real ethics of hard decisions. And these ethical decisions do not occur outside relations of power. According to Roger Simon (1992):

> Questions of justice cannot be addressed outside the way I enter and respond to relations of power and oppression. In other words, for me, ethics are not acted out in the spirit of human isolation but rather mirror the responsibilities of relationship rather than the obligations encumbered within an autonomous self-sufficient moral reason. (p. 26)

What Simon is therefore arguing is the need to understand ethics not as part of a fixed moral code that guides the behavior of the individual but rather as part of a contingent way of thinking and acting that is always in relation to social, cultural, and political relations.

Simon (1992) confronts these questions when he speaks of his "project of possibility" as "the situated refusal of the present as definitive of that which is possible." Such an educational vision that is "capable of narrating stories of possibility" is "constrained within an ethical imagination that privileges diversity, compassionate justice, and securing of the conditions for the renewal of human life" (p. 30). The point here, then, is that ultimately we have to fall back on an ethical vision of responsibility to others. Similar to Foucault's comment that we are not seeking to establish a political position but rather to explore new schemas of politicization (← chap.

1), so perhaps the question here must also be one not of establishing a moral position but of seeking new frames of ethical thought and conduct, or, as Kearney (1988) puts it "the ethical demand to imagine *otherwise*" (p. 364). Such a vision, of course, demands a major rethinking of what applied linguistics might be about. Instead of being a canon of normative knowledge about language acquisition, teaching methods, translation, and so on, it becomes a project to address the ethical demands of language education, of the global spread of English, of the available choices in translation, of language in the workplace, of the complexities of literacy.

TOWARD A POSTCRITICAL PEDAGOGY

Doing critical work is dangerous work. The memories and narratives we may seek to introduce into our classes or research may indeed be dangerous memories. The effects of what we do may be profound. Graman (1988), for example, lists some of the changes that came about in the lives of some of his students as a result of his teaching:

> One became ostracized from his religious group because of his new perspective on Nicaragua. He later began to ask himself profound questions that will probably have a lasting effect on his intellectual and ethical life. Another student spoke of the willpower she gained in the dialogic class which enabled her to seek a divorce she had wanted for years. (p. 447)

We should not believe, therefore, that critical work is some easy road to empowerment or emancipation. We may be heading down a dangerous route with our students or our research, and we need to think very carefully where things may lead and whether we can justify ethically what we are engaged in. But for those who say we are just language teachers or just applied linguists and should not involve ourselves with such concerns, I say that we already are involved. We cannot bury our heads in the sand as liberal-ostrichist applied linguistics has done in the past. What we need is better ways of thinking about what we do.

I have tried to present in this chapter a number of ways in which critical applied linguistics may help inform various pedagogical approaches. I argue in this chapter for a view of the classroom as a microcosm of the larger social and cultural world, reflecting, reproducing, and changing that world. Everything outside the classroom, from community and national language policies to social and cultural contexts of schooling, may have an impact on what happens in the classroom. But I also argue that we need to understand the classroom itself as a social domain, not merely a reflection of the larger society beyond the classroom walls but also as a place in which social relations are played out and therefore a context in which we need to directly address questions of social power. As Auerbach (1995) points out, such relations between the social and the classroom can be seen at many levels, including curriculum, instructional content, materials, and language choice.

Everything in the classroom, from how we teach, what we teach, how we respond to students, to the materials we use and the way we assess the students, needs to be seen as social and cultural practices that have broader implications than just pieces of classroom interaction. For Auerbach (1995), thus, these concerns point in two directions: On the one hand, classrooms need to "include explicit analysis of the social context" outside the classroom, and on the other hand, "students must be involved in making pedagogical choices inside the classroom" (p. 28). In any educational domain, therefore, we need to focus on the cultural politics of what we do and understand the implications of our own and our students' pedagogical choices as both particular to the context and related to broader domains. The challenge is to understand this relation and to find ways of always focusing on the local while at the same time keeping an eye on the broader horizons. And, this view that our classroom walls are permeable means that what we do in our classrooms is about changing the worlds we live in. Thus, we also need to have ways of thinking about and beyond the relations between structure and agency, how micro actions on one level may be part of macro forces on another, and how within the macro forces of society we are still able to change, resist, act with some degree of autonomy.

I have been critical in this chapter of critical pedagogy as it has developed as a canon of work in the texts of Giroux, McLaren, and Kanpol. Among other things, this is part of my argument that critical work should always remain critical and skeptical. The moment we start to accept unquestioningly the work of critical pedagogy, critical literacy, critical discourse analysis, or critical language awareness, we are no longer engaged in a critical project. Nevertheless, a couple of caveats are in order. First, as with my discussion in previous chapters of critical domains, I have presented what I see as a core of mainstream critical work as if this were fairly unproblematically representative of the domain. But *critical discourse analysis* and *critical pedagogy* are also terms used with much broader coverage than implied by this approach. Indeed, the question remains open as to whether we should see critical pedagogy as what is produced in the texts of Giroux, McLaren, and others or whether we see it as the broad totality of many of the critical writers discussed in this chapter.

And second, it is worth noting that, as Gore (1993) recalls, "it was through critical pedagogy that I first found a language with which to name my frustrations with dominant approaches to education" (p. xiii). A similar point is made in Johnston's (1999) remarks (cited earlier) that despite its shortcomings, critical pedagogy gave him "insights into and understandings of the educational process that I would not otherwise have had" (p. 564). Indeed, this experience is very similar to my own since it was through critical pedagogy that I started to develop a critical approach to language and education. I think it is very important to keep this observation in mind. Our pathways to forms of critical work may be very diverse: My own pathway would take another book to tell, but it would certainly include reading Marx, Marcuse, and critical pedagogy. Even if I now distance myself from some of these perspectives, these were the stepping-stones I used on the way. Just as the end goal of critical applied linguistics is a shifting space, so too are the possible pathways.

Lather (1995) argues for "post-critical pedagogies," which she sees as going beyond the "largely male inscribed liberation models of critical pedagogy" (p. 177) and opening up a relation between postmodernism, feminism, and pedagogy. Such postcritical pedagogies must clearly be seen in relation to the feminist, antiracist, and so on (post)linguistics and postcolonial performative approaches I discussed earlier (← chaps. 3 and 4). Lee (1997) also pulls these strands together when she argues that:

> Contemporary poststructuralist, feminist and postcolonial theories argue for the theoretical and political necessity of diversity and differentiation. There is an urgent need, in the contemporary politics of literacy and curriculum, to confront liberal-democratic notions of equality with rigorous questions of difference. (p. 429)

These arguments take us into a postcritical view of language education that attempts to deal with the postcolonial challenge of dealing with the Other, the poststructuralist requirement to understand how discourses operate across multiple sites, constructing our worlds and subjectivities, and the postmodern challenge to deal with the particularities and complexities presented by trying to take differences seriously (these configurations are summarized in Fig. 5.1). The politics of difference is the topic of the next chapter.

postcolonialism and anti-essentialist theory of linguistic performativity ——→	postcolonial performativity
poststructuralism, politics and linguistic analysis ——→	feminist, anti-racist, etc., postlinguistics
postmodernism and difference in transformative education ——→	postcritical pedagogy

FIG. 5.1. Reconfiguring the posts.

The Politics of Difference

Difference, Identity, and Language Learning
    Identity and Subjectivity
Language, Gender, Sexuality, and Difference
    Dominance and Difference
    Performing Gender Through Language
Dealing With Difference: Inclusivity, Issues,
      and Engagement
    Toward Engaged Research
Conclusion: Embodied Differences

I suggested earlier (← chap. 2) that an important distinction between different approaches to politics and knowledge concerned the question of difference. One position argues against overdifferentiation and stresses instead a shared humanity and universal human characteristics. From this point of view, it is exactly the emphasis on difference that leads to bigotry, conflict, even genocide. As I suggest at a number of points in this book, however, such a position is tied on the one hand to a modernist emancipatory position that fails to recognize that it is exactly its own forms of hegemonic knowledge production that are part of the problem; and, more importantly here, on the other hand, this position works against the ethical imperative to engage with the profundity of human difference. I argue that it is only through an attempt at *engagement* that we can take up Kearney's (1988) challenge for an ethical response to an other (see ← chap. 5). As he suggests, once we have gone beyond the restrictions of a modernist view, "we may be in a position to discover another kind of relation be-tween self and other—one more human than humanism and more faithful to otherness than onto-theology" (p. 363).

This chapter, and my approach to critical applied linguistics, starts with these concerns: Much of applied linguistics is averse to any serious engagement with otherness, neglecting the real possibilities of difference. There are two main ways in which difference is neglected. On the one hand, there are approaches to research and practice that negate differ-ence: The central focus is on the control, regulation, and denial of forms of otherness. Most typically, this view is seen in positivistic approaches to research such as those that dominate second language acquisition. If this approach takes as its underlying rationale the unimportance of difference for the understanding of generalizations, other approaches suggest a far greater role for a notion of difference. But the overriding problem from this perspective is that difference becomes reified and fixed through static definitions of Otherness, particularly in terms of categories of gender and culture. On the other hand, then, there are approaches to practice and re-search that acknowledge difference but do so along static and predefined forms of differing.

This chapter suggests that applied linguistics is rife with problematic constructions of otherness, and therefore explores the importance of the politics of difference for critical applied linguistics. While the major con-texts for this exploration will be second language acquisition, identity and language pedagogy, these consideration are clearly important for all do-mains of applied linguistics. Arguing that "asymmetries, inequities, rela-tions of domination and dependence exist in every act of translating," for example, Venuti (1997, p. 4) makes a case for an approach to translation based on an ethics of difference. Such a stance on the one hand "urges that translations be written, read, and evaluated with greater respect for lin-guistic and cultural differences" (p. 6); on the other hand, it aims at "minoritizing the standard dialect and dominant cultural forms in Ameri-can English" in part as "an opposition to the global hegemony of English" (p. 10). For Venuti, the assimilationary processes of translation, whereby texts are constructed to eradicate difference, raise serious ethical and po-litical concerns that need to be resisted: "The heterogenous discourse of minoritizing translation resists this assimilationist ethic by signifying the linguistic and cultural differences of the text—within the major language" (p. 12). Ultimately, an ethics of difference in translation, similar to an ethics of difference in other domains of critical applied linguistics, "re-forms cultural identities that occupy dominant positions in the domestic culture" (p. 83). Such a focus, then, becomes a major concern for critical applied linguistics: Not only does it need to focus on forms of power, to lo-cate itself within an adequate view of language politics, and to respond to the ethics of difference, but it also needs to develop a transformative ele-ment that seeks to reform cultural identities.

DIFFERENCE, IDENTITY, AND LANGUAGE LEARNING

In the last chapter (← chap. 5), I discussed classrooms as social and cultural spaces. The onus in that discussion was on understanding language classrooms both as part of a larger social and cultural domain and as social and cultural domains in themselves. As we also saw in the last chapter, there have been a number of attempts to develop critical pedagogical approaches that breach this gap between the classroom and the world outside. But even if one accepts an understanding of the classroom (or the language learning context more generally) as always social and cultural, it may nevertheless be possible to maintain another dichotomy between the social and cultural context of learning and the psychological processes of learning. Thus, it could be argued that it's all very well to consider classrooms as social contexts, but we still need to get on with the real work of looking at cognitive processes, at how students learn language. Such a dichotomization between the social and the psychological, however, obscures the ways in which social, cultural, and political relations are tied up with questions of identity, subjectivity, and difference.

Unfortunately, studies of how people learn a second language have been constricted by the narrow purview of mainstream second language acquisition (SLA) work. The issues of language learning have been cast as questions to do with the acquisition of morphemes, syntax, and lexis, with pronunciation or communicative competence, and the learner has been cast as a one-dimensional acquisition device. From this perspective, learners are viewed according to a mechanistic metaphor, as a sort of language learning machine. The writing on this topic is full of metaphors such as *input, output, information processing,* and so on. It has also operated with a positivistic research methodology in which the emphasis has been on the quantification of results achieved by experimental or quasi-experimental studies. Typically from this perspective, an attempt is made to study minute aspects of learning in a controlled environment. As a result, studies in second language acquisition have tended to ignore the context of learning, viewing learning environments and learners as settings in which "variables" need to be controlled. From this perspective, issues to do with identity would be sidelined under a category such as "learner variables." Furthermore, language tends to be seen as a fixed object to be acquired rather than as a semiotic system full of variations and struggles. Even basic considerations of variability posed by mainstream sociolinguistics pose challenges to the fixed code fallacy of SLA; the broader considerations raised by a world Englishes perspective (see ← chap. 3) pose more serious challenges, especially in terms of norms, targets, and interlanguage (Sridhar & Sridhar, 1986); and, the more radical postcolonial performative vision of language I am trying to develop here makes the whole paradigm look very suspect.

There has also been considerable debate recently over the benefits of a diversity of approaches or a more limited range of options in studying

SLA (see also → chap. 7). Thus, in response to various attempts to secure a firm agreement on what should and should not count as SLA theory and research (Beretta, 1991; Beretta, Crookes, Gregg, & Long, 1994; Long, 1990), including Gregg's (1993) call only to let "a couple of flowers bloom," others such as Block (1996), Firth and Wagner (1997), and Lantolf (1996) have made a case to let "all the flowers bloom" (Lantolf, 1996). Lantolf suggests that SLA "presents a lopsided and uncritical view of both itself and the scientific tradition from which it arises, and it precipitously dismisses those who would challenge it" (p. 716). These calls for a plurality of approaches to the study of SLA, which might then include modes of analysis that could account for social context, power or identity, have been angrily denounced (Gregg, Long, Beretta, & Jordan, 1997). Although these researchers may be right in their suspicion of a diversity-for-diversity's-sake argument, the failure to account for the politics of their own knowledge production takes us back to some of the problems I outlined earlier (← chap. 2) about the politics of knowledge. It is interesting to reflect on the possibility that just as Newmeyer (1986) observes that "it is hardly surprising that the success of generative grammar in any country has been inversely proportional to the depth of tradition of Marxist scholarship there" (p. 114), so we might suggest that the success of SLA research has been inversely proportional to the depth of critical applied linguistic scholarship.

This mainstream SLA approach to the study of language learning has contributed some useful insights into ways in which grammatical items are acquired, how a first language may affect a second language, or the relative roles of formal instruction and more natural acquisition, but it has had virtually nothing to say about learners as people, or contexts of learning, or the politics of language learning more generally. Norton Peirce (1995) takes SLA research to task for the unhelpful dichotomization between learners and contexts, the uncritical theorizing of social contexts, and the failure to look at questions of power and access. Rampton (1995b) also points out that current work in SLA "could probably benefit from an enhanced sense of the empirical world's complex socio-cultural diversity" (p. 294). Gebhard (1999) argues for a "sociocultural perspective" on language development that takes as a starting point "an understanding that the origin and structure of cognition are rooted in daily social and cultural practices in which an individual participates" (p. 544). From this point of view, SLA is seen as "an institutional phenomenon shaped by cultures and structures at work in educational systems" (p. 545). This includes understanding that "the origin and structure of L2 (Second Language) learners' sociolinguistic knowledge are rooted in the daily social and cultural practices in which they engage;" that "individual characteristics of learners are not descriptors of their internal mental state in any static or politically neutral way;" that "an analysis of context encompasses attention to the ways in which L2 users are physically positioned in relation to others in schools;" and that "schools are structured cultural spaces that play a role in the distribution of discourse practices and the production and reproduction of social orders" (p. 554). This view of language learning as an "institutional phenomenon" clearly ties in with the discussion of the role of education (← chap. 5) in social reproduction.

Identity and Subjectivity

If, on the one hand, mainstream positivist approaches to language learning have thus tended to efface questions of difference as irrelevant to an understanding of underlying aspects of cognition, other approaches to issues in TESOL have tended to operate with shallow and static notions of difference and identity: Difference has tended to be thought of in terms of "culture," and culture has then been seen as a defining and deterministic category. As Ruth Spack (1997) has observed, TESOL and applied linguistics is full of generic labels such as *foreign, other, different,* or *limited* to describe the learners in English classrooms. Indeed, there seems something deeply Othering about labels such as *TE/SOL* (Teaching English to Speakers of Other*ed* Languages) or LOTE (Languages Other Than English, an Australian acronym that I prefer to substitute with LOBE: Languages Othered by English). And when students are described in cultural terms, this tends to be done in terms of an "archaic view of culture" in which "a fixed profile of particular traits for a particular cultural group" (Spack, 1997, p. 768) is repeated over and over again. Thus, it is assumed that Japanese students behave this way or that Italian students write that way. As I have argued at length elsewhere (Pennycook, 1998a), this view of cultural *fixity* is part of a long history of colonial othering that has rendered the cultures of others fixed, traditional, exotic, and strange, whereas the cultures of English (America, Europe) are unexplored givens or moving, modern, and normal. Possibly the locus classicus of this work remains the cultural thought patterns dreamed up by Robert Kaplan (1966) in which "Oriental" students thought in spirals and Westerners in a straight line.

Such "maps of the Other" can be seen as instances of Orientalism. Drawing on the work of Said (1978), Susser (1998) convincingly shows how a great deal of writing on ESL/EFL in Japan can be described as Orientalist. Analyzing writing on Japan according to the Said-inspired categories of *Othering* (dichotomous productions of Self and Other, East and West, Confucian and Christian), *stereotyping* (fixed assumptions about Japanese as group oriented, hierarchical, authoritarian, passive, silent), *representing* Japan typically as homogeneous and harmonious, and *essentializing* by talking of *Japan,* and *the Japanese,* Susser concludes his comprehensive study of texts on Japan by suggesting that "there is considerable Orientalism in the ESL/EFL literature on Japan" (p. 63). As he points out, the issue "is not that there are occasional stereotypes or factual errors .... These fictions have been woven into a pervasive discourse that shapes our descriptions and then our perceptions of Japanese learners and classrooms" (p. 64).

Kubota (1999) also looks critically at ways in which Japanese and other cultures are constructed in relationship to ELT. She points to the ways in which attempts to understand cultural difference in language education:

> have tended to dichotomize Western culture and Eastern culture and to draw rigid cultural boundaries between them. They have given labels such as *individualism, self-expression, critical and analytic thinking,* and *extending knowledge* to Western cultures on the one hand, and *collectivism, harmony, indirection, memorization,* and *conserving knowledge* to Asian cultures on the other. (p. 14)

As Kubota points out, such views are based on a form of cultural determinism that reproduces colonial relations of self and other (Pennycook, 1998a). Distinctions such as extending knowledge versus conserving knowledge, for example, reproduce the distinction between changing, developing, and modern cultures on the one hand and static, conservative, and traditional cultures on the other. As Kubota goes on to show, the Japanese themselves have also played a role here with their own particular productions of the uniqueness of Japanese culture.

It is this construction of cultural difference that is opposed by the postmodernist and poststructuralist arguments against essentialism that I discussed earlier (← chaps. 4 and 5), and it is the particular ways in which the construction of the Other is tied to a history of colonial and racist relations that postcolonialism takes as one of its principal concerns (← chap. 3). This TESOL construction of the Other overlooks the possibility that students have "multiple identities and draw on multiple resources" (Spack, 1997, p. 768) of culture. Such a flat and deterministic view of culture is shallow, therefore, not just because it deals in very superficial ways with cultural difference but also because it deals with limited forms of difference. As I argue in this chapter, however, identities and differences are multiple, diverse, and interrelated.

Nevertheless, some work has sought to explore a more complex range of questions in the context of SLA. McKay and Wong's (1996) study of adolescent Chinese immigrant students in the United States is based on an understanding of learners as complex social actors:

> Contrary to the kind of generic, ahistorical, "stick figure" of the learner painted in much literature on second-language learning and many teacher training programs, learners are extremely complex social beings with a multitude of fluctuating, at times conflicting, needs and desires. They exist in extremely complex social environments that consist of overwhelmingly asymmetrical power relations and subject the learners to multiple discourses. (p. 603)

They develop this understanding of learner identities in response to Norton Peirce's (1995) call to develop a "concept of the language learner as having a complex social identity that must be understood with reference to large and frequently inequitable social structures which are reproduced in day-to-day social interactions" (p. 579).

Such issues, it is worth noting, have many of the hallmarks of what I define as critical applied linguistics: They challenge what they see as reductionist tendencies in applied linguistics; they attempt to develop relations between language learning and larger views of society; and they make power an essential dimension of understanding that relationship. As Bonny Norton (Peirce) points out in the introduction to the long overdue special edition of *TESOL Quarterly* that dealt with identity and second language learning, there are many ways in which this can be understood, particularly in terms of social or cultural identity. She prefers the former, which she takes to mean "the relationship between the individual and the larger social world, as mediated through institutions such as families, schools, workplaces, social services and law courts" (Norton, 1997, p. 420). She prefers to avoid notions of cultural identity—which she sees as referring to identity based on a sense of a shared group or language—because of the tendency for this to become homogeneous and fixed. Nevertheless, as she acknowledges, it is possible for cultural identity to be understood in a much more flexible way than as predetermined by some notion of cultural or ethnic affinity.

Indeed, most of the interesting work currently starting to emerge on language and identity tends to see the social and cultural as interlinked and the formation of our identities as produced in a dynamic relation between fixed pregiven categories of identity and the different positions we take up in discourses. Thesen (1997) sees identity as:

> the dynamic interaction between the fixed identity categories that are applied to social groupings (such as race, gender, ethnicity, language, and other, more subtle representations that are activated in certain discourse settings) and the way individuals think of themselves as they move through the different discourses in which these categories are salient. (p. 488)

As Duff and Uchida (1997) put it:

> Sociocultural identities and ideologies are not static, deterministic constructs that EFL teachers and students bring to the classroom and then take away unchanged at the end of the lesson or course .... Nor are they simply dictated by membership in a larger social, cultural, or linguistic group .... Rather, in educational practice as in other facets of social life, identities and beliefs are co-constructed, negotiated, and transformed on an ongoing basis by means of language. (p. 452)

And it is this crucial role that language plays in the construction of identity that makes the relation to second language learning so important.

Although I have been discussing these issues so far in terms of identity, Norton Peirce has tended to prefer to use the notion of subjectivity. Arguing that most psychological work in second language education tends to deal with fairly homogenous concepts of identity, to theorize desire in terms of notions such as motivation, and to ignore relations of power altogether, she has worked to show how language learners take up different subject positions in different discourses (Norton Peirce, 1995). *Subjectivity* and *subject positions* are terms used in poststructuralist work. Subjectivity refers to the ways in which our identity is formed through discourse. Our identity or identities, therefore, are not pregiven wholes but are rather conflictual and multiple. As Lather (1992) explains, from this point of view, subjectivity is seen:

> both as socially produced in language, at conscious and unconscious levels, and as a site of struggle and potential change. In poststructuralist theories of the subject, identity does not follow unproblematically from experience. We are seen to live in webs of multiple representations of class, race, gender, language and social relations; meanings vary within one individual. (p. 101)

So, following Weedon (1987), Norton Peirce (1995) uses a notion of identity as multiple, constructed through discourse, and a site of struggle (Norton, 1997; Norton Peirce, 1995). From this point of view, the person takes up different subject positions within different discourses, and language—or discourse—is a crucial element in the formation of subjectivity.

Thesen (1997), however, takes both Norton Peirce and McKay and Wong (1996) to task for giving fixed labels to the discourses they see as important and thus deciding already how people are positioned. "Peirce's determinism," she suggests, "despite her emphasis on agency, arises from her reliance on single identity markers, for example, *primary caregiver* or *multicultural citizen*" (p. 505). The problem here is that although Norton Peirce and Wong and McKay are interested in looking at how identity or subjectivity may be multiple and in flux, when they describe the different discourses in which people take up subject positions (the different choices people have), we are left at least with the appearance of fairly static identity markers, as if *primary caregiver* or *multicultural citizen* were themselves not multiple and contested. Norton Peirce (1995) has also been criticized by Price (1996) for failing to theorize how it is that agency operates, how it is that people actually come to take up positions within discourses. As he suggests, "her concern with resistance, power, and silence rests ultimately on an appeal to individual capacities and does not explore far enough the way the individual subject/learner is implicated in social and discourse practices" (p. 336). As Price suggests, Norton Peirce (1995) tends to assume that students can choose to take up particular positions in discourses. This both presupposes that these students have access to these discourses and can make some sort of choice to enter into them.

Thesen (1997) warns us that the naming of discourses and subject positions may tend to give them a unitary and deterministic category, while

Price (1996) warns against too voluntaristic a version of agency that allows for choice between different discourses. At this point, we are not only back at one of the basic concerns of critical theory (see, for example, ← chap. 5), but we are also confronting some of the hardest current questions in critical applied linguistics. Does it make sense to talk of choice in taking up a discursive position when the argument is also that discourses construct our subjectivities? How can we talk about subject positions without reinscribing subjectivity into a fixed form of identity? How is it that students learn discourses in the process of learning a second language? How is it that students come to take up subject positions in discourses in a second language? How can we actually oppose discourses? According to Price (1999):

> Discourse acquisition is a matter of engagement in a productive process rather than a mastery over and reproduction of constitutive discourse properties. This production is performative in that subject, discourse, and its reality are produced in the moment of instantiation. (p. 589)

Here, then, we have a highly challenging proposition that discourse acquisition has to do with engagement and performativity in the moment of production. It is a shame that the pursuit of such questions has so long been held back by the shackles of mainstream SLA research.

Once we start to see identities not so much as fixed social or cultural categories but as a constant ongoing negotiation of how we relate to the world, then we have to acknowledge that second language classrooms, speech therapy sessions, literacy in the workplace, applied linguistics courses, or the process of translating have a great deal to do with questions of identity formation and transformation. If we take seriously the idea that engagement in discourse is part of the continuing construction of identity, then the context of second language education raises significant issues in the construction and negotiation of identity. As Brian Morgan (1997) shows in the discussion of his ESL class in a Chinese community center in Toronto:

> Each ESL classroom is a unique, complex, and dynamic social environment .... Each classroom ... becomes a resource for community development, where students re-evaluate the past (i.e., the rules of identity) in the context of the present and, through classroom reflection and interaction, forge new cultural traditions, histories, and solidarities that potentially improve their life chances for the future. (pp. 432–433)

As his students explored different possibilities of intonation, different possible identities were presented, taken up, rejected, or negotiated. "ESL teachers should pay close if not equal attention to the historical and local conditions that influence identity formation when contextualizing language activities in the classroom" (p. 447).

As Clark and Ivanič (1997) suggest, furthermore, academic writing conventions are not mere questions of learning the ways of the academic community: They also touch on fundamental questions of power and identity. Once again, we can observe here the need to connect the apparently insignificant micro relations of language work to macro relations of politics and identity. I have tried to tackle some of these questions in the context of plagiarism, arguing that "avoiding plagiarism" needs to be seen not as some academic convention students need to master but rather as a complex constellation of issues to do with concepts of the author and textual ownership, questions of language learning and saying things in "one's own words," cultural and educational orientations toward text and memorization, and, therefore, questions of language and identity (Pennycook, 1996a). On the one hand, then, we have classroom practices that aim to change and modify identities toward particular goals: "We need to stop emphasizing only linguistic and technical competence. We spend most of our classroom time trying to make students repeat another's words fluently, trying to erase the traces of their identities shown in their accents" (Cox & Assis-Peterson, 1999, p. 449). On the other hand, we have a constant series of changes, redefinitions, renegotiations of identity.

Thus, as Morgan (1997) argues:

> Identity work in an ESL classroom is not just descriptive or interpretive but fundamentally transformative .... Wherever and however meanings are expressed, shared, challenged, or distorted, language practices are always implicated in how people define who they are and how they subsequently act upon the possibilities such meanings convey. (p. 432)

This process of transformation is well illustrated by Ibrahim's (1999) study of how a group of French-speaking immigrant and refugee continental African youths "become Black" as they engage with possible forms of language and identity in their school in Canada:

> Once in North America ... these youths were faced with a *social imaginary* ... in which they were already Blacks. This social imaginary was directly implicated in how and with whom they identified, which in turn influenced what they linguistically and culturally learned, as well as how they learned it. What they learned ... is *Black stylized English* (BSE), which they accessed in and through Black popular culture. (p. 351)

From this point of view, then, engagement with particular languages and cultures must also be about identity formation. Identities or subjectivities are constantly being produced in the positions people take up in discourse. So, the question of possibilities, of what different possible forms of difference we create, acknowledge, or oppose, is a crucial one whether viewed from the point of view of students, teachers, or researchers.

LANGUAGE, GENDER, SEXUALITY, AND DIFFERENCE

If it has been important to develop a more dynamic understanding of the construction and production of difference based on cultural categories, the domain of gender and sexuality has also been in need of development within (critical) applied linguistics. Forms of discrimination against women in and through language are widely attested: Women are stereotyped as talkative while at the same time they are frequently silenced or ignored; many languages have a range of derogatory terms for women; women are relegated to the private rather than public language domains; women's use of language frequently bears signs of lower social status; women's ways of talking are not accorded respect; language systems themselves encode basic gender inequalities. Clearly, language is an important site of the reproduction of gendered inequality, but to understand how gender and sexuality may relate to a range of issues in applied linguistics, we need to consider carefully what models of language, power, and identity we are using. One of the problems here is that applied linguistics has tended to operate with the rather limited constructs produced through mainstream work on language and gender. It is to questions of difference in terms of language, gender, and sexuality that I therefore turn in this section.

Dominance and Difference

An initial reaction to questions of language and gender might suggest a straightforward connection: Men have power, which will be reflected in their language; women do not have power, which will be reflected in their language (or their silences). Indeed this is how Lakoff (1990) appears to view this relation:

> Men's language is the language of the powerful. It is meant to be direct, clear, succinct, as would be expected of those who need not fear giving offense, who need not worry about the risks or responsibility. It is the language of people who are in charge in the real world. Women's language developed as a way of surviving and even flourishing without control over economic, physical or social reality. (p. 205)

As the earlier discussion of language and power (← chap. 3) suggests, however, a view in which power is held absolutely by some people and not by others, a relation that in turn is reflected by language, is not adequate for more complex understandings of language use.

Other work on language and gender has complicated this picture to some degree. The predominant understanding of language and gender since the 1970s has divided the argument into two camps: dominance or difference (see Table 6.1). As Coates (1998) explains, "research which takes a dominance perspective interprets the differences between women's and men's linguistic usage as reflexes of the dominant-subordinate relationship holding between men and women" (p. 413). So in this view, language use between people of different genders reflects different social power. Although this had the advantage of making research on language and gender from the outstart a political question, it had the drawback of making women's language nothing but a negative reaction to men's. In the same way that critiques of language and social class were accused of suggesting a "deficit" model of language (← chap. 5), so a view of language and gender that proposed that women's language always occurred as a weaker response to male language was seen as positing a deficit view of women's language as a weaker and inferior version.

Research from a "difference perspective, by contrast, sees the differences between women's and men's linguistic usage as arising from the different sub-cultures in which women and men are socialized" (Coates, 1988, p. 413). So in this view, men are socialized with men, and women with women, and the miscommunication between the two is a form of cultural miscommunication. This latter position has been popularized by the work of Deborah Tannen (1990) in books such as *You Just Don't Understand: Women and Men in Conversation.* The advantage of this approach is that it was able to look at women's language as a cultural behavior (and thus as different) and not as a social reflex. The disadvantage was that it tended to re-

TABLE 6.1

Dominance, Difference, and Performativity

	Dominance	*Difference*	*Performativity*
Gender and power	Men have power; women lack power	Men and women are socialized separately	Gender and sex are not given categories, and they interrelate with other forms of power
Gender and language	Men's language is more powerful than women's	Men and women use language differently and misunderstand each other	People perform gendered identities through language
Possibilities for change	Change society (and power) or teach women to use powerful language	Teach men and women to understand their competitive and cooperative ways	Show how genders are performed, not essential, parts of identities

move the political dimension from the equation, focusing on difference as a result of differing socialization rather than unequal social power.

The move to understand women's language as separate but different was therefore a move to "celebrate women's ways of talking" (Coates, 1998, p. 413). But, as critical reviews of Tannen's work suggested (Cameron, 1995; Troemel-Ploetz, 1991), a view that located gender relations merely in terms of miscommunication between two subcultures was a dangerously apolitical view of language and gender, ignoring as it did questions of power. And since, as Cameron (1995) makes clear, suggestions for change based on this difference model of language tended simply to celebrate difference and thus ignore all the inequitable gendered relations of society, any proposal for change "based on the 'difference' model is a good deal less radical than its exponents imagine" (p. 198).

The dominant/dominated framework—although at times perhaps a clear descriptor of fundamental inequalities—is generally too clumsy and limited to understand a broader set of social relations. As Johnson (1997) points out, there has been a tendency to construct an "all-purpose male oppressor" who "talks too much, interrupts and generally dominates conversations with women" (p. 11). Once we understand the ways in which social lives and questions of gender, class, ethnicity, age, health, knowledge, education, and so on intersect, it seems clear that we need ways of understanding how power works in diffuse ways in different moments. On the other hand, the difference view of culture as somehow being outside the domain of power is equally problematic. The notion of *cultural politics,* the idea that different ideas, beliefs, visions of the world, and so on are in competition with each other, suggests that culture is always produced in relations of power. At the very least, therefore, the dominance position has needed greater complexity, while the difference position has needed more politics.

The previous criticism of the tendencies in linguistics and applied linguistics to deal all too often with static and fixed labels of identity, however, suggests the need for more flexible and mobile frameworks of difference here. Studies of language and gender have tended to work with a simple and essentialist dichotomy between men and women whereby either men have power (reflected in their language) and women do not (reflected in their language or silence) or men use language in one way and women in another. Discussing the range of contradictory advice to women as to whether they should therefore use language as men do or accept and value their own language as different, Cameron (1995) suggests that in "this whole contradictory discourse, the most important common factor is simply the idea of an eternal opposition between 'masculine' and 'feminine' styles." Thus, any kind of change "based on the a priori acceptance of an all-pervading gender duality will end up being co-opted to reactionary ends, because the starting assumption is itself reactionary" (p. 200).

Johnson (1997) points to two main problems with most work to date on language and gender. First, both the so-called dominance and difference models "are characterized by almost exclusive *problematization of women*" (p. 10) with to date almost no attempt to understand men as anything other than a one-dimensional male oppressor. And second, there is the continuing difficulty that "the implicit assumption that men and women are binary opposites, and that speech constitutes a symbolic reflection of that opposition, is inherently problematical both from the point of view of language *and* gender" (p. 11). As Johnson goes on to argue, much work in language and gender has simply worked with the assumption of a dichotomy between men and women and then attempted to find linguistic correlates, the main objective of this work therefore being "to verify presumed oppositions between male and female language usage" (p. 11). As Cameron (1997) shows, once one goes looking for such correlates, it is not hard to find them since much language data of this sort can be interpreted in favor of such preconceived assumptions of difference. Johnson (1997), thus, also suggests that work on language and gender may be far more mainstream than it supposes. This argument reiterates some of the points I make throughout this book that so-called critical work that does not problematize its assumptions about power, its dichotomous ways of thinking (men–women; dominant–dominated; oppressed–oppressors; haves–have-nots; and emancipated–unemancipated) remains far less radical than it claims. It may indeed be seen ultimately as reactionary.

A similar concern emerges in some approaches to feminist pedagogy. Exploring the "particular quality of the teaching and learning interactions that take place within a multicultural 'women's space,'" Sanguinetti (1992/3, p. 10) rejected Freirean problem-posing approaches (Auerbach & Wallerstein, 1987; ← chaps. 4 and 5) as too directive and patronizing, too oriented toward a model of liberation. Critical pedagogy, following Ellsworth (1989), she also takes to task for its rationalist and masculinist orientations (← chap. 5). But questioning whether Ellsworth, by "constructing a polemic" against critical pedagogy isn't "perhaps utilising a rational 'masculinist' discursive form based on an 'either/or' negation of the other's meaning," Sanguinetti contrasts Ellsworth's critique with the "lovingly constructive theorising about pedagogy" (p. 25) in Belenky et al's (1986) *Women's Ways of Knowing* and Grumet's (1988) *Bitter Milk*. Although all-women classes may indeed create safe and nurturing spaces, Sanguinetti here starts to construct a problematic gendered essentialism: "the non-traditional, non-academic, women's culture in which women's ways of relating are able to flourish and which create an ideal learning environment" (p. 28). Foucault and Ellsworth she takes to task for viewing power as omnipresent. In her feminist vision of ESL, by contrast, this "masculinist model" is rejected in favor an understanding of how "solidarity between students, and students and teachers can be based on the feminine model of love and connection" (p. 34). To fall back on a "feminine model of love and connection" as a model for critical English language teaching is, similar to the essentialist and binary models of language and gender discussed earlier, ultimately a conservative move because of its essentialist assumptions. And to argue that women create some inherently nurturing space becomes, from this view, a reactionary argument since it reproduces a static vision of women as mothers and nurturers (Schenke, 1991).

Performing Gender Through Language

Attempts constantly to construct fundamental differences between men and women may be seen, as Weedon (1987) and Moi (1985) suggest, as part of an essentialist view of gender. Judith Butler's (1990) key book, *Gender Trouble: Feminism and the Subversion of Identity,* has pointed to the flaws in much of the basic thinking about gender. For the most part, she says, "feminist theory has assumed that there is some existing identity, understood through the category of women, who not only initiates feminist interests and goals within discourse, but constitutes the subject for whom political representation is pursued" (p. 1). Following Foucault's argument that subjects are not pregiven entities but are *produced* in discourse (also compare the discussion of identity in the previous section), Butler argues that "the feminist subject turns out to be discursively constituted by the very political system that is supposed to facilitate its emancipation" (p. 2). Thus, she is arguing that rather than *women* being a pregiven category in search of emancipation, it is a product of those very discourses that speak of women. She goes on to critique the ways in which feminism has too often assumed a universal essence for women that exists across time and culture in opposition to a universal condition of patriarchy:

> The political assumption that there must be a universal basis for feminism, one which must be found in an identity assumed to exist cross-culturally, often accompanies the notion that the oppression of women has some singular form discernible in the universal or hegemonic structure of patriarchy or masculine domination. (p. 3)

This is the point where feminism has been confronted by the postcolonial critique of its own colonialism, its tendency to marginalize other forms of difference under an assumed commonality of womanhood.

Butler (1990) goes on to show how that favorite trope of language and gender studies that sex is biological but gender is culturally constructed cannot hold since, as she puts it:

> Gender is not to culture as sex is to nature; gender is also the discursive/cultural means by which "sexed nature" or "a natural sex" is produced and established as "prediscursive," prior to culture, a politically neutral surface *on which* culture acts. (p. 7)

Thus, there is a cultural matrix through which we view sex, gender, and desire, leading to the continued assumption that gender follows from sex (e.g., male bodies lead to masculinity) and that desire (sexuality) follows from both. As studies of the interrelations between sexed bodies (identity in terms of physical characteristics), gender (identity in terms of social, cultural, and psychological constructions), and sexuality (identity in terms of socioerotic orientation toward other sexed and/or gendered bodies) suggest, such categories are complex and slippery. Zita's (1992) discussion of the problems posed by the postmodern possibility of accepting the claim to be a "male lesbian" (a physical man who feels himself/herself a woman but is attracted to women) shows the diverse spaces opened up by suggesting that not only sexual orientation and gender but also the body may be open to multiple readings.

From here, Butler (1990) argues that gender is not a noun, something we do or have, but rather "gender proves to be performative—that is constituting the identity it is purported to be. In this sense, gender is always a doing, though not a doing by a subject who might be said to preexist the deed" (p. 25). Gender, then, is "the repeated stylization of the body, a set of repeated acts within a highly regulatory frame that congeal over time to produce the appearance of substance, of a natural sort of being" (p. 33). This idea of gender as performative ties in both with the discussion in the previous section of identity as a performative category and with the concept of using English in terms of postcolonial performativity (← chap. 3). This allows us to view language as productive and performative. Language is a doing, "not a doing by a subject who might be said to preexist the deed" but "the repeated stylization of the body, a set of repeated acts within a highly regulatory frame that congeal over time to produce the appearance of substance, of a natural sort of being," the appearance of using English as a natural sort of language.

Such an understanding of gender and desire has been crucial for queer theory in its attempts to go beyond *gay/lesbian* labels and instead to work with more flexible understandings of identity. Thus, as Jagose (1996) explains, queer theory challenges the type of identity politics implicit in labels such as *gay* and *lesbian,* and although acknowledging the gains achieved by mobilizing around such categories, seeks to move into a more complex understanding that "questions that those descriptors are self-evident" (p. 126). Relating Butler's thinking to questions of language and gender, Cameron (1997) argues that the focus needs to be not so much on gender differences as the difference gender makes. The question then becomes not how language use reflects pregiven gender/sex differences but how the construction of difference is related to the production of dominance: "Whereas sociolinguistics traditionally assumes that people talk the way they do because of who they (already) are, the postmodernist approach suggests that people are who they are because of (among other things) the way they talk" (Cameron, 1997, p. 49). The point then becomes, echoing Butler's rethinking of Austin (1962, how to do things with words), how to do gender with language: "What is important in gendering talk is the 'performative gender work' the talk is doing; its role in constituting people as gendered subjects" (Cameron, 1997, p. 59). This view has major implications not merely for questions of gender and sexuality but for all understandings of difference, identity, and power. Indeed, Cameron (1995) suggests that for gender here, "we could substitute any apparently fixed and substantive social identity label" (p. 16).

It is only very recently that these concerns have started to emerge within TESOL. Nelson (1999) argues that while a "lesbian and gay framework has been very useful politically in mobilising for civil rights, it may be less useful pedagogically" (p. 373). She goes on to argue for the importance of using queer theory since it "shifts the focus from gaining civil rights to analysing discursive and cultural practices, from affirming minority sexual identities to problematising all sexual identities" (p. 373). Thus, Nelson argues, "queer theory may provide a more flexible, open-ended framework for facilitating inquiry, particularly within the intercultural context of ESL, than lesbian and gay theory does" (p. 377). As revealed by her analysis of a discussion in an ESL class about the implications of two women walking down the road arm in arm, the complex relations among sexual identities, social norms, cultural difference, and language learning lead to an array of overlapping, contradictory, and competing positions and positionings around questions of sexuality in this ESL class. As she suggests, "sexual identity was more than just the topic of discussion. Even as the participants talked about lesbians or gay men, they were positioning themselves and each other in terms of sexual identity" (p. 388). It is to issues of possible pedagogical and research take-up of questions of difference that I now turn.

DEALING WITH DIFFERENCE: INCLUSIVITY, ISSUES, AND ENGAGEMENT

If we acknowledge that questions of identity and power are closely linked to language and are therefore key concerns for critical applied linguistics, it is important to consider research and pedagogical responses to forms of difference. What available identities or subject positions do we make available in our classes? And how might we both create more possibilities and find ways of working with students' identity formation? How do the types of identities that we construct in our research affect the ways in which applied linguistics constructs the Other? It may be useful to draw a distinction between three levels of response: inclusivity, issues, and engagement (see Table 6.2). The issue in inclusivity is to make sure that people of different backgrounds are represented in our texts, our classroom possibilities, and our approaches to research. As Dendrinos (1992), Jewell (1998), and others have pointed out, the content of ESL textbooks and many ESL classes is

TABLE 6.2
Inclusivity, Issues, and Engagement

	Inclusivity	Issues	Engagement
Focus	A pedagogy of inclusion of diversity	Discussion of issues to do with diversity	Centrality of formations of identity to research and pedagogy
Mode	Representations of diversity in texts, curricula, and classrooms	Tolerance and rational understanding	Genealogy, memory work, and desire

still "a world in which young, heterosexual, middle-class, well-educated people live in big houses and travel and shop incessantly" (Jewell, 1998, p. 4). This struggle for more diverse representation of other possibilities may be seen as a struggle for inclusivity, pressing for the inclusion of women in a diversity of roles, people from different social and ethnic backgrounds, gay and lesbian couples and parents, single parents, and so on.

One of the major silences to date in TESOL has been sexual orientation. As Nelson (1993) suggests, there remain many basic attitudes in TESOL that need to be shifted, including a general assumed heterosexism; a belief that questions of sexual preference have no place in ESL; a belief that students from other countries would find questions of sexual orientation too controversial and that dealing with such questions would be moving into unjustifiable tampering with people's social lives; a sexist acknowledgment of gay men in ESL but ignorance of lesbian teachers; and a tendency for straight teachers to assume gay and lesbian issues are not their concern and should only be addressed by gay and lesbian teachers themselves. As Nelson convincingly argues, all these assumptions need to be questioned. Gay and lesbian teachers and students are denied the possibility of expressing and using those parts of their identities linked to their sexual orientation: "Because of heterosexism, those of us who are involved in gay culture often feel we must hide any expression of that culture" (p. 144); students often have many and interesting things to say about sexuality; it is the responsibility of all teachers to bring questions of sexuality to bear on their work for we all have sexual orientations.

Jewell's (1998) study of a transgendered student in an ESL class shows how she struggles to find possible spaces to speak and roles to identify with: "For Jackie, sexuality is fundamental to social identity. Like her, some people actively promote a gay or transgendered identity, but this is clearly not reflected in ESL textbooks and their rigid consideration of sex-roles and relationship possibilities in society" (p. 9). More generally, Jewell suggests "precisely because there are gay students in our classes, we need to incorporate their stories, experiences and ideas into the classroom dialogue, so that they, too, feel as worthy and represented as any other student in that space" (pp. 6–7). There is a danger, however, that such arguments remain at the level of what Britzman (1995) terms "pedagogies of inclusion" (p. 158) that aim to include authentic images of others. Although this may allow for a greater range of possibilities in classrooms, it may also be more oriented toward legitimation or incorporation of difference rather than engagement with difference. In terms of research, it is akin to including greater diversity in our samples to be more representative.

A slightly different focus aims not so much at inclusivity as at overt discussion. This is an attempt not just to have difference as a background possibility in the textbooks but also to raise more overtly such *issues* as a content focus in class. Thus, we may find textbooks or curricula include sections on gay marriages or women in the workforce. Although this does seem to put issues of difference on the agenda, there are at least two limitations here. First, much of what is presented occurs within an overarching liberal agenda of alternatives and social issues, thus suggesting that the central concern is appreciating or tolerating diversity. Fundamental questions of identity get slotted into a framework of issues so that one week we may be dealing with "The Environment" or "Animal Rights" and another with issues of gender or sexuality. There is also a tendency to deal with a fixed set of dichotomous possibilities (nature or nurture; is homosexuality normal?; Pennycook, 1997b). So, although an issues focus may bring questions of difference into the curriculum, it leaves these as isolated concerns for discussion, unconnected in any clear ways to the context of the class, the lives of the students, or the language they are learning.

Second, this issues focus tends to operate from a mixture of liberalism and emancipatory modernism, suggesting that by rational discussion of questions of difference, we will arrive at greater tolerance or understanding. As Ray Misson (1996) argues with respect to homophobia, and Fazal Rizvi (1993) in the context of racism, to develop antihomophobic or antiracist education requires much more than simply some rational, intellectual explanation of what's wrong with racism and homophobia. Rather, we need an engagement with people's investment in particular discourses, that is, in questions of *desire*: "Our subscription to certain beliefs is not just a rational or a socially-determined thing, but we invest in them because they conform to the shape of our desires" (Misson, 1996, p. 121). The point here, then, is that critical education that aims to change how things are needs to engage with people's investments and desires, not just to try to explain on some intellectual plane. From the point of view of research, this is rather like the scientific leftist approach (← chap. 2) that aims for social transformation through the tools of modernist science.

A third possibility is what we might term an *engagement focus* (compare the discussion ← chap. 5 of an engaged postmodernism). This is an approach to language education and other areas of critical applied linguistics that sees issues such as gender, race, class, sexuality, postcolonialism, and so on as so fundamental to identity and language that they need to form the basis of curricular organization, pedagogy, and research. As Nelson (1999) suggests, "queer-informed inquiry also has the advantage of allowing for a range of sexual identities to be referred to or discussed throughout curricula rather than in relation to certain so-called gay topics" (p. 377). Arleen Schenke (1996) has strongly criticized what she calls "the tired treatment of gender and 'women's lib' in many of our ESL textbooks" (p. 156). In place of these worn-out, liberal, issues-based approaches, she proposes what she calls a "practice in historical engagement," a focus on "the struggle over histories (and forgetting) in relation to the cultures of English and to the cultures students bring with them to the classroom already-knowing" (p. 156). From this point of view, then, questions of difference, identity, and culture are not merely issues to be discussed but are about how we have come to be as we are, how discourses have structured our lives. Questions of gender or race, therefore, make up the underlying rationale for the course. "Feminism," Schenke argues, "like antiracism, is thus not simply one more social issue in ESL but a way of thinking, a way of teaching, and, most importantly, a way of learning" (p. 158).

This engagement focus, then, links questions of identity, politics, and language directly and sees different formations of identity as intertwined. For Schenke (1991), a feminist pedagogy of ESL can be engaged through "a *genealogical* practice in memory work." Similar to Butler's (1990) call for "*a feminist genealogy* of the category of women" (p. 5), Schenke is arguing against an essentialized notion of women and instead seeking to work from a feminist perspective that acknowledges the complex interrelations between constructions of gender and other socially and culturally constructed forms of identity or subjectivity. From this point of view, there is no neutral, nurturing, womanly space outside relations of power, only the need to constantly work through and against certain operations of power. As with Nelson's (1999) understanding of the interrelations between sexuality, gender, and cultural difference, or Ibrahim's (1999) interweaving of questions of race, gender and popular culture, Schenke is here getting at the multiplicity of concerns in any pedagogical moment.

Toward Engaged Research

As Ibrahim (1999) suggests:

> If learning is an engagement of one's identity, a fulfillment of personal needs and desires (of being), and an investment in what is yet to come, any proposed ESL pedagogy, research, or praxis that fails to culminate in these ... is therefore bound to be unsuccessful, if not plainly damaging. (p. 366)

This is equally a question for research, therefore, as it is for pedagogy. Research in critical applied linguistics needs to respond to four basic criteria (see Table 6.3): a mode of working that opposes essentialist categories and attempts to engage seriously with difference; the inclusion of participants' interests, desires, and lives; a focus on the workings of power; and an orientation toward transformative goals. Research from a critical applied linguistic perspective, then, needs to respond to the same antiessentialist concerns outlined earlier. Ben Rampton's (1995b) research on what he calls "language crossing"—the use of language varieties from groups to which one does not normally "belong"—operates with the sort of flexible concept of identity that I argue for here. Drawing on Paul Gilroy's (1987) critique of ethnic absolutism (compare earlier discussions of essentialism), Rampton talks of crossing as involving "the active ongoing construction of a new inheritance from within multiracial interaction itself" (p. 297). Here again, we can see a notion of identity construction rather than preexisting deterministic categories of identity. And, processes of identity construction are firmly located within social, cultural, and historical relations.

Second, linking research with students' lives and concerns has been a major focus of Auerbach's (1994) development of participatory action research, which promotes research by students on the matters that concern them as a means to bring the outside world into the classroom and to take the classroom into the outside world (also see Rivera, 1999). Similarly, Norton Peirce (1995), following Heath's (1983) suggestions for involving students and teachers in researching the literacy practices of their communities, argues for "classroom based social research" to "engage the social identities of students in ways that will improve their language learning outside the classroom and help them claim the right to speak" (p. 26). Following Corson's (1997) argument for critical realism in applied linguistics, a philosophical position that takes the perspectives of participants as real, Jewell (1998) notes that "using a combination of traditional empirical research alongside students' writings or speakings of their lived experiences in relation to ESL" can bring about a "clearer picture of the array of actual actors who use English" (p. 5).

TABLE 6.3
Engaged Research

	Difference	*Participation*	*Power*	*Change*
Four elements of critical applied linguistics research	Engaging with difference and opposing essentialism	Working with participants' interests, desires, and lives	A focus on the workings of power in context	Orientation toward transformative goals; catalytic validity

Third, in the same way that I (1999a) have suggested that certain domains of TESOL are more oriented toward critical work, so particular constellations of power may be more readily researched in particular domains. Thus, research discussed in this and the previous chapter (← chap. 5) focuses on issues to do with race and gender (Ibrahim, 1999), sexual identity (Jewell, 1998; Nelson, 1999), social class (Lin, 1999), and so on. Sunderland (1994) presents a list of gendered topics in ELT waiting to be researched. From another perspective—a postcolonial critical ethnography—Canagarajah (1993) looks at how students resist English and English teaching methods in particular periphery classrooms. Canagarajah defines *critical ethnography* as:

> an ideologically sensitive orientation to the study of culture that can penetrate the noncommittal objectivity and scientism encouraged by the positivistic empirical attitude behind descriptive ethnography and can demystify the interests served by particular cultures to unravel their relation to issues of power. (p. 605)

Particular contexts may be more suited to an analysis of relations of power.

And finally, such research needs to have transformative goals, aiming not just to describe but also to change (also see Pennycook, 1994a). As a number of critical researchers point out, the critical agenda and the openness to a diversity of research approaches should not render research less rigorous. In this context, Lather (1991) discusses the notion of *catalytic validity,* or "the degree to which the research process re-orients, focuses and energizes participants toward knowing reality in order to transform it" (p. 68). Whereas Guba and Lincoln's (1989) notion of *catalytic authenticity* "refers to the degree to which something is actually done" as a result of research (Lynch, 1996, p. 65), catalytic validity requires that research be judged not merely in terms of whether something is done but according to the degree to which such action may be seen as socially transformative, as part of an ethical and political vision of change. Catalytic validity is an important concept for critical applied linguistics.

CONCLUSION: EMBODIED DIFFERENCES

By raising the issue of the politics of difference, this chapter deals with a number of significant themes for critical applied linguistics. Looking at identity as something we perform through language rather than as something reflected in language helps get away from the essentialized identities of much applied linguistic work. Indeed, following the arguments of Butler, Cameron, and Johnson, it becomes evident that following essentialized categories of identity will tend to work against supposedly progressive ends. The notion of performativity is therefore crucial since, as Jagose (1996) puts it, "debates around performativity put a denaturalising pressure on sex, gender, sexuality, bodies and identities" (p. 90). The emphasis on performativity and the lived experiences of language users has also enabled the return of the body. One of the most challenging aspects of Butler's argument is that the distinction between biologically sexed bodies and culturally produced identity and sexuality cannot hold: Even the body is a cultural script. But a danger here, as with overtextualized versions of poststructuralism, postmodernism or postcolonialism, is that the body gets written out of the picture altogether as just another collection of signs, another ephemeral text. And yet it is precisely against the removal of the body that so much critical, and especially feminist, work has fought, arguing that from the inception of Cartesian mind–body dualism (who washed Descartes' socks?), academic work has floated in a disembodied state that has been able to ignore exactly all those embodied aspects of life—gender, sexuality, ethnicity, disability—that matter.

So the body has reemerged not as a static signifier of identity but as a surface onto which identities are inscribed, as a place where our subjectivities are generated and embodied. Foucault (1980a, 1980b) has been useful here, with his call that we should consider the effects of power on the body. Indeed, Foucault suggests the body may be a more useful location to study power than some notion of ideology. Bourdieu's (1991; ← chap. 5) notions of habitus and embodied cultural capital are also useful here since Bourdieu insists our cultural habits are not mere cognitive apparitions but rather are written onto our bodies. As Threadgold (1997) suggests, at this point we can see how a social order is "*both* imbricated in language, textuality and semiosis *and* is corporeal, spatial, temporal, institutional, conflictual, and marked by sexual, racial and other differences" (p. 101). Crucially, as this notion of the body is taken up, we need to address our investment and desire in beliefs and ways of doing things not as some rational, intellectual mistake, as many views of ideology and emancipation seem to imply, but rather as part of what our bodies have become. As Ibrahim (1999) shows, as the youths he studied become Black, they learn both *the talk* and *the walk*.

Such a position refocuses the task of transformative critical work. No longer can this be seen solely in terms of rational discussion or critical awareness. Narrative or memory work in pedagogy and research is not just about telling stories but is about accounting for how our bodies and desires got here. This is also why, in a critical applied linguistics class I taught in Melbourne a few years ago, we had to stop at a certain point in our discussions of CDA, of language politics, of different sorts of feminist pedagogy, of multiliteracies and we had to tell our stories, relate our own discursive and corporeal critical histories, recreate how it was that we came to be and to see ourselves as critical. This, therefore, is another crucial element of engagement: As we work to engage critically, poetically, historically, hermeneutically, and narratively (Kearney, 1988), we need to find ways of engaging with lives, bodies, and desires (also see Fuery, 1995). And this is also why critical applied linguistic teaching and research is more about a way of thinking and being than about a series of issues. I raise this concern again (→ chap. 7).

Chapter 7

Applied Linguistics
With an Attitude

Critical Themes
Guidelines for a Critical Praxis
  Critical Notes for the Fridge Door
Critical Applied Postlinguistics, Postcritical Applied
    Linguistics, or Applied Linguistics With an Attitude

It is time to regroup. In this concluding chapter, I try to pull together some of the main themes covered in preceding chapters. There are two principal domains: First, I deal with the main arguments I have made about the politics of knowledge, language, text, pedagogy, and difference (critical themes). Second, I return to the question of why critical applied linguistics matters and how it can work as a form of critical praxis (guidelines for a critical praxis). While these two sections are largely consolidatory in nature, the final part of this chapter argues for the opposite, for the need to avoid turning critical applied linguistics into a new discipline. Through a consideration of the role critical applied linguistics can play in different courses on applied linguistics, I argue ultimately for critical applied linguistics as a form of antidisciplinary praxis, for critical applied linguistics as applied postlinguistics, for critical applied linguistics as applied linguistics with an attitude.

164

CRITICAL THEMES

Throughout this book, I compare different constellations of knowledge, language, and politics. I sketched (← chap. 2) four possible positions: the liberal ostrichist, anarcho-autonomous, emancipatory modernist, and problematizing practice. The intriguing anarcho-autonomous position, characterized by anarcho-syndicalist politics on the one hand and an autonomous, rationalist, and realist approach to knowledge on the other, is neither common nor of much use for critical applied linguistics, and I do not therefore pursue it further in the other chapters. The other three, however, form a recurring theme throughout the book, and whereas I stress again that I view these only as handy simplifications of complex interrelated views of knowledge and politics, I find them useful for explaining different ways of approaching (critical) applied linguistics (see Table 7.1). Applied linguistics, I suggest, has been dominated by a bland egalitarianism that does not help us in framing questions of inequality, language, and power. Often based in liberal pluralist politics and structuralist approaches to academic work, the approach advocates the isolation of politics from academic work. Thus, the structuralism of linguistics and sociolinguistics that permits the view that all dialects are equal is also the view that has not allowed for an adequate understanding of how languages are complexly related to social and cultural factors, ignoring, therefore, profound questions of social difference, inequality, and conflict. From a critical applied linguistic perspective, this denial of its own politics, this refusal to take into account broader social and political concerns, makes this an ostrich-like (head in the sand) approach to applied linguistics.

Liberal ostrichism can be seen to run through many of the mainstream approaches to applied linguistics that are critically analyzed in this book. Mainstream approaches to sociolinguistics and language planning have inadequate theories of the social, suggesting that language simply reflects rather vague social categories; this position accepts and even celebrates the inevitability of the global spread of English while rather lamely calling for support for other languages; in terms of text analysis, the liberal framework suggests that texts are always open to interpretation and that critical analysis is therefore an imposition of an ideological standpoint; liberal approaches to schooling, meanwhile, construct education as a neutral context of knowledge transaction in which everyone has a chance to succeed; finally, liberal approaches to difference tend to adhere to a humanist stance that suggests diversity is a superficial covering over essential human similarities, and by so doing, this view has led to many static forms of Othering in applied linguistics.

I characterize what I call mainstream approaches to critical applied linguistics as forms of emancipatory modernism. Unlike the autonomous-leftist view described earlier (and ← chap. 2), which eschews connections between politics and language study, this nonautonomous-leftist approach

TABLE 7.1
Frameworks of Politics, Epistemology, and Applied Linguistics

Framework	Politics & Epistemology	Critical Views & Flaws	Forms of Analysis
Liberal ostrichism	Liberal pluralism, structuralism, and bland egalitarianism; critical distance and the isolation of politics from academic work	Inadequate social theory; inability to deal with questions of social difference, inequality, and conflict; language reflects reality	Emphasis on the individual, openness of textual meaning, benefits of English, possibilities of schooling, and fixity of difference
Emancipatory modernism	Scientific leftism: neo-Marxist politics and scientific analysis; macro structures of domination	Powerful critiques of structural inequality; limited by deterministic social vision, ideology, and emancipation	Linguistic imperialism and language rights; critical readings of texts; education as reproduction; inclusionary approach to difference; emancipation
Problematizing practice	Grounded local politics in conjunction with poststructuralism, postmodernism, and postcolonialism	Skepticism about science and knowledge; micro relations of power; no clear political position; possible relativism, irrealism, and overemphasis on discourse	Language productive; resistance and appropriation; analysis of the social through language; engagement with history and difference; catalytic validity

to questions of language, knowledge, and power aims specifically to relate language study to leftist politics. On the one hand, it tends to share a similar belief in rationality, realism, and scientific endeavor, including the old Marxist divide between science and ideology; on the other hand, it directly relates its political analysis to the study of language use. This position is one held by many of those who might typically be seen as falling within the rubric of critical applied linguistics. While this emancipatory modernist framework provides an important basis for critical applied linguistic work, its use of neo-Marxist analyses of power, science, ideology, and awareness has various limitations: It tends to operate with a clumsy material version of power located in dominant groups; it views ideology in a way that is opposed in too simple terms to a knowable reality; in unreflexive fashion, it suggests that scientific knowledge of reality can help us escape from the falsity of ideology; and thus, it offers us a rationalist and realist model of emancipation.

Again, we can see emancipatory modernist approaches to (critical) applied linguistics in many domains. This version of sociolinguistics relates language to class or gender in concrete and critical terms, while in the context of the global spread of English, it raises concerns to do with linguistic imperialism and language rights; the tendency in emancipatory modernist frameworks is to locate language in inequitable but static and deterministic social conditions. In terms of textual analysis, it provides us with both critical literacy and critical discourse analysis, which insist on relating textual meanings to broader social, economic, and political concerns. Such approaches nevertheless run into difficulties because of the tendency toward the social determination of meaning, the focus on texts rather than reactions to texts, and the suggestion that awareness of textually encoded ideologies can lead to emancipation. Critical approaches to education emphasize the ways in which schooling reproduces inequality; critical pedagogy offers a generally modernist emancipatory solution to this by emphasizing the importance of an inclusionary vision of student voice. The modernist emancipatory approach tends to deal with difference, therefore, only in terms of an inclusionary aspect of its vision of critical democracy rather than as an engagement with a broader notion of possibility.

The fourth position, although also viewing language as fundamentally bound up with politics, nevertheless articulates a profound skepticism about science, truth claims, and the possibility of an emancipatory position outside ideology. This position, which we might call a critical applied linguistics as problematizing practice position, draws on poststructuralist, postmodernist, and postcolonial perspectives, viewing language as inherently political, understanding power more in terms of its micro operations in relation to questions of class, race, gender, ethnicity, sexuality, and so on, and arguing that we must also account for the politics of knowledge. Rather than continuing to see scientific endeavor as a means to further critical work, this view sees science—or *claims to scientificity*—as part of the problem. But this position has also been critiqued for its lack of firm political grounding, its relativism, its theoretical obscurity, and its obsessions with discourse and subjectivity.

Despite its possible pitfalls, this was often the position toward which I argue in each chapter. In terms of the politics of language, it suggests that language is productive as well as reflective of social relations and points to the need to understand how people resist and appropriate forms of language oppression. Warning against empty celebration of hybridity and difference, I suggest the notion of postcolonial performativity might give us a way forward here. This allows us to view language as productive and performative, to view the use of English in a postcolonial world as both a set of repeated acts within a regulatory frame that have congealed over time to produce the appearance of substance and as a site of resistance to and appropriation of norms and forms of standardized discourse. In terms of the politics of texts, I suggest that a form of postlinguistics as situated political practice might give us ways to search for the political/discursive (subtextual), social/historical (pretextual), and local/contingent (contextual) ways in which texts and readers produce (intertextual) meanings in relation across texts.

A problematizing stance on schooling takes up questions of resistance and is skeptical about the notion that awareness can lead to emancipation. A postcritical pedagogy draws on a notion of an ethically engaged postmodernism that can help us move away from the sort of essentialism that has so clogged the arteries of applied linguistics, with the clumsy insistence on gendered and cultural identities. This position also seems to offer more possibilities for engaging with difference through views on identity and subjectivity as multiple and contradictory. The spaces opened up by queer theory have finally started to make gender and sexuality not static categories of difference but rather shifting spaces of engagement with desire and the body. Furthermore, research can open its doors to acknowledge not only multiple ways of knowing but also the need to be responsive to catalytic validity, a form of validity that asks how effective research is in bringing about social and political change.

GUIDELINES FOR A CRITICAL PRAXIS

Two questions worth addressing again at this point are: Why critical applied linguistics? and How can it help carry a notion of praxis forward? In answer to the first, it is worth making several points. First, it is worth recalling a point I make much earlier (← chap. 1): An understanding of language as central to human life, and as fundamentally tied up with the cultural politics of the everyday, demands that we have not some bland version of liberal-ostrichist applied linguistics but rather a political vision that locates our work more centrally. Since critical applied linguistics deals with many domains of significant language use, from translation to language in professional settings, from language use in the media to the global spread of English, we stand, as James Gee argued, at the very heart of the most crucial educational, cultural, and political issues of our time. And, this is one additional meaning of *critical*: Critical applied linguistics is concerned with some of the most critical issues of our time.

Second, as I argue in greater detail, although to some extent I present my own version of critical applied linguistics here rather than attempting merely to introduce different options, I do so only as a means to raise and engage in significant discussions over what it means to do critical work. Thus, I am very wary of trying to establish critical applied linguistics as some canon of knowledge and texts with its gurus and gatekeepers. I want to avoid from the outset some of the rigidities and dogmas that have become attached to areas such as critical pedagogy, critical discourse analysis, or critical literacy. Rather, I see critical applied linguistics as a way of thinking, a way of going about applied linguistics that constantly seeks to push our thinking in new and provocative ways. I hope that a book such as this, although possibly setting forth a certain agenda for doing critical applied linguistics, will also produce debate, discussion, argument, dissent.

At the same time, however, I also intend to imply a solidity to work in critical applied linguistics that allows it to move away from a status secondary to other areas. This is a problem that tends to beset applied linguistics in general, leading to a constant sense of interdisciplinarity, which in its weaker form means we are always borrowing from elsewhere. Critical applied linguistics runs the danger of becoming a subdiscipline of applied linguistics that borrows from critical theory or poststructuralism as well as applied linguistics. As Gunther Kress (1996) observes, however, a key challenge lies in "moving beyond the client status of critical language projects in relation to other disciplines" (p. 15) and in developing adequate theories of our own. I want to push this idea further and suggest that the dynamic potential of critical applied linguistics and the extreme importance in the world of areas that it deals with should make this area not some secondary mishmash of other areas but rather a constellation of key ideas and themes that others should be looking to for inspiration. Applied linguistics has for too long gone about trying to solve its own problems without creating sufficiently interesting theory, research, or praxis to be of much interest to other domains. A dynamic critical applied linguistics, by contrast, ought to be an area that people in cultural studies, literary theorists, educationalists, sociologists, anthropologists, psychologists, political scientists, and many others can look toward for leading ideas in critical domains.

Third, it is important to have a sense of the terms of these debates because we appear to be going through a moment of struggle in applied linguistics. It was a number of years ago that Chris Candlin (1990), in a plenary address to the 8th World Congress of Applied Linguistics (AILA) in 1987 asked "What Happens When Applied Linguistics Goes Critical?" Candlin argued for a critical dimension to applied linguistics for two main reasons: first, because applied linguistics had started to lose touch with the problems and issues around language faced by ordinary language users. Applied linguistics, he argued, was becoming an arcane, sectarian, and theory-oriented discipline that was increasingly distanced from the everyday concerns of language use. Second, he suggested, a critical dimension was needed to reveal

hidden connections ... between language structure and social structure, between meaning-making and the economy of the social situation, but also
connections between different branches of the study of language and their
relationship to our central objective, the amelioration of individual and
group existences through a focus on problems of human communication. A
study of the socially-constituted nature of language practice. (pp. 461–462)

Although Candlin's view differs in a number of ways from my own (for
Candlin, it is social relevance rather than political engagement that drives
the critical project), this attempt to make applied linguistics matter, to re-
make the connections between discourse, language learning, language
use, and the social and political contexts in which these occur, at least set a
useful agenda for applied linguistics.

The 1999 AILA convention, by contrast, was most notable for a series of
rearguard actions, including Prabhu's (1999) attack on "misapplied linguistics" and defense of objectivist applied linguistics and Long's (1999)
plea to prevent the proliferation of theories in second language acquisition.
Most notable, however, was Widdowson's (1999) attack on critical applied
linguistics as "hypocritical applied linguistics." It seems to me, however,
that if we are to use a dichotomy between critical and hypocritical applied
linguistics (which I do not in fact wish to perpetuate), then it is the liberal-ostrichist version that indeed is the hypocritical one on (at the very
least) two important grounds. Hypocrisy number one: It is common from
this stance to acknowledge the significance of political concerns (inequality, poverty, racism, etc.) but to argue that these have nothing to do with academic or applied linguistic concerns. This is a hypocritical denial of
political responsibility. Hypocrisy number two: Many of the attacks on
critical applied linguistics suggest little understanding of critical theory or
the debates that surround poststructuralism, postmodernism, or
postcolonialism. One does not have to agree with critical standpoints, but it
is important at the very least to engage in the argument on a reasonable basis of understanding of the issues. This is a hypocritical denial of academic
responsibility. I hope that even if this book does not persuade, it may at
least help inform debate.

Finally, it is important to consider critical applied linguistics within a
global context. The principal concern here is whether the sort of critical
applied linguistics I discuss has sufficient relevance for a diversity of contexts. Is it perhaps just an Anglo-European view on the world? One thing
is clear: Applied linguists around the world do not need another generation of British, American, or Australian "experts" trotting about the world
telling them how to do their work. Heaven forbid that critical applied linguistics should take up a position similar to the patronizing discourses of
applied linguistics, telling the rest of the world what it isn't doing right.
Although always cautious about these global relations, my experience has
been that the sort of critical applied linguistics I am trying to develop here

has many resonances with other people's work. It is by no means the same and may not be called the same thing, but there appear to be many parallels between the sort of critical applied linguistics I am working on here and the agendas of many others around the world. As I travel and talk to people around the world—in parts of Africa, Asia, Europe, and South America—I have found strong connections between what I propose and the directions (critical) applied linguistics is moving in elsewhere. Just to take the example of South American work, from Brazil (Cox & Assis-Peterson, 1999; de Souza, 1994; Jordão, 1999; Moita Lopes, 1998; Signorini & Cavalcanti, 1998) to Chile (Farias, 1999), there is both a separate tradition of critical work and a resonance with the ideas here. Indeed, it is in the central institutions of the United Kingdom and United Steates, with their vested interests in keeping things as they are, where most resistance to critical applied linguistics can be found. The rest of the world has been doing it a lot longer than I have.

Critical Notes for the Fridge Door

In answer to the second question—How might this inform praxis?—I return to the guiding principles that have emerged for me in the last few years. As I emphasize in this book, these notions cannot be reduced to techniques; neither should they be seen as prescriptions. Rather, I offer them as framing ideas for critical praxis, or as critical notes for the fridge door.[1] Two central concerns here have been with the notion of what it means to be critical and how theory, practice, and a critical orientation to work can be allied in a notion of critical praxis. As I argue earlier, critical applied linguistics needs a sense of *critical* that is part of a definitive form of politics. The critical here is a political critique and not merely a way of thinking. But, as suggested by Foucault (1980b), this is not a question of establishing a given political standpoint but rather of imagining and bringing into being new schemas of politicization (← chap. 1). Thus, the political and indeed the ethical can be seen less in terms of a dogmatic claiming of moral and political certitude and more in terms of an ability to politicize anew. Closely related to this is a notion of critical applied linguistics as a problematizing practice; this is a version of critical theory that becomes, as Dean (1994) puts it, a restive problematization of the given (← chap. 1), a constant questioning of our assumptions both within and beyond applied linguistics. This also links to the demand to understand critical applied linguistics as "an open-ended construction that is contested, incessantly perspectival and multiply-sited" (Lather, 1995, p. 177; ← chap. 5). And, it is a way of thinking that is always reflexive about itself,

---

[1]I apologize to anyone for whom this is not an obvious metaphor. For those without fridges, or those who do not use the fridge door as a place to stick daily reminders of things that need to be done, this notion may be opaque.

aware of the limits of knowing (Spivak, 1993; ← chap. 1). This reflexivity about itself is a crucial part of why this book is a critical introduction to critical applied linguistics, for while critical applied linguistics should be a crucial part of any applied linguistic enterprise, I also think we need to be aware of the limits of our knowing.

It has also been important to go beyond a practice/theory dichotomy. This book is not about some sort of critical applied linguistic theory that can now be applied or translated into practice. This is an insidious divide that runs throughout much of applied linguistics (Clarke, 1994). By and large, it is suggested that applied linguists develop theories or do research that can then be applied in classrooms or other settings. Thus, at the end of an article, we are often pushed by editors or reviewers to write that section that explains the pedagogical implications of our work. I suggest in this book (← chap. 1), by contrast, that a notion of praxis may help us avoid this divide. From this point of view, applied linguistics in all its contexts is a constant reciprocal relation between theory and practice, or preferably, "that continuous reflexive integration of thought, desire and action sometimes referred to as 'praxis'" (Simon, 1992, p. 49).

A central task for critical applied linguistics, I suggest, is not only to find ways of thinking about relations between the micro contexts of everyday language use and the macro concerns of society, culture, politics, and power but also to go beyond this kind of dialectical two-tiered model (← chaps. 3 and 5). And in our search for an understanding of language and power, it is important that we do not seek closure too quickly by assuming a given structure of power and then trying to map language onto it. Rather, as Foucault suggests (← chap. 4), power needs to remain as that which must be explained. At the same time, however, we need ways out of some of the dilemmas created by the pluralizations of the posts. Here we need to start to understand how our knowledge is situated. This implies both an understanding of our own locations, our bodies, and the histories that are written onto them and also hermeneutic, genealogical/historical, and narrative understandings of knowledge that can develop a sense of what we do in critical applied linguistics as both located and in motion (← chap. 6). Important too is an understanding of when to act with what sorts of knowledge, and thus to have available Spivak's notion (← chap. 3) of the strategic use of essentialism since it allows us to consider when we want to question identities, realities, rights, or languages and when we need to operationalize more fixed and concrete notions for strategic purposes.

The crucial engagement with ethics and the need for a notion of preferred futures brings us back to Roger Simon's (1992) notion of "the situated refusal of the present as definitive of that which is possible" (p. 30). Such an educational vision that is "capable of narrating stories of possibility" is "constrained within an ethical imagination that privileges diversity, compassionate justice, and securing of the conditions for the renewal of human life" (p. 30; ← chap. 5). In the same way that Foucault presents us with the need to seek new schemas of politicization, this is not about establishing a fixed and normative moral position but rather of seeking new frames of ethical thought and conduct, or as Kearney (1988) puts it, "the ethical demand to imagine *otherwise*" (p. 364). Such a vision, of course, demands a major rethinking of what applied linguistics might be about. Instead of being a canon of normative knowledge about language acquisition, teaching methods, translation, and so on, it would need to become an education in starting to address the ethical demands of language education, the global spread of English, the complexities of literacy, the violence of texts, the politics of translation.

CRITICAL APPLIED POSTLINGUISTICS, POSTCRITICAL APPLIED LINGUISTICS, OR APPLIED LINGUISTICS WITH AN ATTITUDE

One of the paradoxes of critical work emerges from the question of what happens when critical work goes mainstream. Is critical work always destined, by definition, to be marginal; or is it conceivable that everyone might start to do critical work? And if they did so, would it still be critical? Could critical applied linguistics become mainstream applied linguistics, or is that oxymoronic? On the one hand, the object of this book is certainly to argue for more critical applied linguistics. Yet at the same time, we need to acknowledge that as more people start doing critical applied linguistics, it will inevitably get watered down. Critical pedagogy is a good example of this, having started out as a radical critique of education and having become at times nothing but student-centered pedagogy. Versions of critical literacy, by becoming tied to a very specific genre approach to education, have similarly lost their critical edge. Critical discourse analysis may be starting to go the same way.

But the mainstreaming or watering down of critical work can only apply if it becomes solidified and static. And this brings us to a reiteration of an issue I try to stress throughout this book. The purpose here is not to establish and define critical applied linguistics as a discipline, a domain, a field. Rather, the purpose is to provide a glimpse of the *movable praxis* that is critical applied linguistics. I see critical applied linguistics as a constantly shifting and dynamic approach to questions of language and education rather than a method, a set of techniques, or a fixed body of knowledge. And rather than viewing critical applied linguistics as a new form of interdisciplinary knowledge, I prefer to view it as a form of *anti*disciplinary knowledge, as a way of thinking and doing that is always questioning, always seeking new schemas of politicization. To the extent that this view of critical applied linguistics emphasizes the importance of working through the various *post* perspectives, and to the extent that I also argue that this critical applied linguistics needs to avoid any static model building and instead is an approach to language and knowledge that is always in motion, it might already be time to call this either postcritical applied linguistics, following the notion of postcritical pedagogy (← chap. 5), or critical applied postlinguistics, following the notion of postlinguistics as the use of linguistic tools within a poststructuralist framework (← chap. 4). Or perhaps, as I suggest next, it is time just to talk of applied linguistics with an attitude.

To envisage how critical applied linguistics may both appear and disappear, be consolidated and yet remain flexible, it may be useful to consider its potential role in university courses in applied linguistics. We might consider five possibilities (see Table 7.2). The first I call the absent model, the business-as-usual approach to applied linguistics in which the sort of critical concerns I outline in this book are given no space. While the weight of critical concerns related to applied linguistics makes such a position increasingly untenable, it still remains in many versions of applied linguistics, particularly in the narrow version of applied linguistics viewed in terms of translating linguistic theory for language teachers. In the highly commercialized world of English language teaching, courses that try to make applied linguistics an apolitical study of language and teaching methodology are common. Indeed, from this point of view, critical applied linguistics is hypocritical applied linguistics (Widdowson, 1999).

TABLE 7.2
(Critical) Applied Linguistics (CALx) in the Curriculum

CALx Role in the Curriculum	Implications	Problems
Absent	No critical perspectives anywhere in the program	Denial of political and academic responsibility
Week 13	A critical week added on to standard courses; present but peripheral	Fails to engage in any substantial way with critical perspectives
The critical course	A CALx course as part of the program; more significant but optional	Although allowing for serious engagement, maintains the critical as separate; solidifies content
Critical courses	Several critical courses that may no longer label themselves as such	No longer peripheral or isolated but remains an optional concern
Applied linguistics with an attitude	CALx as an ethical, epistemological, and political attitude toward all issues in applied linguistics	From peripheral to pervasive but potentially can disappear

Yet, while some may eschew the notion of critical applied linguistics, there is now sufficient work pursued under the critical rubric in areas that interlink with applied linguistics (critical discourse analysis, critical literacy, critical pedagogy) that it has become increasingly difficult to continue without some acknowledgment of the critical. Thus, many applied linguists have started to include such work as part of their courses: A course in discourse analysis may include a week or two on critical discourse analysis; a subject on literacy might include work in critical literacy; and courses on methodology, curriculum, or teacher education may look at the work done in critical pedagogy. This I term the week 13 model (assuming a 13-week semester), where standard applied linguistics courses acknowledge the critical as one approach and tend to do so at the end of the course. Although it is an improvement on the absent model, it is also very limited: It operates with a liberal, inclusive framework that renders critical work an add-on; it only dips in to critical work in desultory fashion and thus fails to explore basic questions to do with ideology, power, or subjectivity; and it tends to shuffle the critical week off toward the end of the semester so that its position remains peripheral.

A more serious approach attempts a sustained engagement with critical applied linguistics by making it part of the curriculum. This is what I did some years ago at the University of Melbourne when I started teaching a course in critical applied linguistics. In some ways, this was similar to taking everyone else's week 13 away from them again and sticking them together. Thus, we now had a course that dealt with critical discourse analysis, critical literacy, critical language awareness, gender, sexuality and ESL, critical language testing, and so on. This was an exciting course that finally allowed sustained semester-long engagement with critical work. As the course developed, we found we had to range not only over the critical domains as outlined but also over many background areas, from Habermas to Foucault, from ideology critique to postcolonialism. Yet such a course also has its drawbacks: It runs the danger of isolating critical applied linguistics as a particular and separate approach to language-related domains, and thus it can help in the creation of noncritical approaches in other subjects. It also runs the danger of solidifying critical applied linguistics into a recognizable subject matter.

A fourth approach is where critical applied linguistics becomes more diffuse. Now instead of one course taught and labeled as *critical applied linguistics,* it starts to operate through different courses. In my current context at the University of Technology, Sydney, for example, we teach courses such as Language and Power and Critical Literacies, which range across numerous concerns and contexts. From this point of view, rather than a consolidation of critical work under one heading, it starts to become more diverse. There are a number of advantages to this: It allows greater possibilities of coverage and of approaches, and it means that critical applied linguistics is no longer one elective that you can take or not take but rather is part of several courses and starts to form a more substantial part of the curriculum. Even with this more serious engagement, however, critical applied linguistics still remains something you may or may not do. It is no longer a peripheral occurrence (the critical week) or an isolated subject (the critical course), but it remains an optional concern.

The final model, then, continues this process of diffusion away from isolated moments of criticality and instead moves toward a critical approach infusing a whole area. Thus, the imperative to develop broader, more ethically accountable, and more transformative frameworks of knowledge in applied linguistics suggests the possibility not of peripheral critical work but of pervasive critical work. From this point of view, we can start to envision critical applied linguistics less in terms of models or methodologies and more in terms of an ethical, epistemological, and political attitude toward all questions in language education, literacy, translation, or language use in the workplace. Discussing the ways in which a notion of critical literacy still allows for uncritical literacy, and leads toward rigid and stultifying concepts of what critical literacy may be, Bill Green (1997) argues for the need to reclaim literacy as always already political from the outset:

> We must ask, finally, again and again: What is the status of the *critical* in the concept and the project of "critical literacy?" As the disciples begin to gather around, it becomes all the more imperative to question the "critical," to open up the debate, and to admit that nothing is certain or safe, and that this too is just a Fiction, albeit one that can and does have effects on the world .... Might it not be the case, instead, that the necessary effort must now go into reclaiming literacy as, *from the outset,* always already political? [Such a view] throws the very project of "critical literacy" into disarray, or at least into history, because it means now that we can work, strategically, from the outset with a politicized understanding of literacy, with the view that any literacy worth the name (and worth working with and struggling for—worth spending time on) ... is always already political, and moreover, an instrument and a resource for *change,* for challenging and changing the Wor(l)d. (p. 240–241)

Substituting critical applied linguistics for critical literacy into this argument, we can then start to see the need always to question the status of the critical, to open up the debate, and to admit that nothing is certain or safe, that the necessary effort might now go into reclaiming applied linguistics as, *from the outset,* always already political. This throws the very project of critical applied linguistics into disarray, or at least into history, because it means now that we can work, strategically, from the outset with a politicized understanding of applied linguistics, with the view that any applied linguistics worth the name (and worth working with and struggling for—worth spending time on) ... is always already political and, moreover, an instrument and a resource for *change,* for challenging and changing the wor(l)d. Following Bill Green, then, critical applied linguistics might be seen not so much as an alternative approach to applied linguistics but rather as applied linguistics with an attitude. And this is where I would like to leave this introduction to critical applied linguistics, at a moment not of model building, theory construction or programmatic posturing, but rather at a moment of dissolution, of pulling apart. Whatever use critical applied linguistics may be, it cannot be tied to my vision of how it may work. I have tried to hold it still long enough to describe, but now I would rather cast it adrift.

References

Althusser, L. (1971). *Lenin and philosophy and other essays*. London: New Left Books.

Appadurai, A. (1990). Disjuncture and difference in the global cultural economy. In M. Featherstone (Ed.), *Global culture: Nationalism, globalization and modernity* (pp. 295–310). London: Sage.

Ashcroft, B., Griffiths, G., & Tiffin, H. (1989). *The empire writes back: Theory and practice in post-colonial literatures*. London: Routledge.

Atkinson, D. (1997). A critical approach to critical thinking in TESOL. *TESOL Quarterly, 31,* 71–94.

Auerbach, E. (1993). Reexamining English only in the ESL classroom. *TESOL Quarterly, 27,* 9–32.

Auerbach, E. (1995). The politics of the ESL classroom: Issues of power in pedagogical choices. In J. Tollefson (Ed.), *Power and inequality in language education* (pp. 9–33). New York: Cambridge University Press.

Auerbach, E. (1999, October). *Border skirmishes: The power of literacies vs. the literacies of power.* Keynote speech, Rocky Mountain TESOL Conference, Las Cruces, NM.

Auerbach, E. (2000). Creating participatory learning communities: paradoxes and possibilities. In J. K. Hall & W. Eggington (Eds.), *The sociopolitics of English language teaching* (pp. 143–164). Clevedon, UK: Multilingual Matters.

Auerbach, E. (n.d.). Invited and rejected manuscript, cut from B. Cope & M. Kalantis (Eds.), *Multiliteracies: Literacy learning and the design of social futures.* London: Routledge.

Auerbach, E., & Wallerstein, N. (1987). *ESL for action: Problem- posing at work.* Reading, MA: Addison Wesley.

Austin, J. L. (1962). *How to do things with words.* Cambridge, MA: Harvard University Press.

Bailey, R. (1991). *Images of English: A cultural history of the language.* Ann Arbor: The University of Michigan Press.

Barrett, M. (1991). *The politics of truth: From Marx to Foucault.* Stanford, CA: Stanford University Press.

Baynham, M. (1995). *Literacy Practices.* London: Longman.

Bee, B. (1993). Critical literacy and the politics of gender. In C. Lankshear & P. Mc-Laren (Eds.), *Critical literacy: Politics, praxis and the postmodern* (pp. 105–132). Albany: State University of New York Press.

Belenky, M., Clinchy, B., Glodberger, N., & Tarule, J. (1986). *Women's ways of knowing: The development of self, voice and mind.* New York: Basic Books.

Benesch, S. (1996). Needs analysis and curriculum development in EAP: An example of a critical approach. *TESOL Quarterly, 30,* 723–738.

Benesch, S. (1999). Thinking critically, thinking dialogically. *TESOL Quarterly, 33,* 573–580.

Benson, P. (1997). The philosophy and politics of learner autonomy. In P. Benson & P. Voller (Eds.), *Autonomy and independence in language learning* (pp. 18–34). London: Longman.

Beretta, A. (1991). Theory construction in SLA: Complimentarity and opposition. *Studies in Second Language Acquisition, 13,* 493–511.

Beretta, A., Crookes, G., Gregg, K. R., & Long, M. H. (1994). A comment from some contributors to Volume 14, Issue 3. *Applied Linguistics, 15,* 347.

Bernstein, B. (1972). Social class, language and socialization. In P. P. Giglioli (Ed.), *Language and social context: Selected Readings* (pp. 157–178). Harmonds- worth: Penguin.

Bex, T., & Watts, R. J. (Eds.). (1999). *Standard English: The widening debate.* London: Routledge.

Bhatt, A., & Martin-Jones, M. (1992). Whose resource? Minority languages, bilingual learners and language awareness. In N. Fairclough (Ed.), *Critical language awareness* (pp. 285–302). London: Longman.

Block, D. (1996). Not so fast: Some thoughts on theory culling, relativism, accepted findings and the heart and soul of SLA. *Applied Linguistics, 17,* 63–83.

Bourdieu, P. (1986). The forms of capital. In J. G. Richardson (Ed.), *Handbook of theory and research for the sociology of education* (pp. 241–258). Westport, CT: Greenwood.

Bourdieu, P. (1991). *Language and symbolic power.* Oxford, UK: Polity.

Bowles, S., & Gintis, H. (1976). *Schooling in capitalist America.* New York: Basic Books.

Britzman, D. (1995). Is there a queer pedagogy? Or, stop reading straight. *Educational Theory, 45,* 151–165.

Brookfield, S. (1987). *Developing critical thinkers.* Milton Keynes: Open University Press.

Brutt-Griffler, J., & Samimy, K. (1999). Revisiting the colonial in the postcolonial: Critical praxis for nonnative English-speaking teachers in a TESOL program. *TESOL Quarterly, 33,* 413–431.

Burnett, L. (1962). *The treasure of our tongue.* London: Secker & Warburg.

Butler, J. (1990). *Gender trouble: Feminism and the subversion of identity.* New York: Routledge.

Butler, J. (1997). *Excitable speech: A politics of the performative.* New York: Routledge.

Cameron, D. (1990). Demythologizing sociolinguistics: Why language does not reflect society. In J. Joseph & T. Taylor (Eds.), *Ideologies of language* (pp. 79–96). London: Routledge.

Cameron, D. (1995). *Verbal hygiene.* London: Routledge.

Cameron, D. (1997). Performing gender identity: Young men's talk and the construction of heterosexual masculinity. In S. Johnson & U. H. Meinhof (Eds.), *Language and masculinity* (pp. 47–64). Oxford, UK: Blackwell.

Canagarajah, A. S. (1993). Critical ethnography of a Sri Lankan classroom: Ambiguities in student opposition to reproduction through ESOL. *TESOL Quarterly, 27,* 601–626.

Canagarajah, S. (1999a). On EFL teachers, awareness, and agency. *ELT Journal, 53,* 207–214.

Canagarajah, S. (1999b). *Resisting linguistic imperialism in English teaching.* Oxford, UK: Oxford University Press.

Canale, M., & Swain, M. (1980). Theoretical bases of communicative approaches to second language teaching and testing. *Applied Linguistics, 1*(1), 1–47.

Candlin, C. (1990). What happens when applied linguistics goes critical? In M. A. K. Halliday, J. Gibbons, & H. Nicholas (Eds.), *Learning, keeping and using language* (pp. 461–486). Amsterdam: John Benjamins.

Chomsky, N. (1971). *Problems of knowledge and freedom.* New York: Pantheon.

Chomsky, N. (1974). Human nature: Justice versus power [Dicussion with M. Foucault]. In F. Elder (Ed.), *Reflexive water: The basic concerns of mankind* (pp. 133–198). London: Souvenir Press.

Chomsky, N. (1979). *Language and responsibility.* New York: Pantheon.

Chrisman, L., & Williams, P. (1994). Colonial discourse and post-colonial theory: An introduction. In P. Williams & L. Chrisman (Eds.), *Colonial discourse and postcolonial theory. A reader* (pp. 1–20). New York: Columbia University Press.

Christie, F. (1998). Learning the literacies of primary and secondary schooling. In F. Christie & R. Misson (Eds.), *Literacy and schooling* (pp. 47–73). London: Routledge.

Clark, R. (1992). Principles and practice of CLA in the classroom. In N. Fairclough (Ed.), *Critical language awareness* (pp. 117–140). London: Longman.

Clark, R., & Ivanič, R. (1997). *The politics of writing.* London: Routledge.

Clarke, M. (1994). The dysfunctions of the theory/practice discourse. *TESOL Quarterly, 28*(1), 9–26.

Coates, J. (Ed). (1998). *Language and gender: A reader.* Oxford, UK: Blackwell.

Cope, B., & Kalantzis, M. (1993). The power of literacy and the literacy of power. In B. Cope & M. Kalantzis (Eds.), *The powers of literacy: A genre approach to teaching writing* (pp. 63–89). London: The Falmer Press.

Cope. B., & Kalantzis, M. (Eds.). (2000). *Multiliteracies: Literacy learning and the design of social futures.* London: Routledge.

Cope, B., Kalantzis, M., Kress, G., Martin, J., & Murphy, L. (1993). Bibliographical essay: Developing the theory and practice of genres based literacy. In B. Cope & M. Kalantzis (Eds.), *The powers of literacy: A genre approach to teaching writing* (pp. 231–247). London: The Falmer Press.

Corder, S. (1973). *Introducing applied linguistics.* Harmondsworth: Penguin.

Corson, D. (1997). Critical realism: An emancipatory philosophy for applied linguistics? *Applied Linguistics, 18,* 166–188.

Coulmas, F. (1998). Language rights—interests of state, language groups and the individual. *Language Sciences, 20,* 63–72.

Cox, M. I. P., & de Assis-Peterson, A. A. (1999). Critical pedagogy in ELT: Images of Brazilian teachers of English. *TESOL Quarterly, 33,* 433–451.

Crawford, A. (1999). "We can't all understand the whites' language": An analysis of monolingual health services in a multilingual society. *International Journal of the Sociology of Language, 136,* 27–45.

Crystal, D. (1997). *English as a global language.* Cambridge, UK: Cambridge University Press.

Davies, B. (1989). *Frogs and snails and feminist tails.* Sydney, Australia: Allen & Unwin.

Dean, M. (1994). *Critical and effective histories: Foucault's methods and historical sociology.* London: Routledge.

de Beaugrande, R. (1997). Theory and practice in applied linguistics: Disconnection, conflict or dialectic? *Applied Linguistics, 18,* 279–313.

Delpit, L. (1988). The silenced dialogue: Power and pedagogy in educating other people's children. *Harvard Educational Review, 58,* 280–298.

Delpit, L. (1995). *Other people's children: Cultural conflict in the classroom.* New York: The New Press.

Dendrinos, B. (1992). *The EFL textbook and ideology.* Athens, Greece: N.C. Grivas.

de Souza, L. M. (1994). Post colonial literature and a pedagogy of revisioning: The contribution of Wilson Harris. *Claritas, 1,* 55–61.

Dua, H. (1994). *Hegemony of English.* Mysore, India: Yashoda Publications.

Duff, P., & Uchida, Y. (1997). The negotiation of teachers' sociocultural identities and practices in postsecondary EFL classrooms. *TESOL Quarterly, 31,* 451–486.

Ellsworth, E. (1989). Why doesn't this feel empowering? Working through the repressive myths of critical pedagogy. *Harvard Educational Review, 59,* 297–324.

Fairclough, N. (1989). *Language and power.* London: Longman.

Fairclough, N. (1992a). The appropriacy of "appropriateness." In N. Fairclough (Ed.), *Critical language awareness* (pp. 33–56). London: Longman.

Fairclough, N. (1992b). *Discourse and social change.* Oxford, UK: Polity.

Fairclough, N. (1992c). Introduction. In N. Fairclough (Ed.), *Critical language awareness* (pp. 1–29). London: Longman.

Fairclough, N. (1993). Critical discourse analysis and the marketization of public discourse. *Discourse and Society, 4,* 133–168.

Fairclough, N. (1995). *Critical discourse analysis.* London: Longman.

183

Fairclough, N. (1996). Technologisation of discourse. In C. R. Caldas-Couthard & M. Coulthard (Eds.), *Texts and practices: Readings in critical discourse analysis* (pp. 71–83). London: Routledge.

Fairclough, N. (2000). Multiliteracies and language: Orders of discourse and intertextuality. In B. Cope & M. Kalantzis (Eds.), *Multiliteracies: Literacy learning and the design of social futures* (pp. 162–181). London: Routledge.

Fairclough, N., & Wodak, R. (1996). Critical discourse analysis. In T. van Dijk (Ed.), *Discourse analysis* (pp. 258–284). London: Sage.

Fanon, F. (1963). *The wretched of the earth* (C. Farrington, Trans.). Harmondsworth: Penguin. (Original work published 1961)

Farias, M. (1999, April). *Enfoques críticos en el proceso de enseñanza/aprendizaje de lenguas extranjeras* [Critical approaches to the process of teaching/learning foreign languages]. 7th Symposium for tertiary foreign language teachers. Mendoza, Argentina.

Featherstone, M. (1990). Global culture: An introduction. In M. Featherstone (Ed.), *Global culture: Nationalism, globalization and modernity* (pp. 1–14). London: Sage.

Firth, A., & Wagner, J. (1997). On discourse, communication, and (some) fundamental concepts in SLA research. *Modern Language Journal, 81,* 285–300.

Foley, G. (1999). *Learning in social action: A contribution to understanding informal education.* London: Zed Books.

Foucault, M. (1974) Human nature: Justice versus power [Discussion with N. Chomsky]. In F. Elder (Ed.), *Reflexive water: The basic concerns of mankind* (pp. 133–198). London: Souvenir Press.

Foucault, M. (1979). *Discipline and punish: The birth of the prison.* New York: Vintage.

Foucault, M. (1980a). *The history of sexuality: Volume 1: An introduction.* New York: Vintage.

Foucault, M. (1980b). *Power/knowledge: Selected interviews and other writings, 1972–1977.* New York: Pantheon.

Foucault, M. (1991). *Remarks on Marx.* New York: Semiotext(e).

Fowler, R. (1996). On critical linguistics. In C. R. Caldas-Couthard & M. Coulthard (Eds.), *Texts and practices: Readings in critical discourse analysis* (pp. 3–14). London: Routledge.

Fowler, R., Kress, G., Hodge, R., & Trew, T. (Eds.). (1979). *Language and control.* London: Routledge.

Freire, P. (1970). *Pedagogy of the oppressed.* New York: Continuum (M. B. Ramos, Trans.).

Freire, P., & Macedo, D. (1987). *Literacy: Reading the word and the world.* South Hadley, MA: Bergin & Garvey.

Friedman, J. (1990). Being in the world: Globalization and localization. In M. Featherstone (Ed.), *Global culture: Nationalism, globalization and modernity* (pp. 311–328). London: Sage.

Frye, D. (1999). Participatory education as a critical framework for an immigrant women's ESL class. *TESOL Quarterly, 33,* 501–513.

Fuery, P. (1995). *Theories of desire.* Melbourne, Australia: Melbourne University Press.

Galtung, J. (1980). *The true worlds. A transnational perspective.* New York: The Free Press.

Gebhard, M. (1999). Debates in SLA studies: Redefining SLA as an institutional phenomenon. *TESOL Quarterly, 33,* 544–557.

Gee, J. P. (1993). Postmodernism and literacies. In C. Lankshear & P. McLaren (Eds.), *Critical literacy: Politics, praxis and the postmodern* (pp. 271–296). Albany, NY: State University of New York Press.

Gee, J. P. (1994). Orality and literacy: From *The Savage Mind* to *Ways With Words.* In J. Maybin (Ed.), *Language and literacy in social practice* (pp. 168–192). Clevedon, UK: Multilingual Matters.

Gee, J. (1996). *Social linguistics and literacies: Ideologies in discourse.* London: Taylor & Francis.

Gee, J. (2000). New people in new worlds: networks, the new capitalism and schools. In B. Cope & M. Kalantzis (Eds.), *Multiliteracies: Literacy learning and the design of social futures* (pp. 43–68). London: Routledge.

Gee, J., Hull, G., & Lankshear, C. (1996). *The new work order: Behind the language of the new capitalism.* Sydney, Australia: Allen & Unwin.

Giddens, A. (1979). *Central problems in social theory: Action, structure and contradiction in social analysis.* Berkeley, CA: University of California Press.

Giddens, A. (1982). *Sociology: A brief but critical introduction.* London: Macmillan.

Gilroy, P. (1987). *There ain't no black in the union jack.* London: Hutchinson.

Giroux, H. (1983). *Theory and resistance in education: A pedagogy for the opposition.* South Hadley, MA: Bergin & Garvey.

Giroux, H. (1988). *Schooling and the struggle for public life: Critical pedagogy in the modern age.* Minneapolis: University of Minnesota Press.

Goldstein, T. (1996) *Two languages at work: Bilingual life on the production floor.* Berlin: Mouton de Gruyter.

Gore, J. (1993). *The struggle for pedagogies: Critical and feminist discourses as regimes of truth.* New York: Routledge.

Graman, T. (1988). Education for humanization: Applying Paulo Freire's pedagogy to learning a second language. *Harvard Educational Review, 58,* 433–448.

Green, B. (1997). Reading with an attitude; or Deconstructing "Critical literacies." Response to Allan Luke and Peter Freebody. In S. Muspratt, A. Luke, & P. Freebody (Eds.), *Constructing critical literacies: Teaching and learning textual practice* (pp. 227–242). St Leonards, NSW: Allen & Unwin.

Gregg, K. R. (1993). Taking explanation seriously: Or, let a couple of flowers bloom. *Applied Linguistics, 14,* 276–294.

Gregg, K. R., Long, M., Jordan, G., & Beretta, A. (1997). Rationality and its discontents in SLA. *Applied Linguistics, 18,* 539–559.

Grumet, M. (1988). *Bitter milk: Women and teaching.* Amherst: University of Massachusetts Press.

Guba, E., & Lincoln, Y. (1989). *Fourth generation evaluation.* Newbury Park, CA: Sage.

Habermas, J. (1972). *Knowledge and human interests.* London: Heinemann.

Habermas, J. (1984). *The theory of communicative action.* Boston: Beacon.

Habermas, J. (1985). Psychic thermidor and the rebirth of rebellious subjectivity. In R. Bernstein (Ed.), *Habermas and modernity* (pp. 67–77). Cambridge, MA: MIT Press.

Habermas, J. (1998). *On the pragmatics of communication.* Cambridge, MA: MIT Press.

Hall, S. (1994). Encoding/decoding. In. D. Graddol & O. Boyd-Barrett (Eds.), *Media texts: Authors and readers* (pp. 200–211). Clevedon, UK: Multilingual Matters.

Halliday, M. (1978). *Language as social semiotic.* London: Arnold.

Hanson, J. (1997, July). The mother of all tongues. Review of D. Crystal, *English as a Global Language,* Cambridge: Cambridge University Press. *Times Higher Education Supplement,* 1288, p. 22.

Haraway, D. (1988). Situated knowledges: The science question in feminism and the privilege of partial perspective. *Feminist Studies, 14*(3), 575–599.

Harland, R. (1987). *Superstructuralism: The philosophy of structuralism and post-structuralism.* London: Routledge.

Harris, R. (1981). *The language myth.* London: Duckworth.

Harris, R. (1997). Fighting the many enemies. A review of *Oxford English dictionary additions series volume three* and J. Honey *Language is power: The story of standard English and its enemies. The Times Higher 1296 September 5 1997,* 19.

Hatim, B., & Mason, I. (1997). *The translator as communicator.* London: Routledge.

Haugen, E. (1972). *The ecology of language: Essays by Einar Haugen* (A.S. Dil Ed.). Stanford, CA: Stanford University Press.

Heath, S. B. (1983). *Ways with words: Language, life and work in communities and classrooms.* Cambridge, UK: Cambridge University Press.

Herman, E. S., & Chomsky, N. (1988). *Manufacturing consent: The political economy of the mass media.* New York: Pantheon.

Hodge, R., & Kress, G. (1988). *Social semiotics.* Cambridge, MA: Polity.

Hogben, L. (1963). *Essential world English.* London: Michael Joseph.

Honey, J. (1983). *The language trap: Race class and the "standard English" issue in British schools.* Kenton, UK: National Council for Educational Standards.

Honey, J. (1997). *Language is power: The story of standard English and its enemies.* London: Faber and Faber.

Ibrahim, A. (1999). Becoming Black: Rap and hip-hop, race, gender, identity and the politics of ESL learning. *TESOL Quarterly, 33,* 349–369.

Ivanič, R. (1990). Critical language awareness in action. In R. Carter (Ed.), *Knowledge about language and the curriculum: The LINC reader* (pp. 122–132). London: Hodder & Stroughton.

Jäger, S., & Jäger, M. (1993). *Aus der Mitte der Gesellschaft* [From the middle of society]. Duisburg, Germany: Diss.

Jagose, A. (1996). *Queer theory.* Melbourne: Melbourne University Press.

Janks, H. (1997). Critical discourse analysis as a research tool. *Discourse: Studies in the Cultural Politics of Education, 18,* 329–342.

Janks, H., & Ivanič, R. (1992). Critical language awareness and emancipatory discourse. In N. Fairclough (Ed.), *Critical language awareness* (pp. 305–331). London: Longman.

Jenkins, R. (1992). *Pierre Bourdieu.* London: Routledge.

Jewell, J. (1998). A transgendered ESL learner in relation to her class textbooks, heterosexist hegemony and change. *Melbourne Papers in Applied Linguistics, 10,* 1–21.

Johnson, S. (1997). Theorizing language and masculinity: A feminist perspective. In S. Johnson & U. H. Meinhof (Eds.), *Language and masculinity* (pp. 8–26). Oxford, UK: Blackwell.

Johnston, B. (1999). Putting critical pedagogy in its place: A personal account. *TESOL Quarterly, 33,* 557–565.

Jordan, G., & Weedon, C. (1995). *Cultural politics: Class, gender, race and the modern world.* Oxford, UK: Blackwell.

Jordão, C. (1999). Critical pedagogy and the teaching of literature. *Acta Scientarium, 21,* 9–14.

Kachru, B. (1990). World Englishes and applied linguistics. *World Englishes, 9,* 3–20.

Kachru, B. (1996). The paradigms of marginality. *World Englishes, 15*(1), 241–255.

Kanpol, B. (1990). Political applied linguistics and postmodernism: Towards an engagement of similarity within difference. A reply to Pennycook. *Issues in Applied Linguistics, 1,* 238–250.

Kanpol, B. (1994). *Critical pedagogy: An introduction.* Westort, CT: Bergin & Garvey.

Kanpol, B. (1997). *Issues and trends in critical pedagogy.* Cresskill, NJ: Hampton Press.

Kaplan, R. (1966). Cultural thought patterns in intercultural education. *Language Learning, 16,* 1–20.

Kearney, R. (1988). *The wake of imagination.* Minneapolis: University of Minnesota Press.

Kramsch, K. (1993). *Context and culture in language teaching.* Oxford: Oxford University Press.

Krashen, S. (1981). *Second language acquisition and second language learning.* Oxford: Pergamon.

Kress, G. (1990). Critical discourse analysis. *Annual review of applied linguistics* [W. Grabe, Ed.], Vol. 11, pp. 84–99.

Kress, G. (1993). Genre as social process. In B. Cope & M. Kalantzis (Eds.), *The powers of literacy: A genre approach to teaching writing* (pp. 22–37). London: The Falmer Press.

Kress, G. (1996). Representational resources and the production of subjectivity: Questions for the theoretical development of critical discourse analysis in a multicultural society. In C. R. Caldas-Coulthard & M. Coulthard (Eds.), *Texts and practices: Readings in critical discourse analysis* (pp. 13–31). London: Routledge.

Kress, G., & Hodge, R. (1979). *Language as ideology.* London: Routledge.

Kress, G., & van Leeuwen, T. (1990). *Reading images.* Geelong, Australia: Deakin University Press.

Kubota, R. (1999). Japanese culture constructed by discourses: Implications for applied linguistics research and ELT. *TESOL Quarterly, 33,* 9–35.

Kumaravadivelu, B. (1999). Critical classroom discourse analysis. *TESOL Quarterly, 33,* 453–484.

Labov, W. (1970). The logic of nonstandard English. In F. Williams (Ed.), *Language and poverty: Perspectives on a theme* (pp. 153–189). Chicago: Markham.

Lakoff, R. (1990). *Talking power: The politics of language.* New York: Basic Books.

Lankshear, C. (with J. P. Gee, M. Knobel, and C. Searle). (1997). *Changing literacies.* Buckingham, UK: Open University Press.

Lantolf, J. (1996). SLA theory building: Letting all the flowers bloom! *Language Learning, 46,* 713–749.

Lather, P. (1991). *Getting smart: Feminist research and pedagogy with/in the postmodern.* New York: Routledge.

Lather, P. (1992). Postmodernism and the human sciences. In S. Kvale (Ed.), *Psychology and postmodernism* (pp. 88–109). London: Sage.

Lather, P. (1995). Post-critical pedagogies: A feminist reading. In P. McLaren (Ed.), *Postmodernism, postcolonialism and pedagogy* (pp. 167–186). Albert Park, Australia: James Nicholas Publishers.

Lee, A. (1996). *Gender, literacy, curriculum: Rewriting school geography.* London: Taylor & Francis.

Lee, A. (1997). Questioning the critical: Linguistics, literacy and curriculum. In S. Muspratt, A. Luke, & P. Freebody (Eds.), *Constructing critical literacies: Teaching and learning textual practice* (pp. 409–432). Sydney, Australia: Allen and Unwin.

Lin, A. (1999). Doing-English-lessons in the reproduction or transformation of of social worlds? *TESOL Quarterly, 33,* 393–412.

Liu, J. (1999). Non-native-English-speaking professionals in TESOL. *TESOL Quarterly, 33*(1), 85–102.

Long, M. (1990). The least a second language acquisition theory needs to explain. *TESOL Quarterly, 24,* 649–666.

Long, M. (1996). Ebonics, language and power. *University of Hawai'i Working Papers in ESL, 15,* 97–122.

Long, M. (1999, August). *Theories and theory change in SLA.* Keynote address to the 12th World Congress of Applied Linguistics, AILA '99, Tokyo.

Loomba, A. (1998). *Colonialism/postcolonialism.* London: Routledge.

Luke, A. (1988). *Literacy, textbooks and ideology: Postwar literacy instruction and the mythology of Dick and Jane.* London: The Falmer Press.

Luke, A. (1996). Genres of power? Literacy education and the production of capital. In R. Hagen & G. Williams (Eds.), *Literacy in society* (pp. 308–338). London: Longman.

Luke, A. (1997a) Critical approaches to literacy. In V. Edwards & D. Corson (Eds.), *Encyclopedia of language and education, vol. 2 literacy* (pp. 143–151). Dordrecht, Netherlands: Kluwer Academic Publishers.

Luke, A. (1997b). The material effects of the word: Apologies, "Stolen Children" and public discourse. *Discourse: Studies in the Cultural Politics of Education, 18,* 343–368.

Luke, A., & Freebody, P. (1997). Critical literacy and the question of normativity: An introduction. In S. Muspratt, A. Luke, & P. Freebody (Eds.), *Constructing critical literacies: Teaching and learning textual practice* (pp. 1–18). Sydney, Australia: Allen and Unwin.

Luke, A., McHoul, A., & Mey, J. L. (1990). On the limits of language planning: Class, state and power. In R. B. Baldauf, Jr., & A. Luke (Eds.), *Language Planning and Education in Australasia and the South Pacific* (pp. 25–44). Clevedon, UK: Multilingual Matters.

Luke, A., & Walton, C. (1994). Teaching and assessing critical reading. In T. Husen & T. Postlethwaite (Eds.), *International encyclopedia of education* (2nd ed., pp. 1194–1198). Oxford, Uk: Pergamon.

Lynch, B. (1996). *Language program evaluation: Theory and practice.* Cambridge: Cambridge University Press.

Markee, N. (1990). Applied linguistics: What's that? *System, 18,* 315–324.

McCarthy, T. (1978). *The critical theory of Jürgen Habermas.* London: Hutchinson.

McClintock, A. (1994). The angel of progress: Pitfalls of the term 'postcolonialism.' In P. Williams & L. Chrisman (Eds.), *Colonial discourse and postcolonial theory: A reader* (pp. 291–304). New York: Columbia University Press.

McCormick, K. (1994). *The culture of reading and the teaching of English.* Manchester, UK: Manchester University Press.

McGee, T. G. (1995). Eurocentrism and geography: Reflections on Asian urbanization. In J. Crush (Ed.), *Power of development* (pp. 192–207). London: Routledge.

McKay, S. L., & Wong, S. C. (1996). Multiple discourses, multiple identities: Investment and agency in second language learning among Chinese adolescent immigrant students. *Harvard Education Review, 3,* 577–608.

Mclaren, P. (1989). *Life in schools: An introduction to critical pedagogy in the foundations of education.* New York: Longman.

Mey, J. (1985). *Whose language? A study in linguistic pragmatics.* Amsterdam: John Benjamins.

Mills, S. (1997). *Discourse.* London: Routledge.

Milroy, J. (1999). The consequences of standardisation in descriptive linguistics. In T. Bex & R. Watts (Eds.), *Standard English: The widening debate* (pp. 16–39). London: Routledge.

Misson, R. (1996). What's in it for me?: Teaching against homophobic discourse. In L. Laskey & C. Beavis (Eds.), *Schooling and sexualities: Teaching for a positive sexuality* (pp. 117–129). Geelong, Australia: Deakin Centre for Education and Change.

Moi, T. (1985). *Sexual/textual politics: Feminist literary theory.* London: Methuen.

Moita Lopes, L. P. de (1998). A transdisciplinaridade é possível em lingüística aplicada? [Is transdisciplinarity possible in applied linguistics?]. In I. Signorini & M. Cavalcanti (Eds.), *Lingüística aplicada e transdisciplinaridade* (pp. 113–128). Campinas, Brazil: Mercado de Letras.

Morgan, B. (1997). Identity and intonation: Linking dynamic processes in an ESL classroom. *TESOL Quarterly, 31,* 431–450.

Morgan, B. (1998). *The ESL classroom: Teaching, critical practice and community development.* Toronto, Canada: University of Toronto Press.

Mühlhäusler, P. (1996). *Linguistic ecology: Language change and linguistic imperialism in the Pacific region.* London: Routledge.

Nandy, A. (1983). *The intimate enemy: Loss and recovery of self under colonialism.* Delhi, India: Oxford University Press.

Nelson, C. (1993). Heterosexism in ESL: Examining our attitudes. *TESOL Quarterly, 27,* 143–150.

Nelson, C. (1999). Sexual identities in ESL: Queer theory and classroom inquiry. *TESOL Quarterly, 33,* 371–391

New London Group. (1996). A pedagogy of multiliteracies: Designing social futures. *Harvard Educational Review, 66,* 60–92.

Newmeyer, F. (1986). *The politics of linguistics.* Chicago: University of Chicago Press.

Niranjana, T. (1991). Translation, colonialism and the rise of English. In S. Joshi (Ed.), *Rethinking English: Essays in literature, language, history* (pp. 124–145). New Delhi, India: Trianka.

Norton, B. (1997). Language, identity, and the ownership of English. *TESOL Quarterly, 31,* 409–430.

Norton Peirce, B. (1995). Social identity, investment, and language learning. *TESOL Quarterly, 29,* 9–31.

Norton Peirce, B., & Stein, P. (1995). Why the "Monkeys passage" bombed: Tests, genres, and teaching. *Harvard Educational Review, 65*(1), 50–65.

Parakrama, A. (1995). *De-hegemonizing language standards.* New York: Macmillan.

Patterson, A. (1997). Critical discourse analysis: A condition of doubt. *Discourse: Studies in the Cultural Politics of Education, 18,* 425–435.

Peirce, B. N. (1989). Toward a pedagogy of possibility in the teaching of English internationally. *TESOL Quarterly, 23,* 401–420.

Pennycook, A. (1989). The concept of method, interested knowledge and the politics of language teaching. *TESOL Quarterly, 23,* 589–618.

Pennycook, A. (1990). Towards a critical applied linguistics for the 1990's. *Issues in Applied Linguistics, 1,* 8–28.

Pennycook, A. (1991). A reply to Kanpol. *Issues in Applied Linguistics, 2,* 305–312.

Pennycook, A. (1994a). Critical pedagogical approaches to research *TESOL Quarterly, 28,* 690–693.

Pennycook, A. (1994b). *The cultural politics of English as an international language.* London: Longman.

Pennycook, A. (1994c). Incommensurable discourses? *Applied Linguistics, 15,* 115–138.

Pennycook, A. (1996a). Borrowing others' words: Text, ownership, memory and plagiarism. *TESOL Quarterly, 30,* 201–230.

Pennycook, A. (1996b). TESOL and critical literacies: Modern, post or neo? *TESOL Quarterly, 30,* 163–171.

Pennycook, A. (1997a). Cultural alternatives and autonomy. In P. Benson & P. Voller (Eds.), *Autonomy and independence in language learning* (pp. 35–53). London: Longman.

Pennycook, A. (1997b). Vulgar pragmatism, critical pragmatism, and EAP. *English for Specific Purposes, 16,* 253–269.

Pennycook, A. (1998a). *English and the discourses of colonialism.* London: Routledge.

Pennycook, A. (1998b). The right to language: Towards a situated ethics of language possibilities. *Language Sciences, 20,* 73–87.

Pennycook, A. (1999a). Introduction: Critical approaches to TESOL. *TESOL Quarterly, 33,* 329–348.

Pennycook, A. (1999b). Pedagogical implications of different frameworks for understanding the global spread of English. In C. Gnutzmann (Ed.), *Teaching and learning English as a global language: Native and non-native perspectives* (pp. 147–156). Tübingen: Stauffenberg Verlag.

Perry, T., & Delpit, L. (Eds.). (1998). *The real ebonics debate: Power, language, and the education of African-American children.* Boston, MA: Beacon Press.

Phillipson, R. (1992). *Linguistic imperialism.* Oxford: Oxford University Press.

Phillipson, R. (1998). Globalizing English: Are linguistic human rights an alternative to linguistic imperialism? *Language Sciences 20,* 101–112.

Phillipson, R. (1999). Voice in global English: Unheard chords in Crystal loud and clear [Review of the book *English as a global language*]. *Applied Linguistics, 20,* 265–276.

Phillipson, R., Rannut, M., & Skutnabb-Kangas, T. (1994). Introduction. In T. Skutnabb-Kangas & R. Phillipson (Eds.), *Linguistic human rights: Overcoming linguistic discrimination* (pp. 1–22). Berlin, Germany: Mouton de Gruyter.

Phillipson, R., & Skutnabb-Kangas, T. (1995). Linguistic rights and wrongs. *Applied Linguistics, 16,* 483–504.

Phillipson, R., & Skutnabb-Kangas, T. (1996). English only worldwide or language ecology? *TESOL Quarterly, 30,* 429–452.

Poster, M. (1989). *Critical theory and poststructuralism: In search of a context.* Ithaca, NY: Cornell University Press.

Poynton, C. (1993a). Grammar, language and the social: Poststructuralism and systemic-functional linguistics. *Social Semiotics, 3,* 1–21.

Poynton, C. (1993b). Naming women's workplace skills: Linguistics and power. In B. Probert & B. Wilson (Eds.), *Pink collar blues* (pp. 85–100). Melbourne: Melbourne University Press.

Poynton, C. (1996, October). *Language and difference.* Plenary address to the 21st Annual Conference of the Applied Linguistics Association of Australia, University of Western Sydney, Nepean.

Prabhu, N. S. (1999, August). *Misapplied linguistics.* Paper presented at the 12th World Congress of Applied Linguistics, AILA '99, Tokyo.

Prain, V. (1997). Multi(national)literacies and globalising discourses. *Discourse: Studies in the Cultural Politics of Education, 18,* 453–467.

Price, S. (1996). Comments on Bonny Norton Peirce's "Social identity, investment, and language learning": A reader reacts. *TESOL Quarterly, 30,* 331–337.

Price, S. (1999). Critical discourse analysis: Discourse acquisition and discourse practices. *TESOL Quarterly, 33,* 581–595.

Radway, J. (1984). *Reading the romance: Women, patriarchy and popular literature.* Chapel Hill: University of North Carolina Press.

Rajagopalan, K. (1999). Of EFL teachers, conscience, and cowardice. *ELT Journal, 53,* 200–206.

Rampton, B. (1995a). *Crossing: Language and ethnicity among adolescents.* London: Longman.

Rampton, B. (1995b). Politics and change in research in applied linguisitics. *Applied Linguistics, 16,* 233–256.

Rassool, N. (1998). Postmodernity, cultural pluralism and the nation-state: Problems of language rights, human rights, identity and power. *Language Sciences, 20,* 89–99.

Richards, J., Platt, J., & Weber, H. (1985). *Longman dictionary of applied linguistics.* London: Longman.

Rivera, K. (1999). Popular research and social transformation: A community based approach to critical pedagogy. *TESOL Quarterly, 33,* 485–500.

Rizvi, F. (1993). Children and the grammar of popular racism. In C. McCarthy & W. Crichlow (Eds.), *Race, identity, and representation in education* (pp. 126–139). New York: Routledge.

Roberts, C., Davies, E., & Jupp, T. (1992). *Language and discrimination: A study of communication in multi-ethnic workplaces.* London: Longman.

Rockhill, K. (1994). Gender, language and the politics of literacy. In J. Maybin (Ed.), *Langauge and literacy in social practice* (pp. 233–251). Clevedon, UK: Multilingual Matters and The Open University.

Said, E. W. (1978). *Orientalism.* London: Routledge & Kegan Paul.

Sanguinetti, J. (1992/3). Women, "employment" and ESL: An exploration of critical and feminist pedagogies. *Prospect, 8*(1&2), 9–37.

Schenke, A. (1991). The "will to reciprocity" and the work of memory: Fictioning speaking out of silence in E.S.L. and feminist pedagogy. *Resources for Feminist Research, 20,* 47–55.

Schenke, A. (1996). Not just a "social issue": Teaching feminist in ESL. *TESOL Quarterly, 30,* 155–159.

Shohamy, E. (1997, March 10). *Critical language testing and beyond.* Plenary address to the American Association of Applied Linguistics, Orlando, FL.

Signorini, I., & Cavalcanti, M. (Eds.). (1998). *Lingüística aplicada e transdisciplinaridade* [Applied and transdisciplinary linguistics]. Campinas, Brazil: Mercado de Letras.

Simon, R. (1992). *Teaching against the grain: Essays towards a pedagogy of possibility.* London: Bergin & Garvey.

Singh, J. (1996). *Colonial narratives/cultural dialogues: "Discoveries" of India in the language of colonialism.* London: Routledge.

Skutnabb-Kangas, T. (1988). Multilingualism and the education of minority children. In T. Skutnabb-Kangas & J. Cummins (Eds.), *Minority education: From shame to struggle* (pp. 9–44). Clevedon, UK: Multilingual Matters.

Skutnabb-Kangas, T. (1998). Human rights and language wrongs—a future for diversity? *Language Sciences, 20,* 5–28.

Skutnabb-Kangas, T., & Phillipson, R. (Eds.). (1994). *Linguistic human rights: Overcoming linguistic discrimination.* Berlin, Germany: Mouton de Gruyter.

Smith, N. (1999) *Chomsky: Ideas and ideals.* Cambridge, UK: Cambridge University Press.

Spack, R. (1997). The rhetorical construction of multilingual students. *TESOL Quarterly, 31*(4), 765–774.

Spivak, G. C. (1993). *Outside in the teaching machine.* New York: Routledge & Kegan Paul.

Sridhar, K. K., & Sridhar, S. N. (1986). Bridging the paradigm gap: Second language acquisition theory and indigenized varieties of English. *World Englishes, 5*(1), 3–14.

Street, B. (1984). *Literacy in theory and practice.* Cambridge, UK: Cambridge University Press.

Street, B. (1995). *Social literacies: Critical approaches to literacy in development, ethnography and education.* London: Longman.

Sunderland, J. (Ed.). (1994). *Exploring gender: Questions and implications for English language education.* Englewood Cliffs, NJ: Prentice-Hall.

Susser, B. (1998). EFL's othering of Japan. *JALT Journal, 20,* 49–82.

Talbot, M. (1992). The construction of gender in a teenage magazine. In N. Fairclough (Ed.), *Critical language awareness* (pp. 174–200). New York: Longman.

Talbot, M. (1995). *Fictions at work: Language and social practice in fiction.* London: Longman.

Tannen, D. (1990). *You just don't understand: Women and men in conversation.* New York: Morrow.

Thesen, L. (1997). Voices, discourse, and transition: In search of new categories in EAP. *TESOL Quarterly, 31,* 543–560.

Thomas, N. (1994). *Colonialism's culture: Anthropology, travel and government.* Oxford, UK: Polity.

Thompson, J. (1991). Editor's introduction. In J. B. Thompson (Ed.), *Language and symbolic power (Pierre Bourdieu)* (pp. 1–31). Oxford, UK: Polity.

Threadgold, T. (1997). *Feminist poetics: Poiesis, performance, histories.* London: Routledge.

Threadgold, T., & Kamler, B. (1997). An interview with Terry Threadgold on critical discourse analysis. *Discourse: Studies in the Cultural Politics of Education, 18,* 437–451.

Tollefson, J. (1989). *Alien winds: The re-education of America's Indochinese refugees.* New York: Praeger.

Tollefson, J. (1991). *Planning language, planning inequality: Language policy in the community.* London: Longman.

Troemel-Ploetz, S. (1991). Selling the apolitical: Review of Deborah Tannen's *You just don't understand. Discourse and Society, 2,* 489–502.

Tsuda, Y. (1994). The diffusion of English: Its impact on culture and communication. *Keio Communication Review, 16,* 49–61.

Usher, R., & Edwards, R. (1994). *Postmodernism and education.* London: Routledge.

van Dijk, T. (1993a). *Discourse and elite racism.* London: Sage.

van Dijk, T. A. (1993b). Principles of critical discourse analysis. *Discourse and Society, 4*(2), 249–283.

Venuti, L. (1997). *The scandals of translation: Towards an ethics of difference.* London: Routledge.

Walkerdine, V. (1990). *Schoolgirl fictions.* London: Verso.

Wallace, C. (1992). Critical literacy awareness in the EFL classroom. In N. Fairclough (Ed.), *Critical language awareness* (pp. 59–92). London: Longman.

Walsh, C. (1991). *Pedagogy and the struggle for voice: Issues of language, power, and schooling for Puerto Ricans.* Toronto, Canada: OISE Press.

Watkins, M. (1999). Policing the text: Structuralism's stranglehold on Australian language and literacy pedagogy. *Language and Education, 13*(2), 118–132.

Weedon, C. (1987). *Feminist practice and poststructuralist theory.* Oxford, UK: Basil Blackwell.

Weiler, K. (1992). Teaching, feminism, and social change. In M. Hurlbert & S. Totten (Eds.), *Social issues in the English classroom* (pp. 322–337). Urbana, IL: NCTE.

Widdowson, H. (1980). Models and fictions. *Applied Linguistics, 1,* 165–170.

Widdowson, H. (1998). The theory and practice of critical discourse analysis. Review article. *Applied Linguistics, 19,* 136–151.

Widdowson, H. G. (1999, August). *Coming to terms with reality: Applied linguistics in perspective.* Plenary address to the 12th World Congress of Applied Linguistics, AILA '99, Tokyo.

Wiggins, M. E. (1976). The cognitive deficit difference controversy: A Black sociopolitical perspective. In D. Harrison & T. Trabasso (Eds.), *Black English: A seminar* (pp. 241–254). Hillsdale, NJ: Lawrence Erlbaum Associates.

Wiley, T., & Lukes, M. (1996). English-only and standard English ideologies in the U.S. *TESOL Quarterly, 30*(3), 511–536.

Williams, G. (1992). *Sociolinguistics: A sociological critique.* London: Routledge.

Williams, G. (1998). Children entering literate worlds: Perspectives from the study of textual practices. In F. Christie & R. Misson (Eds.), *Literacy and schooling* (pp. 18–46). London: Routledge.

Wodak, R. (1996). *Disorders of discourse.* London: Longman.

Wodak, R., de Cillia, R., Reisigl, M., & Leibhart, K. (1999). *The discursive construction of national identity* (A. Hirsch & R. Mitten, Trans.). Edinburgh: Edinburgh University Press.

Young, R. (1990). *White mythologies: Writing history and the West.* London: Routledge.

Young, R. (1995). *Colonial desire: Hybridity in theory, culture and race.* London: Routledge.

Zita, J. (1992). Male lesbians and the postmodernist body. *Hypatia, 7*(4), 106–127.

Author Index

A

Althusser, L., 121
Appadurai, A., 70
Ashcroft, B., Griffiths, G., & Tiffin, H., 70
Atkinson, D., 4, 25,
Auerbach, E., 77, 100, 102–103, 115, 121, 131, 138–139
Auerbach, E., & Wallerstein N., 15, 154
Austin, J. L., 157

B

Bailey, R., 56,
Barrett, M., 41,
Baynham, M., 77,
Bee, B., 100–101,
Belenky, M., Clinchy B., Goldberger N., & Tarule, J., 154
Benesch, S., 16, 25, 131
Benson, P., 95, 116, 120–122
Beretta, A., 144
Beretta, A., Crookes, G., Gregg, K. R., & Long, M. H., 144
Bernstein, B., 122

Bex, T & Watts, R. J., 47
Bhatt, A., & Martin-Jones, M., 96,
Block, D., 144
Bourdieu, P., 28, 123–126, 163
Bowles, S., & Gintis, H., 121
Britzman, D., 159
Brookfield, S., 4,
Brutt-Griffler, J., & Samimy, K., 15, 125
Burnett, L., 31,
Butler, J., 107, 126, 155–157, 160

C

Cameron, D., 18, 47, 50–51, 53–54, 73, 153–157
Canagarajah, S., 16, 62, 65, 69–71, 116–118, 120, 126–130, 162
Canale, M., & Swain, M., 52
Candlin, C., 169–170
Chomsky, N., 33–36, 43,
Chrisman, L., & Williams, P., 66
Christie, F., 123
Clark, R., 40, 96,
Clark, R., & Ivanic, R., 12, 150
Clarke, M., 3,
Coates, J., 18, 151–152

195

Cope, B., & Kalantzis, M., 77, 97, 99, 103, 131, 133
Cope, B, Kalantzis, M., Kress, G., Martin J., & L Murphy, 96 fn 2
Corder, S., 3
Corson, D., 98–99, 136–137, 161
Coulmas, F., 64
Cox, M.I.P & de Assis-Peterson, A. A., 150, 171
Crawford, A., 19, 54
Crystal, D., 56–58

D

Davies, A., xi–xii
Davies, B., 78
de Beaugrande, R, 3
Dean, M., 7–8, 171
Delpit, L., 78, 95–97
Dendrinos, B., 16, 128–129, 157
de Souza, L. M., 171
Dua, H., 57–58, 71
Duff, P., & Uchida, Y., 147

E

Ellsworth, E., 132

F

Fairclough, N., 13, 28, 37–38, 51–52, 79–94, 109
Fairclough, N., & Wodak, R., 79–80
Fanon, F., 67
Farias, M., 171
Featherstone, M., 70,
Firth, A., & Wagner. J., 144
Foley, G., 110
Foucault, M., 10, 28, 35, 42–43, 83–85, 89–92, 109, 163, 171–172
Fowler, R., 99
Fowler, R., Kress, G., Hodge, R., & Trew T., 79,
Freire, P., 101–102
Freire, P., & Macedo, D., 101
Friedman, J., 126
Frye, D, 15, 103, 131

Fuery, P., 163

G

Galtung, J., 61
Gebhard, M., 144–145
Gee, J., 23, 76–78, 89, 136
Gee, J., Hull, G., & Lankshear C., 19
Giddens, A., 38, 44, 50, 119
Gilroy, P., 161
Giroux, H., 49, 101, 122–123, 126–7, 130
Goldstein, T., 54
Gore, J., 26, 130, 132, 139
Graman, T., 15, 102, 138
Green, B., 176–177
Gregg, K. R., 144
Gregg, K. R., Long, M., Beretta, A., & Jordan, G., 144
Grumet, M., 154
Guba, E and Lincoln Y., 162

H

Habermas, J., 6–7, 42, 87
Hall, S., 111
Halliday, M., 79
Hanson, J., 57
Haraway, D., 134
Harland, R., 90, 104–105
Harris, R., 47, 51,
Hatim, B., & Mason, I., 13, 110
Haugen, E., 60
Heath, S. B., 77, 124, 161
Herman, E. S., & N. Chomsky, 34
Hodge, R., & Kress, G., 79
Hogben, L., 57–58
Honey, J., 28, 31, 47–8,

I

Ibrahim, A., 14–15, 150, 160–162, 163
Ivanic, R., 52

J

Jäger, S., & Jäger, M., 80
Jagose, A., 156, 162
Janks, H., 96,

Janks & Ivanic, 40, 96
Jenkins, R., 125–126
Jewell, J., 157–159, 161–162
Johnson, S., 153–154
Johnston, B., 26, 133–134, 139
Jordan, G., & Weedon, C., 128
Jordão, C., 171

K

Kachru, B., 2, 70
Kanpol, B., 130, 133
Kaplan, R., 145
Kearney, R., 136, 138, 141–142, 163, 173
Kramsch, K., 71
Krashen, S., 3, 78
Kress, G., 13, 36, 84, 86, 94, 97, 133, 169
Kress, G., & Hodge, R., 79
Kress, G., & van Leeuwin, T., 79
Kubota, R, 146
Kumaravadivelu, B., 109, 129

L

Labov, W., 49,
Lakoff, R., 28, 151
Lankshear, C., 76–77
Lantolf, J., 144
Lather, P., 42, 132, 134–135, 140, 148, 162, 171
Lee, A., 76, 98–100, 109–110, 140
Lin, A., 15, 125–126, 162
Liu, J., 15
Long, M., 33, 144, 170
Loomba, A., 66
Luke, A., 12, 75, 88, 98–99, 103–104, 112, 123, 126, 131
Luke, A., &Walton, C., 75
Luke, A., & Freebody, P., 12, 75
Luke, A., Mchoul, A., & Mey, J. L., 17, 55
Lynch, B., 162

M

Markee, N., 3,
McCarthy, T., 87
McClintock, A., 66

McCormick, K., 4, 94, 113
McGee, T. G., 135
McKay, S. L., & Wong, S. C., 146, 148
Mclaren, P., 130
Mey, J., 17, 37–39, 51, 73
Mills, S., 83–84, 108–109
Milroy, J., 32
Misson, R., 159
Moi, T., 155
Moita Lopes, L. P., 171
Morgan, B., 15, 131, 149
Mühlhäusler, P., 60

N

Nandy, A., 66–67
Nelson, C., 15, 157–8, 160, 162
New London Group, 77, 99–100
Newmeyer, F., 34, 144
Niranjana, T., 14, 69
Norton, B., (see also Peirce, Norton Peirce), 15, 147–148
Norton Peirce, 146–148, 161
Norton Peirce, B., & Stein. P., 17,

P

Parakrama, A., 51, 106
Patterson, A., 84, 108,
Peirce, B. N., (see also Norton, Norton Peirce), 52–53, 118, 144
Pennycook, A., xi, 5, 56, 64, 66, 68, 71, 83, 95, 99, 118, 120, 133, 145–146, 159, 162
Perry, T., & Delpit, L., 50,
Phillipson, R., 18, 36, 56, 58, 61–63, 94
Phillipson, R., Rannut, M., & Skutnabb-Kangas, T., 64
Phillipson, R., & Skutnabb-Kangas, T., 18, 60, 63, 70
Poster, M., 6
Poynton, C., 19, 104, 106, 109–110
Prabhu, N. S., 170
Prain, V., 100
Price, S., 94, 148–149

R

Radway, J., 78
Rajagopalan, K., 70,

Rampton, B., 9, 32, 68–9, 144, 161
Rassool, N., 64
Richards, J., Platt, J., & Weber, H., 2
Rivera, K, 15, 103, 131, 161
Rizvi, F., 159
Roberts, C., Davies, E., & Jupp, T., 54
Rockhill, K., 78

S

Said, E. W., 69, 80
Sanguinetti, J., 15, 154
Schenke, A., 15, 155, 160
Shohamy, E., 16–17
Signorini, I., & Cavalcanti, M., 171
Simon, R., 3, 25, 120, 127, 131, 137, 172
Singh, J., 68
Spack, R., 145
Sridhar, K. K. & Sridhar S. N., 143
Skutnabb–Kangas, T., 18, 61–63
Skutnabb–Kangas, T., & Phillipson, R., 63
Smith, N., 34–35,
Spivak, G. C., 8, 14, 43, 72, 172
Street, B., 9, 77
Sunderland, J., 15, 162
Susser, B., 145–146

T

Talbot, M., 78, 96
Tannen, D., 152
Thesen, L., 147–148
Thomas, N., 67
Thompson, J., 123
Threadgold, T., 87, 109–110, 111, 163
Tollefson, J., 17, 18, 59–60, 63, 121
Troemel-Ploetz, S., 153
Tsuda, Y., 58,

U

Usher, R., & Edwards, R, 41, 130–131, 133–135

V

van Dijk, T., 13, 79, 82, 86, 93
Venuti, L., 14, 69, 142

W

Walkerdine, V., 78
Wallace, C., 96
Walsh, C., 15, 103,
Watkins, M., 99
Weedon, C., 25, 109, 148, 155
Weiler, K., 103,
Widdowson, H., 2–3, 4, 29, 33, 94, 111, 170, 174
Wiggins M. E., 48
Wiley, T., & Lukes, M., 48
Williams, Geoff, 123
Williams, Glyn, 6, 17, 38, 45, 50, 53–54, 122
Wodak, R. , 19, 36, 80, 82–88,
Wodak, R. et al., 79

Y

Young, R., 9 fn1, 67, 134

Z

Zita, J., 156

Subject Index

A

Academic writing, 40, 96,
  and identity, 150
Access, 6, 18, 19, 37, 44, 48, 49, 64, 97
  literacy, 78, 99
Agency, 26, 31, 62, 73
  and subjectivity, 148
  and structure, 117–120
  and voice, 101,
  voluntaristic, 149
Anarcho-syndicalism, 33–34
  anarcho-autonomy, 30, 33–36, 43,
    165
Applied Linguistics, 4, 14, 25, 26, 29,
    33, 44, 46, 134, 137, 165,
    169,
  courses in, 174–176
  definitions, 2–3, 115
  and ethics, 136–138
  hypocritical, 29, 33, 170, 174
  lack of history, 68
  mainstream, xi–xii, 30, 41, 62, 114,
    165
  misapplied linguistics, 170
  postcritical, 174

and structuralist linguistics, 106,
  165
  with an attitude, 173–177
Applied postlinguistics, 110–113, 174
Appropriacy, 40, 52–53,
  vs. desirability, 53, 55, 72
Appropriation, 62, 68–71, 167
Australia, 96, 102, 103, 175
  LOTE/LOBE, 145
Autonomy (learner), 95, 120
  political approach to, 116
Awareness, 40, 101–102, 163, 166
  conscientization, 101, 103
  and emancipation, 40, 100, 167

B

Bodies and embodiment, 124–125,
  162–163, 172
British Council, 61
Brazil, 39, 101, 171

C

Canada, 14, 15, 131,
  becoming Black in, 150

Chinese ESL class, 149
Capital, forms of 123–126
   cultural, 123–126
      Embodied, (see habitus)
   economic, 123–126
   linguistic, 123–125
   social, 123–125
   symbolic, 123–126
Capitalism, 34, 37, 58, 62, 66, 87, 89,
      92, 121
   fast capitalism, 78, 99
Catalytic validity, 162, 168
Change, (see transformation)
Chile, 171
Class, 15, 17, 19, 37–39, 42, 48, 51,
      53, 55, 58, 73, 92, 122, 162,
      167
   conception within sociolinguistics,
      51
   class-based language practices,
      49–50, 77–78, 95,
      122–123
      elaborated and restricted code,
         122
   international class of English speak-
      ers, 122
Classrooms, 115–117
   as microcosm of social order,
      115–116
   relative autonomy of, 117–118
Communicative competence, 52, 68,
Communicative language teaching, 95
Compassion, 7
Context, 5, 16–17, 35, 70–71, 76
   classrooms in, 115–117
   of language learning, 143–145
   literacy and social context, 76–78
   text in, 98, 111–112
Critical, meanings of, 4–5, 171
   work, approaches to, 25–26,
      peripheral vs. pervasive, 176
Critical bilingualism, 15, 103
Critical discourse analysis (CDA), xi,
      10–12, 20, 36, 37–38, 78–94,
      105, 169, 173, 175
   conversational control vs ideological
      meaning, 81
   denaturalizing ideologies, 81
   discourse and ideology, 82–84
   knowledge and truth, 84–85
   materialism, 89–93
   order and disorder, 85–89

principles of, 80
production and reception, 93–94
3-D model, 82, 93
as situated political practice. 88
Critical discourse research, 15
Critical ethnography, xi, 16, 71,
      116–117, 162,
Critical language awareness, 11–12, 40,
      94–96
   and emancipation, 40
   explicit pedagogies, 96
      for inclusion and access, 97
Critical language projects, 94, 169
Critical language testing, 16–17, 175
Critical linguistics, 79
Critical literacy/literacies, 12–13, 20,
      75–78, 94–104, 105, 169,
      173, 175–176
   access and inclusion, 76, 97, 105
   critical social literacy, 75
   critical text analysis (see critical dis-
      course analysis)
   Freirean, 15, 76, 101–104, 105, 154
      reading the word and the world,
         101–102
      banking, transmissive education,
         101
      participatory, 102
   genre-based, 95–100, 123
      as pedagogy of deferral, 100,
   literacy as social practice, 76–78
   multiliteracies, 77–78, 99–100, 105
   poststructuralist practice, 76, 105,
      108–113
   situated political practices, 112
   social literacies, 77, 96, 105,
Critical needs analysis, 16
Critical pedagogy, xi, 11–12, 13,
      100–104, 130–133, 167, 169,
      173, 175
   bombastic tendencies, 26
   critical praxis vs. critical theory,
      130–131
   dialogic pedagogy, 131
   as pedagogy of inclusion, 100,
      130–133, 157–159, 167
   postcritical, (see postcritical peda-
      gogy)
   rationalism in, 132–133, 154
   as regime of truth, 132
   and voice, 100–104, 105, 130–131
Critical realism, 161

Critical social inquiry, 5–6, 20,
   social theory, 50–51
Critical sociolinguistics, 6, 11, 18, 22,
   37–39, 51,
Critical Theory, 5, 6–7, 20, 42, 87
   Frankfurt School, 6–7, 87
Critical thinking, 4, 25, 29
   dialogic, 131
Culture, 127, 145–146
   cultural fixity, 145–146
      In ESL/EFL. 145–146
   cultural politics, 127–129, 139, 153
   cultural preferences, 129
   cultural thought patterns, 145
   and colonialism, 67, 145
   cultural capital, (see capital, cultural)

D

Descartes' socks, 163
Descriptivism and prescriptivism, 31,
   51
Desire, 6, 7, 126, 159, 163, 172
Determinism, 25, 28, 30, 62, 66, 89,
   117–120, 126, 167
   and poststructuralism, 108
   and volitionism, 118
Difference, 6, 7, 18, 19, 23, 78
   cultural, 141–150
   and dominance (language and gen-
      der), 151–154
   effaced 48,
   and ethics, 141
   gender and sexuality, 151–157
   pedagogical approaches to, 157–160
   perspective on language and gender,
      152–153
   vs. similarity, 35, 141
Discourse, 26, 78, 107
   adherence of, 56
   big-D, little-d, 89
   discourse analysis, 3, 44,
      critical, (see Critical Discourse
         Analysis)
      French, 79
      historical method, 79
      reading analysis, 79
   discursive mapping, (see
      poststructuralism)
   disorders and orders of, 85–89
   Foucauldian notion of, 83–89, 109

   and identity, 148–149
   vs. ideology, 82–94
   postcolonial, 80
   sociocultural change, 79
Disparity, 6, 7, 18, 19, 78
Diversity, 51, 56, 60, 63–68, 70, 75,
   100,
   inclusivity, 157–158

E

East Timor, 34,
Emancipatory modernism, 4, 7, 22, 30,
   36–42, 92, 165–167
   and colonialism, 68, 70
   and CDA, 84
   and critical pedagogy, 132
   and difference, 141, 159
   emancipation, 30, 37, 39
   emancipatory discourse, 40
   emancipatory knowledge, 42
   limitations, 41–42, 70
Empowerment, 28, 39, 48,
Engagement, 141, 157–162
   with otherness, 142
   pedagogy of, 22, 158–160
   and performativity, 149
   postmodernism and, 135, 168
   research, 160–162
English, xi, 14, 16, 31,
   American, 14.
   Black/African-American Vernacular,
      15, 32, 48–50,
   Black stylized English, 150
   global spread of, 5, 14, 18, 36,
      56–65, 70–71, 122, 134,
      142, 165–166
      and forms of capital, 125
      colonial celebratory position, 56
      diffusion of English, 58
      laissez-faire liberalism, 56
      language rights, 63–64
      linguistic hegemony, 62 (see also lin-
         guistic imperialism)
   literacy in, 78
   standard language, 47–49, 77, 97
   (see also World Englishes)
English as a second language (ESL), 15,
   102, 116, 121, 131, 157–158
English language teaching (ELT), xii,
   2, 14–16, 62

feminist approaches, 154–155,
160
refugee education, 121
and queer theory, 157
teaching methods, 16, 117–118,
129, 162
TESOL, 56, 118, 120, 122,
124–126, 131
TOEFL, 124–125,
textbooks, 16, 116–117, 128–129,
157–158
universal second language, 58
Essentialism, 35, 43, 64, 161, 168
anti-essentialism, 69, 107,134, 146
in research, 161
(see also postmodernism,
poststructuralism)
ethnicity, 143–146
gender, 153–155
strategic use of, 72–73, 172
Ethics, 9, 65, 136–138, 172
ethics of difference, 14, 142
Ethnicity, 42. 50, 54, 69, 128, 167
Europe, 30, 35, 67
EuroAmerican thought, 119, 145,
170
Eurocentrism, 41, 68, 88, 134
(see also Orientalism)

F

Feminism, 5, 8, 12, 13, 28
feminist language teaching, 15, 131,
154–155, 160
memory work, 160
feminist pedagogy, 101–102, 140,
154–155
poststructuralism, 104–110
feminist research, 15
hostility to theory, 25
patriarchy, 25, 73
Fixity, 145–146
fixing the Other, 69
(see also essentialism, Orientalism)

G

Genealogical practice, 160
Gender, 15, 17, 19, 37, 42, 50, 53, 107,
162, 167

and language (see language and gender)
and literacy, 78, 101–102,
and modernity, 87
(see also feminism, sexuality)
Germany, 80
Globalisation, 57–58, 70–71, 100
center-periphery models, 16, 62, 70,
118

H

Habitus, 124–125, 127, 163
(see also capital, cultural)
Heterosexism, 158 (see also queer theory, sexuality)
Heterosis, 9–10, 20, 22
Historical understanding, 6, 68
of language, 68–69, 111
of discourse, 80, 168
identity formation, 149
pedagogy of historical engagement,
160
Homophobia, 159
antihomophobic pedagogy, 159
(see also heterosexism, sexuality)
Hong Kong, 15, 125
Humanism, 5, 34–35, 42, 67, 119, 165
and colonialism, 67
anti-humanism, 31
human nature, 34–35,
Hybridity, 9, 69–71, 167
linguistic, 59, 71

I

Ideal speech situation, 87–88
Identity, 15, 57, 71, 142
formation, 147–150
and language learning, 143–150
politics, 156
social vs cultural, 147
identity work, 150
(see also sexuality, sexual identity)
Ideology, 6, 13, 26, 38
and discourse, 80, 82–94, 108
and subjectivity, 145–150
in CDA, 81, 82–94
as false consciousness, 119
ideological globalization, 70

as obfuscation, 38, 40, 81, 85, 88, 108
ideology critique, 5, 35, 81, 108
vs. science, 36, 166
Imperialism, 26, 61, 66, 70, 73
linguistic (see linguistic imperialism)
Inclusion, pedagogy of, 158–159
vs issues-based, 159
(see also engagement, critical pedagogy)
India, 57–58, 69, 71
Individualism, 60, 95, 119–120
individual choice, 57, 60, 129
individualistic idealism, 103, 131
Institutional power relations, 54, 82, 85
and language learning, 144–145
medical, 19, 54, 82
Intertextuality, 108, 112, 168
Intonation and identity, 149

J

Japan, 69, 145–146

K

Knowledge, 24–45
antidisciplinary, 173
knowledge claims and truth, 84–85
and power, 39, 42,
production, 25
situated knowledge(s), 17, 135, 172
(see also politics of knowledge)

L

Language, 46–73
and dialect, 32,
and gender, 6, 18, 19, 28, 151–157
one-dimensional male oppressors, 153
and power, 18, 47–48, 55, 58, 61–62, 80–82, 98–99, 172
as productive of society, 50, 53, 55, 72, 80, 156
as reflection of society, 18, 39, 45, 53, 55, 62, 156
deficit view of, 47–49, 122, 152
Language crossing, 69, 161

Language learning (see also SLA), 2, 15,
Language policy and planning, 17–18, 55–65, 165–166
neoclassical vs. historical structural, 59–60
Language rights, 18, 22, 59–65
ecology of language, 59–61
Language teaching (see English language teaching)
Language testing (see critical language testing)
ethicality in, 136
Liberalism, 5, 17, 22, 30, 35, 165–166
egalitarianism, 49, 99, 165–166
laissez-faire liberalism, 56–59
liberal complementarity, 56–59
liberal ostrichism, 29–33, 43, 138, 165–166, 168
liberal pluralism, 32, 159, 175
liberal sociolinguistics, 48–55, 165–166
and pedagogy, 95–96, 165–6
structuralism, 50, 165–6
view of meaning, 94, 165–166
Libertarianism, 34
Linguicism, 61
Linguistic imperialism, 18, 22, 36, 59, 61–63, 70–71, 119
Linguistics, 2–3, 30–31, 33–36, 49, 51
and colonialism, 106
critical, 79
diachronic, synchronic, 31,
grammatical models, 98
internal and external, 32, 107
prescriptivism, 51 (see also descriptivism)
structuralism, 30–31, 99, 104–106
systemic functional, 98–99
Literacy, 3, 76–78
as threat and desire, 78
autonomous vs. ideological, 9, 76
critical (see critical literacy)
events, 124
first language, 12, 76
hypodermic effects of, 104
literacy myth, 76
and oracy, 77
practices, 32, 77, 161
workplace, 18, 78
Literary criticism, 4, 29, 31,

M

Marxism, 6, 33, 44
    and ideology, 82–92, 119
    ideological state apparatus, 121
    infrasructure and superstructure,
        38–9, 99, 104–106
    materialism, 39, 89–93, 105–106,
    neo-Marxism, 5, 6, 30, 32, 37–39,
        55, 89, 94, 166
    outflanked 44,
    scientific leftism, 36–38, 84–85
Mentalism, 34
Modernism, Modernity, xii, 7
    neomodernism, 99
    (see also Emancipatory modernism,
        postmodernism)
Mother tongues, 60–64
Multilingualism, 18, 23, 63
    and monolingualism, 18, 58, 63
Multimodality, 105

N

Native and nonnative speakers, xi, 15,
    44, 107, 125
Normativity, 6, 9–10, 44, 50–1
North America, 3, 35, 96, 100

O

Objectivity, 4, 7, 17, 106
    and truth, 38,
Oppression, 17, 26, 39,
    dominant groups, 90
    oppressed and oppressor language,
        37
    limitations of analysis, 38, 107,
        132–133
Orientalism, 14, 69, 145–146
    and Japan, 145–146
    maps of the Other, 145

P

Participatory education, 102 (see also
    research)
    in TESOL, 131
Pedagogy of possibility, 120, 127

project of possibility, 137, 172 (see
    also preferred futures)
Performativity, 126, 155–157
    performing gender, 155–156
    postcolonial (see postcolonial
        performativity)
Plagiarism, 150
Politics and power, 27–29
    politics of difference, 141–163
    politics of knowledge, 24–45, 85,
        144, 167
    politics of language, 36, 46–73,
    politics of language teaching, 116
    politics of pedagogy, 114–140
    politics of texts, 74–113
Popular culture, 15, 150
Positivism, 6, 17, 31, 42, 53, 55, 84,
    87, 142
Postcolonialism, 5, 8, 12, 22, 30, 35,
    65–69, 146, 167
    and colonialism, 14, 66–68
    colonial discourse, 68–69
        colonial-celebratory view, 56–57
    maps of the Other, 145
    postcolonial literature, 67
    postcolonial performativity, 59,
        71–73, 143, 156, 168
    postcoloniality, 66
    postparadigmatic diaspora, 42
    translation, 14, 69
Postcritical pedagogy, 138–140, 168
    and postcolonial performativity, 140
    and applied postlinguistics, 140
Postcritical applied linguistics, 174
Postlinguistics, 22, 75, 108–113, 168
    applied (see applied postlinguistics)
    feminist, 110
    and systemic functional linguistics,
        109–110
Postmodernism, xii, 8, 22, 30, 42,
    133–138, 167
    and education, 133–136
    of engagement, 135, 168
    and ethics, 136–138
        ethical human discourse, 136
    and postcolonalism, 134
    postmodernity, 66, 133–134
    as a way of thinking, 134,
    postmodern problematizing, (see
        problematizing practice)
Poststructuralism, 5, 13, 22, 30, 42, 45,
    55, 92, 104–110, 133, 167

discursive mapping, 5, 111
discursive position, 44, 104
relativism, 88
subjectivity, subject position, 106–107, 147–149
as a way of thinking, 107
Power, 6, 7, 27–29, 165–167
contextual operation of, 123
culture of, 96,
and ethics, 137
Foucault and, 90–92, 112, 123
inequality, 15, 19, 22, 26, 37–39,
and knowledge, 42, 57, 91–92
language and, (see language and power)
and literacy, 78 (see critical literacy)
as productive, 92
Praxis, 3, 20, 130–131, 171–172
movable praxis, 173
Preferred futures, 8–9, 20, 172
Preferred meanings, 111
Problematizing practice, 4–5, 7, 20, 22, 25, 30, 41–44, 107, 167, 171
Puerto Rico, 103

Q

Queer theory, 5, 8, 12, 15, 156–157, 168
in ESL, 157

R

Race, racism, 14–15, 17, 19, 26, 37, 42, 48–9, 53, 54, 67–69, 82, 146, 150, 159, 162
antiracism, 8, 96, 159–160
linguicism, 61
Rationalism, rationality, 6, 7, 25, 29, 30, 33–35, 41, 43, 60, 84, 87, 92, 166–167
and desire, 126, 163
postcolonial challenge, 67–68
rational discussion, 159
Realism, 30, 33–35, 43
Relativism, 30, 88, 92, 94, 167
and postmodernism, 134–135
and poststructuralism, 88, 108
Reproduction, 15, 65, 121–126
of inequality, 37, 121–126, 166–167
and resistance, 65, 126–130

social vs cultural, 121–126
Research, xii, 161
engaged, 160–162
participatory (action) research, 15, 161
Classroom-based social research, 161
Resistance, 6, 16, 62, 65–71, 126–130, 162
and appropriation, 68–71, 167
to knowledge, 26
and power, 91
third spaces, 71

S

Second Language Acquisition (SLA), 3, 43, 120, 142–145, 170
narrow perspective of, 143
sociocultural approach, 144
Self-reflexivity, 8, 20, 30, 172
lack in mainstream critical work, 38, 41, 85, 133, 154
Sexuality, sexual identity, 15, 42, 107, 155–160, 162, 167–168
male lesbian, 156
transgendered identity, 158
Situatedness, 69, 88, 135, 172
situated ethics, 137
situated meanings, 108, 111
situated political practice. 88, 112
(see also context, knowlege)
Social relations, 5–6, 45
consensus vs. conflict 50, 55
inequitable, 6, 17, 18, 33, 39, 50, 86
micro and macro relations, 5, 114–115, 117–118, 172
Social semiotics, 79, 99fn3,
Sociodrama, 103
Sociolinguistics, 6, 17–18, 31–32,
discourse sociolinguistics, 87
conceptions of power, 47–55
liberal, 48–55
mainstream, traditional, 37, 51, 122
static view of society, 53, 154
critical, (see critical sociolinguistics)
view of appropriacy, 52,
Spanish, 13,
South Africa, 19, 54, 96, 118
People's English, 118
Southeast Asia, 121

Sri Lanka, 71, 116–117,
Structuralism, 22, 30–33, 35,
  de Saussure, 30,
  determinism, 89
  egalitarianism, 30–32,
  functionalism, 50
  structural power, 62
  (see also poststructuralism)
Structure and agency, 117–120
  and habitus, 125
  structuration, 119–120
  poststructuration, 120
Subjectivity, 104–107, 147–149
Superstructuralism, 90, 104–106
  (see also Marxism, infrastructure and
    superstructure)

T

Tamil, 71, 116–117, 128
Theory and practice, 3, 172
  (see also praxis)
Theory, animosity to, 25–27
Transformation (see also preferred fu-
    tures), 6–7, 15, 75, 150
  transformative pedagogy, 132
  transformative research, 162
  social agenda, 53, 75, 77, 142
Translation, xii, 2–3, 19, 20, 44, 54, 69,
    110,
  and ethics of difference, 142
  interpreting, 19.

U

United Kingdom (Britain) 54, 82, 171
  infrastructuralism, 90
  Lancaster CDA & CLA, 95–96
United States of America (US), 2, 15,
    30, 34, 50, 121, 124, 171
  Americanization, 70
  California, 78
  Chinese immigrants, 146
  (see also North America)
Universalism, 34–35, 43, 56, 76,
    132–133
  and difference, 141
  and gender, 155
  and relativism, 134–135
  universal grammar, 35
  universal pragmatics, 87–88

V

Validity, 16–17, 162, 168
Vietnam, 34, 39
Voice, 100–105, 130–131
  articulating alternative realities, 130
  (see also critical pedagogy)

W

World Englishes, 70–71, 143
  Essential World English, 57–58
Worldliness of English, 71

DATE DUE

#47-0108 Peel Off Pressure Sensitive